Captain Bligh's Second Chance

Captain Bligh's

Second Chance

An Eyewitness Account of his
Return to the South Seas
By Lt George Tobin

edited by Roy Schreiber

CHATHAM PUBLISHING

LONDON

Introduction and editorial matter © Roy Schreiber 2007
This edition © Chatham Publishing 2007 [2016]

First published in Great Britain in 2007 by
Chatham Publishing
Lionel Leventhal Ltd,
Park House, 1 Russell Gardens,
London NW11 9NN

British Library Cataloguing in Publication Data
Tobin, George
   Captain Bligh's second chance : an eyewitness account of
   his return to the South Seas
   1. Tobin, George - Diaries 2. Bligh, William, 1754–1817 –
   Travel – Oceania 3. Great Britain. Royal Navy – History –
   18th century 4. Providence (Ship) 5. Tahiti – Discovery and
   exploration – British 6. Tahiti - Social life and customs –
   19th century 7. Oceania – Discovery and exploration –
   British
   I. Title II. Schreiber, Roy E.
   996.2

   ISBN-13: 9781861762801
   ISBN-10: 1861762801

ISBN 978 1 86176 280 1

Designed and typeset by JCS Publishing Services, jcs-publishing.co.uk
Printed and bound in Great Britain by Cromwell Press, Trowbridge

Contents

Illustrations

Maps

Plates

(between pp. 56 and 57)
1 The *Providence* and her attendant, the *Assitant*
2 Rock, near the Paarl
3 Sucking fish
4 Flying fish of Sao Tiago, Cape de Verde Islands
5 Bonito
6 Fish of Adventure Bay, Tasmania
7 Near the Paarl Rock, Cape of Good Hope
8 Pintado bird, near Cape of Good Hope
9 Animal of Adventure Bay in Tasmania
10 Wooding place, Adventure Bay, Tasmania
11 In Adventure Bay, Tasmania
12 View from the lowlands to the Northward of Adventure Bay, Tasmania
13 Point Venus, Island of Tahiti
14 The observatory &c. &c., Point Venus, Tahiti
15 Near the mouth of the Ha'apaiano'o River, Island of Tahiti
16 Canoes of Tahiti

(between pp. 120 and 121)
17 On Matavai River, Island of Tahiti, from recollection
18 Fish of Tahiti, aihoua
19 Dolphins
20 A *fare tupapa'u*, with the corpse on it, Island of Tahiti
21 Matavai Bay, and the Island of Tetiaroa, from the hills south of the bay, Tahiti
22 In the district of Ha'apaiano'o, Island of Tahiti, looking towards Matavai
23 The *marae* at Pare, Island of Tahiti, looking towards Matavai

Acknowledgements

I wish to acknowledge the permission and cooperation of the Mitchell Library in the State Library of New South Wales that enabled publication of the Tobin material they hold. From top to bottom, their staff were always courteous, prompt and informative. Carol Hopper Brill kindly provided me with an extensive bibliography of material about marine life and Vic Riemenschneider did the same for birds. I wish to thank them both. Jim Blodgett helped me by translating the one and only Latin phrase that Tobin used, for which he has my thanks as well. Lee Kahan and James Tierney put me on the trail of various eighteenth-century scandals. Paul Herr assisted with geographic information that helped clarify some questions I had. I also wish to single out John Lewis, who proofread the manuscript. He has a talent that I very much appreciate.

Editorial Commentary

Despite his early denials, George Tobin strongly implies that he wrote his memoir for the wider world's enjoyment. He most certainly did not do it for the sake of other naval officers or scholars. That is undoubtedly why he used his brother James, a knowledgeable amateur, as the supposed audience for his reminiscences about the voyage. In accord with that original design, this edition of Lieutenant Tobin's memoirs is also intended for any reader with an interest in Pacific exploration and all the various side paths that such a journal involves.

Since more than two centuries separate the composition and publication of these memoirs, a few adjustments were needed to remain faithful to the original intent. The first concerns English spelling, punctuation, and paragraphing. While eighteenth-century writing is closer to that of the twenty-first century in all these areas than it is to the Elizabethan, it is just far enough different – a word Tobin spelled 'diffirent' – to be annoying to the modern reader. Making the smallest number of editorial changes possible, these aspects of the memoir have been altered to conform to present-day usage. While trying not to interfere unnecessarily with the writing style, this sometimes meant dividing sentences that went on for half a page. Conversely, that also meant occasionally linking brief, sentence-long paragraphs with the following or preceding one.

By and large, the same updating has been done with geographic locations. In this edition Tobin went to Tahiti, not O'Tahytey. With some supplementary reference to a modern world atlas, Isaac Oliver's books *Ancient Tahitian Society* (Honolulu: University of Hawaii Press, 1974) and *Return to Tahiti* (Honolulu: University of Hawaii Press, 1988) along with John Robson, *Captain Cook's World* (London: Chatham Publishing, 2000), provided the bulk of the information and spellings used for the Atlantic and Pacific oceans and their islands.

In two hundred years the conventions for calculating global locations have also changed. While Tobin's age did recognise Greenwich as the prime or zero meridian, it did not use 180° longitude on the other side of the world as the second dividing point between the eastern and western hemispheres; Tobin would describe his ship as located at 200° east longitude rather than 160° west. His era also did not have an international date line. In this volume Tobin's positions and dates are adjusted to fit the modern conventions. In a few cases, for reasons that will be either obvious or noted, his original notations are retained.

Rendering the Tahitian spellings into the twenty-first-century vernacular was a bit more complicated. Until the nineteenth century, Tahitian was not a written language, which meant Tobin wrote down what he heard, not what he saw on paper. Other eighteenth-century visitors did the same and, needless to say, they did not always hear and record things in quite the same way. In addition, like any living language, Tahitian vocabulary has changed over time. Once again, using

Isaac Oliver's work, and a Tahitian–English dictionary, Leonard Clairmont (with Mauu Ariiteuira Teriitahi), *Tahitian–English, English–Tahitian Dictionary* (New York: P. Shalom Publications, 2001), as a supplement, the Tahitian has been brought up to date. The few exceptions are noted or are clear from the context. However, in order to give the reader a sense of what Tobin heard, this edition keeps his original spellings in the few pages of Tahitian vocabulary that he placed in Chapter 7.

Detailed notes and drawings of Tobin's served as the basis for this memoir. Yet, especially when writing about the expedition after it sailed from Tahiti, he left blank spaces for positions and dates that he hoped to fill in from his official naval journal. The Admiralty required this journal-keeping of all officers assigned to Royal Navy vessels. As Tobin states at least twice, it annoyed him that while composing the memoir, he could not use his journal. The reason for his difficulty was that some weeks before the voyage ended, Bligh collected the journals of all the officers and ship's master and then, as ordered, turned them over to the Admiralty when he arrived back in England. Several times over a thirty-year time span, Tobin tried to get Admiralty permission to consult that official journal. They turned him down every time. Two centuries on, the Admiralty, in the form of the National Archive at Kew, has opened this material to the general public. It now classifies the journal as ADM 55/94 and ADM 55/95 and this journal and all the others from the *Providence* voyage are there for the reading. Thanks to this openness, whenever the information Tobin wanted exists in his journal, this edition fills in the blanks.

It should not go unobserved that when the journal and the memoir record information about a position or a date, they rarely contradict each other. The same is true on a scattering of occasions when Tobin provides a narrative of events in the journal that can be compared to the memoir. It is also worth noting that if the journal is read by itself without any reference to the memoir, the reader could easily form the opinion that Tobin almost never left the *Providence*, even during extended anchorages.

There are two sets of notes attached to this version of the memoir. Tobin wrote some notes to expand upon various points he wanted to make, these authorial notes are marked with superscript numbers in the main text and appear in the notes section at the back of the book. Editorial notes, marked with *, †, ‡ etc, appear as footnotes. These notes appear when Tobin uses words no longer in common usage or technical sailing terms. In those instances the *Oxford Universal Dictionary* acted as the source for most of the definitions provided. Editorial notes are also used in order to explain references Tobin made that his contemporaries no doubt understood but a modern reader most likely would not. When he is clearly speculating or reporting sailors' tales or what he calls Cape Stories, no notes are used to correct them. In the rather small number of places where he gives incorrect information as fact, or he could not find the information he wanted to give the reader, a note then provides the correction or addition. All editorial insertions in the text will appear in square brackets.

Lastly, a word about cuts and additions to the text. In two instances Tobin spends more than a page discussing matters that relate to his assignment to the North American coast and that had no relationship to the *Providence* voyage. This material does not appear in this edition of the memoir. Although Tobin was a careful writer, especially when he went from one page to the next, he sometimes repeated the last word on the following page. In about a half a dozen instances, he left out a word. This version of his memoirs contains the needed corrections that it is safe to say Tobin would have made if he had published his text.

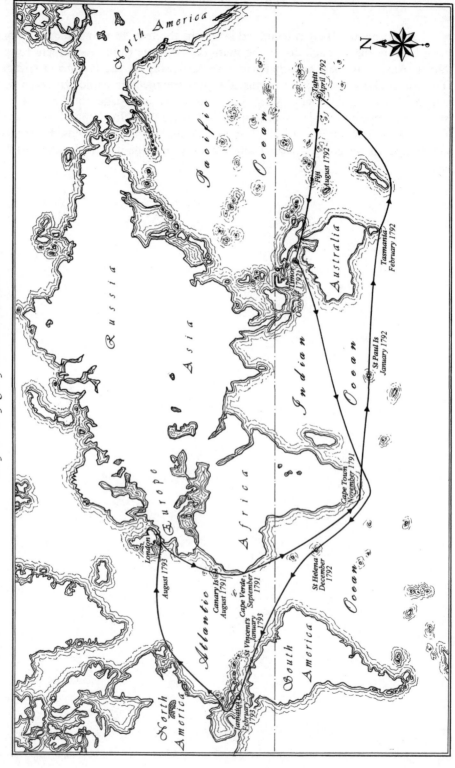

Map 1 Voyage of the Providence

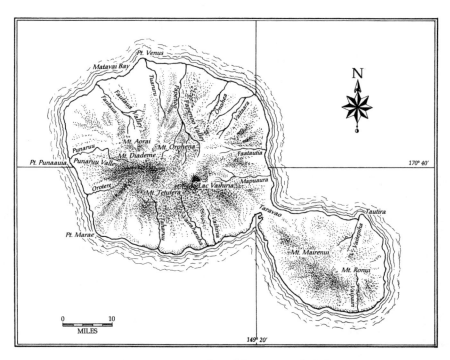

Map 2   Geographical features of Tahiti

Map 3   Regions of Tahiti

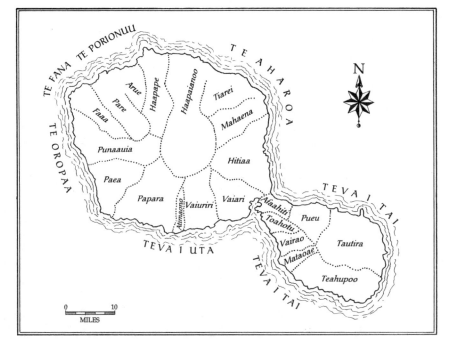

Map 4   Route of the Providence through the Fiji Islands

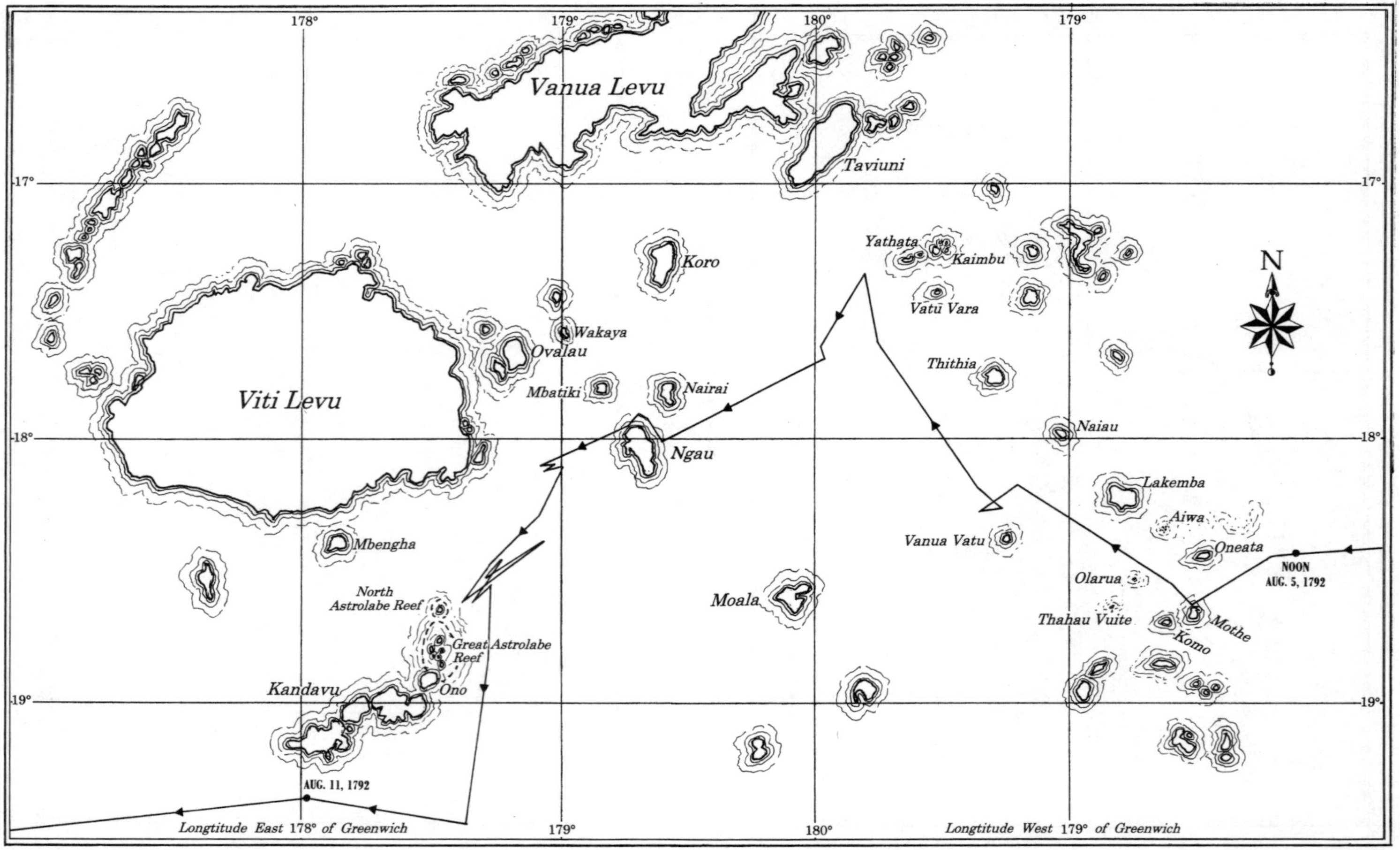

N

Vanua Levu

Viti Levu

Taviuni

Yathata
Kaimbu
Vatu Vara
Thithia

Naiau

Lakemba
Aiwa
Oneata

NOON
AUG. 5, 1792

Mothe
Komo

Olarua
Thahau Vuite

Vanua Vatu

Koro

Wakaya
Ovalau
Mbatiki
Nairai

Ngau

Moala

Mbengha

North
Astrolabe Reef
Great Astrolabe
Reef
Ono

Kandavu

AUG. 11, 1792

Longitude West 179° of Greenwich

Longitude East 178° of Greenwich

17°

18°

19°

179°

180°

179°

178°

Introduction

There never should have been a voyage to Tahiti to collect breadfruit in 1791. Yet, as cinema fans the world over know, two years earlier a mutiny on the *Bounty* meant William Bligh failed to complete his first breadfruit voyage. In April of 1789 nearly half of the ship's crew cast him and eighteen others adrift in a twenty-three-foot launch. With only slight exaggeration one author calculated that a book a year has been written about the mutiny since the event. Certainly, the amount of celluloid footage devoted to the mutiny must be approaching the more than 3,000 miles of the launch's journey. George Tobin picks up the story after most of these other works end, but that leaves something of a gap between the end of the *Bounty* story and the beginning of his memoir.

Bligh arrived back in England on 14 March 1790 and became an instant hero. To have survived the voyage in the launch and returned safely to his homeland was reason enough for his status. He also had the advantage of complete control over how to tell the tale about the mutiny and his subsequent tribulations. The other survivors did straggle back to England over the next few months, and some of them could have told different stories. Bligh was on bad terms with several of these 'loyalist' survivors – notably the master, John Fryer, the carpenter, William Purcell and the gunner, William Peckover. But at this stage they either were not interviewed by the press, or they thought it best not to provoke the newly minted hero by contradicting him. Perhaps Bligh's forcing the court martial of Purcell for his behaviour on the launch helped silence the others. For at least the next three months, Bligh remained a genuine, certified hero. His patron, Sir Joseph Banks, introduced him to George III; all the best salons spoke of him with admiration, and he even became the subject of an 'entertainment' in a London theatre. More important to Bligh, before 1790 ended, he had his behaviour on the *Bounty* vindicated by his own court martial and received a promotion to the rank of post captain in the Royal Navy. It is ironic that, had he been successful with the *Bounty* voyage, the peace-time navy might well have done with him what they did with his great mentor and model, James Cook. After Cook's first voyage, he only received a promotion to the rank of commander. All through his career Bligh seems to have had the gift for turning adversity into good fortune.

While all these events played out in Bligh's life, the navy decided to send out Captain Edward Edwards in the all too appropriately named frigate, *Pandora*, to catch the mutineers. The members of the Admiralty Board then had to decide whether they wished to send yet another an expedition to transplant breadfruit from Tahiti to the West Indies.

Some of the reasons for the failure of the first voyage went back to the board's actions. They showed an initial lack of enthusiasm about this venture that translated into a very meagre budget. As a result, they picked an exceedingly small ship for the first voyage and, despite Bligh's warnings, they refused to give him either marines to help enforce discipline or commissioned officers to help share the responsibility of controlling his tiny vessel. He served as the only commissioned officer on board the *Bounty* with the lowly rank of lieutenant. That meant he had to take full responsibility for the discipline of the crew as well as the navigation and running of the ship. In the end, the Admiralty's excessive zeal for economy proved expensive indeed.

In 1791 they decided to make amends by giving Bligh two ships, nearly half a dozen commissioned officers and a contingent of marines. Perhaps it did not hurt that the new First Lord of the Admiralty, the earl of Chatham, had the prime minister, William Pitt, for a younger brother. Money would be no problem. It also helped that the initial sponsor of the voyage, Sir Joseph Banks, had not lost faith either in the importance of transplanting breadfruit or in his chosen leader for the expedition. Banks had personally selected Bligh for this mission, and to change commanders could have been taken as a tacit admission that he had shown poor judgement in his initial choice. Ever since Banks had gone with Captain Cook on his first voyage, he had attempted to make himself the great patron and benefactor of Pacific explorers. If Bligh failed, so did Banks. Not long after landing the launch on Timor, in his very first letter home, Bligh had not been slow to remind Banks of that situation.

In so far as it is possible to know such things, Bligh had another hold on Banks. On Captain Cook's final voyage, as sailing master of the *Resolution*, Bligh had drawn a series of charts at Cook's direction. They covered both the new discoveries and the track the expedition took. At end of the voyage these charts came into the possession of Henry Roberts and James King. Roberts had been Bligh's master's mate on the *Resolution* and his name appears at the bottom of the printed charts that became part of the official published version of that voyage. King began as a lieutenant on the *Resolution*, but he ended the voyage as commander of its sister ship, *Discovery*. Upon returning to England, he took over the responsibility for writing the story of what happened to the expedition after Cook's death in Hawaii. From reading King's journal entries, he and Bligh had not been friends; judging by Bligh's later commentary, their dislike of one another ran rather deep. Banks became heavily involved with facilitating the publication of the official record of Cook's voyage. Only after the three volumes appeared in 1784 did he discover that King had misled him about the authorship of the charts and that Bligh deserved a percentage of the royalties. Banks was essentially a fair man and that mistake may well have influenced his sense of obligation to Bligh. It may also have helped bring the half-pay naval lieutenant to his attention; Banks would not intentionally injure anyone who willingly acknowledged his patronage. When it became time to select the leader of the new breadfruit voyage, both Banks and the Admiralty chose Bligh. He had his second chance.

Bligh, in turn, had choices to make about who came with him on this new voyage. Given what happened on the *Bounty*, the choice of officers and men obviously had great sensitivity for him. After all, the lead mutineer, Fletcher Christian, had been his personal selection. In the end only one person from the *Bounty* voyage came on the *Providence*, Lawrence Lebogue, the sailmaker. The gunner, William Peckover – who clearly relished Pacific exploration – also applied, but Bligh turned him down; Peckover had had some unhelpful things to say about Bligh at the court martial of the carpenter, Purcell.

For the second and third in command Bligh chose Nathaniel Portlock and Francis Godolphin Bond. Also a veteran of Cook's voyages, Portlock went on to gain considerable experience as a Pacific navigator. Bond's virtues lay closer to home. He was related to Bligh and had risen to the rank of lieutenant. The first of these two individuals commanded the supply vessel, *Assistant*, and the second became first lieutenant on the *Providence*. Bligh had what he hoped would be the right combination of experience and loyalty from those immediately beneath him in rank. This time around, he made the right choices.

Two others on the *Providence* have some claim to special notice. One is the midshipman, Matthew Flinders. He would eventually become another of Banks's Pacific explorers and would devote a good portion of his life to charting the Australian coast. Interestingly enough, it was Captain Thomas Pasley who encouraged Flinders to accompany Bligh. Pasley's nephew was Peter Heywood, one of the *Bounty* mutineers. Despite the fine training as a cartographer and navigator that Flinders acknowledged he received from Bligh, the two of them had major differences. Before the expedition returned to England, Bligh reduced Flinders to the rank of able seaman. It seems they disagreed about which one of them should receive credit for a chart. Twenty years later, ever oblivious to the pain he caused others, Bligh wanted Flinders to dedicate his book about his Australian explorations to his old instructor. Flinders declined.

The other noteworthy character on the *Providence* was the author of this memoir, George Tobin. Although his father made his money as a West Indian planter on the island of Nevis, George was born in Salisbury in 1768. Even though his father made periodic trips to the plantation, George and his two brothers, John (who became a playwright) and James (the supposed audience for whom this memoir was written) stayed in Salisbury for their schooling. In George's case his formal education did not last very long because by 1780, at the age of eleven, his name already appeared in naval records. Although it was not uncommon for the children of rich gentlemen to have their names entered in a ship's book and never serve, it does appear that George actually did join the ninety-gun *Namur* and participated in the so-called Battle of the Saints that took place in 1782.

After the peace with France the following year, in common with Bligh and many other naval personnel, Tobin found himself without a ship. Also in common with his future captain, during this period Tobin served in the merchant navy and made at least one voyage to India and China in 1788. As he says in his memoir, after having passed his lieutenant's examination in November 1790, the *Providence* became his first assignment back in the Royal Navy.

Perhaps he could have done better. Horatio Nelson was a relation of Tobin's and actually offered to help him. His father let the world know that, when it came to pushing his son's advancement in the navy, he considered money no object. Despite all this good will, Tobin's career progressed at a rather leisurely pace. The navy promoted him to the rank of commander in 1798, eight years after becoming a lieutenant. He only became a captain in 1802 through a general promotion that took place during a temporary lull in the Napoleonic Wars. His last active command occurred in 1814 and he did not become an admiral until 1837, the year before his death. Judging from the record that Tobin left of the *Providence* voyage and by other observations of him, he proved a skilful naval officer. Yet, despite occasional commentary about his lowly rank, the young lieutenant seemed to lack that burning ambition for advancement or glory that so much characterized his patrons Bligh and Nelson. Good company of either sex, natural history, literature, sketching and painting all seemed to matter to him, with career ambitions surfacing only periodically. Even by eighteenth-century standards, this attitude marked Tobin out as an unusual naval officer. Perhaps, as the heir to a substantial fortune, he felt no need to prove that he could eat life before it devoured him.

When Tobin reached Tahiti in 1792, he found that many of its inhabitants shared his easy-going disposition. Then, right from the first, he encountered two rather notable exceptions. Although at first glance the chief and his wife with whom Tobin dealt most often seemed like other Tahitians, they possessed very different temperaments. The two of them went by a variety of names, but by the time the *Providence* arrived, the British usually referred to the chief as Pomaurey or Pomare and his wife as Edeea or 'Itia. Both were remarkable people. Physically, in terms of height and weight, they were huge by the standards of their day, but it was their intelligence that was particularly impressive. From their first contact with Europeans some twenty years earlier, they recognised the superiority of western technology over Tahitian, especially in the area of weapons. As a result, they plotted and schemed with each successive European ship's appearance to obtain the fire power necessary to dominate Tahiti and the surrounding Society Islands.

Part of their scheme involved cultivating the British officers who visited their island with increasing regularity since Wallis and Cook had arrived in the late 1760s. Pomare and 'Itia had the good fortune to control territory that included one of the best harbours for European deep-draft ships. By playing generous hosts and supplying the necessities of life to these western mariners, they gradually managed to barter for the firearms they sought. By remaining with the commanders of these vessels virtually every day that they stayed in Tahiti and providing each one of their officers with a special trusted friend or *tiao*, Pomare and 'Itia by and large managed to prevent rival chiefs from gaining access to these westerners. As part of this plan, Tobin became 'Itia's *tiao* and on departing presented her with a firearm. He never realised that this final gift had been the object of her plan from the first.

Virtually every British seaman who left a record of his Tahitian visit during this period came away favourably impressed with the 'king and queen' of Tahiti. Yet the personalities of the couple had little in common with each other. In the case of 'Itia, their high opinion of her had absolutely nothing to do with the sensual stereotype Europeans held of Tahitian women. Quite the contrary, no one ever called her physically attractive. The quality of her mind, her charm and her physical bravery impressed these observers. Tobin responded to her quite sympathetically.

On the other hand, Pomare seemed lazy to him, a reluctant warrior at best and one who visibly shook at the sound of musket fire (as opposed to his wife, who was a crack shot). Tobin records a conversation with Pomare in which the 'king' says that, since George III did not lead armies into battle, why should he do so himself? Few good things about Pomare found their way into Tobin's memoir. Yet, as the British got to know Pomare, many of them, including Cook and Bligh, realised that behind that fat, indolent facade one could find a man of superior political skills and great common sense. By 1800 he and his 'queen' became masters of Tahiti and nearly all the nearby islands.

In the process of gathering daily events that acted as the live sources for his memoirs, Tobin understood that, for accuracy's sake, he needed to disturb the lives of the Pacific Islanders as little as possible. Yet there is no question that he struggled when he saw something that offended his European sense of morality. Tahitian sexual customs gave him a particularly difficult time, such as when a *tiao* offered his wife to his British counterpart, with the wife's willing cooperation. Because of his western background, Tobin began by saying that the islanders should not act that way. But as he thought about the custom, he realised the Tahitians had their own cultural reasons for behaving the way they did. As this turnaround indicates, Tobin increasingly proved a strong believer in the superiority of 'natural man', uncorrupted by civilisation. In this, like so many of his contemporaries, he closely paralleled the views of Voltaire and Rousseau. This idea led him to observe the Tahitians and other people he encountered with a strong willingness to see the best in their societies.

Tobin strongly believed that most of the evils found originated with the Tahitians' European visitors. For that reason, he frequently bemoaned the westerners' corruption of the islanders. The Tahitian ruling class's growing addiction to alcohol, their peculiar ways of wearing foreign clothing and their greed for technological marvels from iron axes to muskets, all saddened and frustrated him. As far as Tobin was concerned, after the *Providence* left, all future European contact was dangerous. Evil could just as easily come from over-zealous missionaries as from unthinking whalers. He feared both would produce disastrous consequences on the Tahitians' mental and physical health. Tobin knew that the population had declined dramatically since Cook's arrival. Already, people with all the best intentions had unintentionally introduced fatal diseases to the Tahitians, and in all likelihood that pattern would continue. Tobin is among the last of his generation to see the Tahitians before they were totally overwhelmed, and before they almost vanished.

As he predicted, by the turn of the century the missionaries and the whalers in ever-increasing numbers made their appearance and neither group shared Tobin's unwillingness to disturb the state of nature as they found it on Tahiti. This memoir is something of a final look at the Tahitian world as the Europeans first experienced it. Those early voyagers treasured the experience. So it is no surprise that Tobin viewed Tahiti as not far removed from paradise. That view would not reappear again for many generations. Even at the end of the nineteenth century, the Tahitian faces Paul Gauguin painted do not show people living in paradise.

Like several well-known Europeans before him, and like Gauguin a century later, Tobin used more than words to record what he saw. He painted a series of sketches using watercolour and ink. Many naval officers of this era attempted sketching everything from a view of a recently discovered island to the animals, plants and people they encountered. Not all of them had talent. That is why the Cook expeditions had professional illustrators such as Parkinson, Hodges and Webber. Even a quick glance at some of the naval personnel's work, such as George Pinnock of Wallis's voyage, shows that employing professionals made sense. As Tobin mentions at the end of his memoir, a professional artist was suppose to go out on this voyage as well, but he became ill and did not sail with them. Tobin tried to fill the gap. When it came to people, no one will ever confuse him with Hodges or Webber. Still, his views of Tahitian life are informative in their detail, even if the human figures are rather basic. Some of his scenic views are quite successful, especially a couple of Adventure Bay. His plants, fish and animals would not have embarrassed Parkinson. The drawings of the water craft of all the cultures he encountered, including his own, are uniformly of high quality.

In recording what Tobin saw of the people he found on Tahiti, this young lieutenant comes through as reflecting the values of his age. This pose is not entirely accidental. Perhaps because he lacked a formal education, he very much wanted to present himself as a well-read, cultured man, despite his occasional protests to the contrary. In order to achieve this goal, throughout the memoir, Tobin relies upon a wide number of authorities to substantiate his point of view, as well as a few poets, for decoration. He had read and quotes from such sources as printed versions of Cook's first two voyages, although interestingly not from the third. Bligh's book about the *Bounty* voyage and mutiny provides additional material. Tobin also uses Alexander Dalrymple's two-volume *Historical Collection of the Several Voyages and Discoveries in the South Pacific* (vol 1 1767, vol 2 1771). Even David Collins's study of the early British settlement in Australia (*Account of the Colony in New South Wales*, London, 1803) and one of Bryan Edward's books about the West Indies (*An Historical Survey of the French Colony in the Island of St*

Domingo, London, 1797) receive a mention. So does at least one book on natural history and a study of Sri Lankan society. Besides books, the *Gentleman's Magazine* and various newspapers also acted as source material. Some of the anonymously authored poetry Tobin includes is a good deal short of first rank, but he compensates, however briefly, with some lines from Thomas Gray and a verse from 'The Island' by Lord Byron.

What Tobin produces in his memoir is a combination of many genres. He is first and foremost a nautical observer and at one point apologises to his brother for boring him with notations about the ship's position and compass variations. In each of the lands he touches, he is also the travel writer who comments on which of the sights to see and which to avoid. Upon setting foot on any shore, virtually the first thing Tobin tried to do was go hiking, preferably to the top of the highest hill. The naturalist comes through strongly on these hikes, where he produces a steady stream of commentary on the world he encounters. But it comes through even more sharply when he is at sea and makes observations about everything from the sea birds, to the jellyfish, to the plant life.

His keenest interests, however, are reflected in his descriptions of the people he finds. He records a wide variety of observations, from the exact shade of their skin colour and texture of their hair, to the cut of their clothes (if any), to the shape of their containers, to the effectiveness of their weapons. He had the instincts of a cultural anthropologist before the profession existed.

Whenever Tobin has extended contacts with individuals, he makes an equally detailed commentary on their personalities. By his own admission he finds the women particularly fascinating, with all that observation implies. When it comes to women from his own country, his views do not even remotely resemble his contemporary, Mary Wollstonecraft. Especially with regard to women's education, his sentiments are far from enlightened. Yet when Tobin observed Tahitians, he proved as capable of giving an insightful analysis of the 'queen's' personality, despite her physical unattractiveness, as he was of giving an equally perceptive one of her remarkably attractive (and frequently naked) younger sister.

Interestingly enough, the one person who does not receive detailed examination is William Bligh. Not yet forty years old, someone whom contemporaries often noted as rather short in both stature and temper, in Tobin's memoir he is a figure seen at a distance, with his actions only occasionally noted. Only one short line is devoted to any aspect of his personality; especially while on Tahiti, Tobin dined with Bligh on a regular basis and must have observed him closely, but nonetheless he remains silent about his captain as a person. True, what little he does have to say about Bligh is positive, and on their return he clearly felt the man was badly treated by the Admiralty. Yet for whatever reason, the attention to detail that Tobin has when writing about the Tahitians is not there when discussing Bligh.

Unlike the first lieutenant, Bond, who wrote home some extraordinarily angry letters about his relative, the captain, Tobin never directly says a negative word about Bligh. Even so, from both Tobin's and Bligh's records of the voyage, one clash between them comes to light. It happened when Tobin fired on a canoe filled with New Guinea tribesmen in the Torres Straits. Blight saw the action as a prelude to potential disaster and said so in his journal. In person he no doubt said so to Tobin, with some force. While never publicly taking issue with his former commander, Tobin spends a good deal of time in his memoir with a description of the ships' navigation of the Torres Straits and in defending his behaviour. Clearly on this second voyage, Bligh had not lost his knack of pushing people too hard for his and their good. At the time, Tobin claims he dealt with his problems by discussing them with his messmates. Later he found a way to deal with these frustrations by writing his memoir. Fletcher Christian and his friends seized the ship.

Another omission comes through in the memoir, and it concerns the aftermath of the mutiny Christian sparked on the *Bounty*. That event and what followed does receive periodic mention. Several of the mutineers and their fate are spoken of directly. But there could have been so much more. As it turned out, one of the Tahitians who returned to the West Indies with the crew of the *Providence* had been a member of the small band of islanders who accompanied Fletcher Christian and all the other mutineers to the island of Tubuai, where they attempted to found a settlement. While Tobin mentions the Tahitian's participation and hearing the stories he told about what happened in this unsuccessful effort, he never gives more than the most cursory observations about what went on there. Since his informant had learned some English and Tobin had learned some Tahitian, the language barrier had nothing to do with this silence. This is especially true since Tobin also reports having at least one discussion about these events with Joseph Coleman, the loyalist armourer on the *Bounty* for whom there was no room on Bligh's launch.

Despite these gaps in the story, Tobin does have a high-spirited tale to tell about adventures that came his way on an expedition that went half-way around the world. In doing so he gives a sense of trying to please an audience; introspective musings make very few appearances. The goal is to entertain his reader, ostensibly his brother James, but in all probability others as well. It is true, as he was willing to acknowledge, that at times he wandered off the subject, but he always found his way back. At his best, he has a clarity of language that is truly surprising for one with his largely informal education. He also has the ability to produce comedy and pathos, even if he is sometimes a bit heavy-handed in the way he goes about it. Although he lacks the polish of a professional storyteller, he can and does make his story a fascinating one. He has written a piece that is reminiscent of James Boswell's *London Journal*, and for a young serving naval officer, that is not bad company to keep.

Roy Schreiber

CHAPTER 1ST

April–October 1791

Appointed to the Providence.—To convey the breadfruit from Tahiti to the West Indies.—Failure of the Bounty in 1787.—Captain William Bligh, and Lieutenant Nathaniel Portlock.—Crews of Providence and Assistant, and kind of vessels.—Messieurs Wiles and Smith Botanists.—Sheerness, Lieut. Thomas Pearce and party of marines.—Reach Spithead.—Leave England.—Three watches.—Vessels separate in a fog, the only instance of their parting during the voyage.—Speak to a whaler.—Our mess.—Promotion.—Arrive at Tenerife.—Transactions there.—Quit Tenerife.—Captain Bligh sick.—Mother Cary's Chickens.—Decks wetted.—Pilot fish.—Cape de Verde Islands.—Log books.—Arrive at Sao Tiago.—Quit Sao Tiago.—Speak to a French brig.—Porpoises.—Men of war birds.—Cross the Equinoctial Line.—Lieutenant Bond in charge of the Assistant.—Shark and dolphins caught.—Advance southward.—Albatrosses, pintado birds.—Porpoise struck.—Luminous appearance of the sea.—Blubbers.—Whales seen.—Bermuda.—Gannets seen.—Arrive at Table Bay, Cape of Good Hope.—

Thetis, off Bermuda January 1797

My dear James –

It is more from a desire of employing some portion of time which begins to be wearisome, I take up my pen than in a belief that the hasty observations in the following sheets will add much to your amusements.

You cannot but remember the anxiety I ever expressed to embark on a voyage to the South Seas; nor was it long after receiving my lieutenant's commission ere Lord Chatham, who then presided at the Admiralty, was considerate enough at the solicitation of my friends, to give me the appointment of third lieutenant of the *Providence*, destined to transport the breadfruit and other plants from Tahiti to our West India colonies.

At times when indolence did not lay its heavy hands on me, it was my custom to commit my ideas to paper, on the various circumstances that occurred as we voyaged along; I am now about to put such fragments, in some sort of connection. And as they are not meant for the 'public eye'. I will not dread the critique of a friend who is aware that, the person addressing him, from between eleven and twelve years of age has nearly the whole time been tossing on an element, giving him claim to indulgence and pardon for those errors with which a nautical education is sufficiently freighted.

The first expedition, towards the close of the year 1787, for conveying the breadfruit and other useful plants to the West Indies having failed, by the unfortunate mutiny on board the *Bounty* in April 1789, it was determined by the government to make a second attempt in so humane and laudable an undertaking. The success of this voyage has fully answered the most sanguine expectations of everyone concerned in it.

Captain William Bligh was again chosen to command the expedition. And, as the navigation in many parts, particularly the straits formed by Australia and New Guinea, was known to be intricate and full of danger, a small brig* under the command of Lieutenant Nathaniel Portlock, an experienced officer and scientific seaman, who had been familiar to voyages of circumnavigation, was appointed to assist him.

The ship selected by Captain Bligh, under the authority of the Admiralty, was a new West Indiaman, built at William Perry's yard Blackwall. She was flush-decked, about four hundred tons burden; of good capacity, and in every respect adapted to the voyage. Our consort was a brig of rather more than an hundred tons burden. They were both coppered and named, the former the *Providence*, her tender the *Assistant*.

In April 1791 the two vessels were commissioned, the *Providence* to be navigated by an hundred men including officers and marines, the *Assistant*, if I remember right, by five and twenty. While at Deptford every attention was paid by the officers of the dockyard to make the ship as commodious as possible. Frames and other conveniences were fitted for carrying the plants after embarking them from Tahiti. As the whole of the after-cabin was allotted to them, it encroached in a great measure on our accommodations.

At this place Messieurs Wiles and Smith joined the ship for the purpose of collecting and superintending the care of the plants during the voyage. Every article that had hitherto been found an anti-scorbutic,† or any way conducive to health in distant voyages, such as sauerkraut, sweetwort, essence of malt, spruce, portable soup, hops, &c. &c. was bountifully supplied us.‡ Two Brodie stoves with funnels to communicate through the cable tiers and more confined parts of the ship were also received on board, as well as a kind of portable oven to re-bake the bread should it be found necessary.[1]

June 22nd

We this day left Deptford, anchoring in the evening at Galleons Reach to take on board the ordnance and ammunition, the former being sixteen four pounders and several swivels. The *Assistant* had six four pounders besides swivels.

---

* brig: a vessel with two masts, square rigged, but carrying also on her mainmast a lower fore and aft sail with a gaff and boom.
† anti-scorbutic: for the prevention of scurvy, contains vitamin C.
‡ Only sauerkraut of the items listed contained vitamin C.

In our way towards the Nore, the ship was found to be so crank* that, stopping at Sheerness, twenty tons of iron ballast, besides some shingle, were taken on board. At this place Lieutenant Thomas Pearce, a sergeant, two corporals, a drummer and fifteen private marines, joined from Chatham barracks.

July 16th

The vessels did not reach Spithead until this day. Here the crew was completed, and in addition to the many wholesome articles received at Deptford, several cases of borecole, or dried cabbage, were sent on board from Haslar Hospital. This was found to be palatable when cooked in various ways.

The day approached fast for our departure from the British shore and civilised society to mingle with the uncultivated children of nature in more distant countries. He must indeed be destitute of reflection and sensibility who has not some connections or attachments to bind him to his native isle. Particularly happy in my relatives and friends, I sorely felt the separation, nor did I look to this voyage of anxious uncertainty without some unpleasant thoughts, but they were soon dissipated. It was a voyage I had eagerly courted and volunteered and my profession taught me that repining was wrong and would avail naught.

August 2nd

Everything being ready for sea, a little after noon the anchors were weighed, and we sailed through the fleet at Spithead with a fine breeze. The wind was variable in the Channel until the 7th, when a departure was taken from the British coast, not without our anxiously casting the last look 'on the hills of our native isle as it receded from the view, until the wat'ry horizon bid the prospect die'.

On the 17th we were advanced southward as far as 42°..09' north latitude, the longitude by account† being 12°..24' west. The thermometer 67½°. The crew were now put at three watches, a measure, the beneficial effects of which was sensibly felt throughout the voyage, and it gives me a real satisfaction to observe that it is becoming very much the custom, even in our ships employed on active service in war.

There was rain on the following night during the whole of which a good fire, with a sentinel to prevent accidents, was kept in the galley, most of the watch taking the benefit of it, a sufficient number being left on deck to attend the halyards‡ and look out. This custom was observed throughout the voyage, as

---

*   crank: liable to lean over or capsize, said of a ship when it has too little ballast to carry full sail.

†   by account: using mathematical calculations.

‡   halyards: used to raise and lower the yardarms to which the sails are attached.

well as enforcing the people to dry their wet clothes which at length became habitual to them. Too much attention cannot be paid to it, as nothing generates sickness so much on board ship as wet or damp clothes.

On the 21st in a thick fog the two vessels were unavoidably not in sight of each other for about two hours, and it was the only instance during the voyage of their having at all separated, notwithstanding the great variety of weather they experienced.

22nd

An English ship was spoken with this day from Southampton bound round Cape Horn on the Southern Whale Fishery. Mr. Harwood, the surgeon, visited her commander who was unwell.

27th

The atmosphere was hazy. In the morning the Pico de Teide of Tenerife appeared in sight. And on the following day with the assistance of our boats, anchored in the road of Santa Cruz in thirty-four fathoms water, mooring with the best bower* in forty seven fathom north by east and south by west, a cable each way. When moored, the east point of the road bore east by north four leagues, the west point, southwest by west six leagues,† the high church of St. Francis west, one mile, and the Pico de Teide, just discernible above the mountains west by north. You must not let these nautical terms annoy you, for although of no importance to you whether the church bore east or west, at some future period it may (as a direction) to me; therefore whenever you meet with latitude, longitude, bearings and distance, or any such phrases, you have only pass them by unheeded.

In noticing the southern whaler on the 22nd, it escaped me to observe that in the subsequent part of the voyage, we had communication with several of these ships. In the Greenland and Davis Straits fishery, the blubber from the whale is packed up in casks and brought to Great Britain, but in the southern fishery, the oil is extracted from it at sea, the ships being provided with boilers for the purpose.

In the course of the passage to Tenerife nothing particular occurred worthy of remark. Harmony prevailed among us, the people were in high health and spirits, and from the preserving attention of their commander, little contrary was to be apprehended. You will perhaps find me tedious, but in what I am about, I wish not to pass over anything that may serve to assist me at any future period should I ever be employed on a similar expedition, and should peace take place, it would meet my choice in preference to the tameness of either the home station

---

*   best bower: large anchor kept on the bow (front) of a ship.
†   league: three nautical miles.

or any of the regular ones abroad. Somewhere I must serve, nor will I rest, however remote the period may be, until I reach the permanent post* of a profession in which I delight, and which I was sanguine enough when embarked on the voyage which now employs my pen, to calculate I should have arrived at ere this.

You were in America or the West Indies when we returned which prevented me making you personally acquainted with my associates 'in travel'. But as I shall have occasion to mention some of them, it will not be amiss to tell you who were the residents of a square, six feet by eight, where cheerfulness was wont to reign. We are now scattered far about. One indeed, my ever valued and lamented friend poor Guthrie, has left us about two years – for I trust a better world. Severe illness obliged him to withdraw his services from the Mediterranean fleet. And on the way to breathe his last among his endearing friends at home, death stopped him short at Innsbruck in Austria, that they might not be witness to the melancholy event.

Our mess was composed of six. We met all strangers to each other. It does not too often happen that, in the confined space of a ship harmony, or even good breeding, is found to exist, nor is it surprising when we reflect on the many abrupt and uncultivated characters among us, but it was my good fortune – and in such a voyage what a consummation attained – to meet with men, who from having mixed in the world, joined to the advantage of some early liberal education, a considerable portion of that general information so absolutely necessary to create sensations different from those produced by the 'torpid narrative of the mere sailor'. Conscious that comfort depended on ourselves, if our tempers were not all cast exactly in the same mould, without much exertion or self-denial they were so disciplined, that we conciliated towards each other in a manner rendering discontent rarely known. The infirmity of the moment was soon banished, and only served, when it did happen, which was seldom, to convince us that good humour and unanimity were guests absolutely necessary to smooth the passage.

We were	Francis Godolphin Bond	1st Lieutenant
	James Guthrie	2nd
	George Tobin	3rd
	William Nicholls	Master
	Edward Harwood	Surgeon
	Thomas Pearce	Lieutenant of Marines

Save the regret occasioned by quitting our friends and country, we were full of hope and spirits.

Our calculations on the Admiralty, in the event of accomplishing the expedition, were rather sanguine. We calculated – erroneously. For your friend, neither his age nor services, gave him room to murmur, but surely his messmate,

---

* post: The full title of a captain in the Royal Navy was post captain.

Bond, from the situation he held, his length of service and former sufferings,[2] might have had more consideration bestowed on him than in the appointment of first lieutenant of a purchased four and twenty gun ship. But I fear that the popularity which attended the equipment of the expedition was considerably diminished towards its completion. You are perhaps unacquainted that about a short twelve month previously to our return, a court martial had been held on the mutineers of the *Bounty*. It does not belong to me to judge of the necessity of such a measure while Captain Bligh was absent. It was thought proper, and it was not difficult to discover on our arrival that impressions had been received by many in the service by no means favourable to him. It is hard of belief that this could have extended to the officers of the succeeding voyage. Yet, we certainly thought ourselves rather in the 'background' – but enough, at present, of this truly melancholy subject.

Before the vessels were anchored in the road at Santa Cruz, we were visited by the master of the port, enquiring after names and destination. Guthrie was soon after sent on shore to learn if the governor would return our salute, as well as to obtain permission for the ships to be supplied with water and refreshments. The governor was at the Grand Canary, but my messmate was politely received by the commandant, who declined a salute, urging as a reason the very great expense it would be to the Spanish government did such a custom prevail. The request to procure water and refreshments was most readily granted. At this island we remained until the 2nd when water being completed, and a supply of wine taken on board, we continued our course to the southward.

The town and road of Santa Cruz have been so often fully described by various voyagers, that I shall not attempt giving you any more than a cursory statement of what I immediately saw, or learnt, during our short stay. The little time I was on shore was chiefly devoted to the necessary duty of the ship.

On passing the northeast part of the island until you approach the town of Santa Cruz, the country bears a most dreary and unprofitable aspect, not a vestige of vegetation is to be seen, but on the very summit of the mountains and on a few spots in the valleys. Above the town it becomes more level, and some patches of cultivation are discernible. The northwest part of the island (I was informed) boasts a more fertile soil, and from the great quantity of fruit and vegetables brought from the neighbourhood of La Orotava, there is little doubt of its being the case. About six miles on the road to this place is the city of Laguna.

The town of Santa Cruz is by no means irregular and has light airy appearance from the shipping. The houses of the better sort of people are spacious, but not at all adapted to the warmth of the climate. In common with all the Spanish and Portuguese settlements, the poorer class of people are numerous, and the most wretched of human beings never failing to solicit the charity of the stranger as he passes them. On the whole island it is computed that there are about sixty-eight thousand inhabitants. A militia is kept up, who every Sunday are mustered and go through their exercise. The garrison of Santa Cruz, the only one on the island, does not amount to three hundred regulars, including officers, who bear a very great proportion to the men. These did not appear in anyway tolerably appointed. The churches and religious sanctuaries are not very numerous. Those I visited boasted the most gaudy ornaments. The chapel to a convent of Dominican friars is remarkable for its cleanliness and neatness. No molestation whatever was given in our visits to any of them, and in passing the different cells, our bows were returned with much politeness and cordiality by their tenants, some of whom appeared of a very advanced age. The church of St. Francis is conspicuous by its high tower and is a good anchoring mark for ships coming into the road.

There is a pier for the convenience of landing goods, to which very fine water for the shipping is conveyed by pipes. On this pier are several pieces of large brass ordnance. This seems to be the resort of the inhabitants of an evening, and notwithstanding there is a cool shaded walk contiguous to it (like your fine exchange at Bristol), it is seldom visited.

Fruit is remarkably reasonable in its price, but of an inferior quality. Grapes brought on board were sold at about half penny the pound, and peaches nearly as moderate. There are besides, pears, apples, figs, bananas, and a few nectarines, and from good authority I learnt that most of the tropical, as well as European, fruits are procurable according to the different seasons. The common as well as the sweet potato are in abundance.

The beef we thought of an inferior quality, and poultry, which is chiefly brought from the Grand Canary, could scarcely be procured. The supply of fish was hardly to be noticed, but at certain seasons many vessels are sent to the African coast on a fishery established there by the Spaniards, returning with them cured, to the Canaries.

The weather during our stay was uncommonly sultry and oppressive, nor did the night air at all make amends for our sufferings in the day. The land breeze, which in most warm latitudes is eagerly courted, is here as much to be dreaded, the rocks acquiring such a degree of heat from the day's sun as to render the air passing over them almost unsupportable. The thermometer in the shade was at 89° which was higher than it ever rose in the subsequent part of the voyage.

Having heard that about the sides, and near the summit of the peak, men were living in a state of religious retirement, I made enquiry respecting it, but was assured that it was not the case, as travellers from curiosity and peasants who gain a livelihood by bringing down ice, are the only visitors. I was much disappointed with respect to the appearance of this celebrated mountain, the surrounding ones no doubt take considerably from its grandeur. It was clothed in snow during the visit of the *Providence*, and when the sun shone on it, had a beautiful effect. Our short stay at Tenerife to my unfeigned mortification, prevented me attempting a journey to Pico de Teide, or indeed any excursion beyond the environs of Santa Cruz.

Quitting Tenerife, a course was shaped for the Cape de Verde Islands. Previously to leaving Santa Cruz Captain Bligh was attacked with an alarming fever, nor was his health perfectly established until within a short period of our reaching the Cape of Good Hope.

September 6th

Besides other aquatic birds, those by seamen called Mother Cary's Chickens were about us in numbers.[3] From what circumstance they acquired this name I could never learn. Seamen, who are in general superstitious, on the appearance of these little birds calculate on stormy weather being near. That a continual intercourse with the sea enables them in some degree to foretell approaching storms cannot be denied, but in the present instance I feel no hesitation in pronouncing that their prophetic knowledge is entirely groundless. I have seen these birds in all countries, climates, and weather, without ever finding the elements in any way disturbed by their appearance. It is of the petrel tribe, web footed, with very long delicately formed legs. In colour, except in the breast being black, it a good deal resembles the common land martin. They seldom settle on the water, but collect in numbers about the wake of a ship, hovering near the surface in search of food. I recollect many years ago, meeting on the coast of Nova Scotia with a dead whale about which were some thousands of these little birds. Many of them settled on the decks of the ship, apparently worn out by hunger.

The weather now became considerably warmer. Wind sails to convey air below were fitted to the different hatchways, and in the evenings the upper deck was always wetted, a custom never neglected by us in very warm latitudes. This not only communicates a coolness below, but is a great preservative for the planks against the acquired heat of the day's sun.

A pilot fish was taken. In shape it is not very unlike a mackerel, yet not so sharp at the head or near the tail. The colour purple and grey, in broad vertical stripes. This fish is seldom seen but when accompanying the shark, from which circumstance it has by seamen acquired the name. The shark is generally attended by one or more of these fish who are busily employed in examining the different food passing near. When many baited hooks have been towing over board, I have seen the pilot fish going and returning without the shark paying any attention, but on meat being thrown into the sea without a hook, the inspection of the pilot fish never failed bringing the shark to his prey. The shark is also frequently attended by sucking fish. These fish adhere so fast to its skin that I have known them taken together.

9th

Early in the morning the Island Sal was seen on the western side of which the ships passed. The latitude observed at noon was 16°..50' north, the centre mountain bearing south 74° east. The thermometer 81½°. In the evening, while the west end of Boa Vista bore south and Sao Nicolau west, northwest, the southeast end of Sal was northeast by east. Sal appeared barren and destitute of verdure, the land hilly and unequal. A very careful lookout was kept in the night for the Leton Rocks, and before the dawn opened, the vessels were brought to.

10th

The Leton Rocks were seen soon after daylight. At noon the latitude was observed in 15°..41' north, when they bore north 42° east about 3 leagues distant. These rocks cannot be too carefully avoided. They form but a small spot, yet a heavy sea breaks on them. Our meridian observation correctly fixed their latitude. Boa Vista appeared hilly and as barren as Sal.

11th

In the morning the island of Sao Tiago was seen, and before noon the vessels were anchored in Port Praia road, having thirteen fathom on a sandy bottom with stones. The ship was steadied with the kedge anchor,* when the fort bore north, northwest by west two miles. The last point east by north ½ north, and the southwest point west by north, one mile distant.

I should have informed you that towards the conclusion of the voyage our log books and journals, at the desire of Captain Bligh, were given up. These, on ships' arrival in England, were deposited in the Admiralty office, nor do I know whether they will ever again reach their proper owners. Hitherto all the efforts I have made to recover them have proved fruitless. In particular voyages of discovery this precaution, however harsh, might for a time be proper to prevent misrepresentation, but in the present case mystery seems so truly unnecessary that I cannot but confess my feelings to be rather sore at the deprivation of them – but 'tis part of our creed to suppose that our rulers are right. We enlist under this impression. The above circumstance may make me frequently incorrect as to dates, particularly subsequently to our departure from Tahiti.

Soon after anchoring at Port Praia, I was sent to wait on the governor. It has already been observed that Captain Bligh was in an ill state of health, and part of my mission was to enquire whether his taking up his residence on shore would be likely to benefit him. A genteel young Portuguese with much politeness offered the use of his house, but at the same time urgently recommended our proceeding to sea, giving a most unfavourable account of the place at that season. A fever, he said, was carrying off five or six daily. The governor, who I found in a very sorry mansion indeed, received me with civility, yet gave me to understand that until the ships had been formally reported, no traffic of any kind could be allowed, but on my representing the very ill state of our commander's health, after some persuasion, allowed a few oranges to be taken on board. In the evening I again paid my respects at Government House, not a little surprised to

---

*   kedge anchor: a small anchor with an iron stock used for mooring or warping (shifting the stern through the direction of the wind) a ship.

find that its tenant had forgotten an appointment he had made to meet me, by taking a ride up the country. The commandant, however, allowed us to return on board with a few more oranges which, with some decayed cocoanuts, was all the fruit to be procured. In this second visit the ragged sergeant of a ragged guard attached himself to our party, full of the most flattering assurances that abundance of every kind of stock and fruit would be brought early on the morrow from the more productive parts of the island.

The very sickly state of Port Praia hurried us to sea that night, without waiting the sergeant's abundant supply. In attempting to weigh the anchor it was found to be so fastened to something at the bottom as to render all our efforts fruitless. It is more than probable it got hooked to one of the anchors left by Commodore Johnstone, or Monsieur de Suffren, in April 1781.*

So short was our visit to Port Praia, my observations respecting it must be very confined. The anchorage seems to be sheltered from every wind but a southern one. No wharf or regular landing place appeared, but the surf did not beat high on the beach. I did not observe a single boat of any kind, which is the more remarkable as great abundance of fish are to be easily caught along the shores, but the inhabitants deny themselves this indulgence from an apprehension that if boats were in common use, their slaves would avail themselves of it by deserting to the African shore.

Fish were so very plentiful that our people caught more than enough for their expenditure with hook and line. The beach seemed to be particularly favourable for hauling the seine.† One fish was remarkable for the brilliancy of its colours being of a bright vermilion, mottled with lively purple spots. Flying fish were numerous and very large; on returning to the ship in the evening one flew into the boat of the following dimensions

	Inches
Length	14½
Length of the upper wings	8
Length of the under wings	3¾
Circumference at the thickest part of the body	5¾

It was the largest flying fish I ever met with in any part of the world. The shape very much resembled the mullet. I have no doubt but excellent sport might be had by shooting them in the air.

I do not know whether it has been noticed, but the flying fish has the peculiarity of the lower part of the tail being full twice the length of the upper. The use of it has been evident to me frequently. I have by the hour watched

---

* Commodore George Johnstone and Monsieur de Suffren, a French naval commander, fought a naval engagement in that harbour during which Johnstone was fortunate enough to beat off Suffren, who had taken him by surprise.

† the seine: a fishing net designed to hang vertically in the water, the ends being drawn together to enclose the fish.

dolphin and bonitos in pursuit of them, when, without wholly immersing themselves, which would have proved fatal, they have dipped in their progressive motion the lower part of the tail on the surface of the water, so as to supply their wings with moisture to support them from falling. I rather think that I never saw a flying fish exceed the distance of an hundred yards without seeking this relief. The flying fish has a remarkably large eye.

The town is situated on a cliff not far from the beach, bearing a most wretched appearance. More than three parts of the inhabitants appeared to be Africans or the produce of African parents. The houses teemed with misery and sickness, and even the governor's was not equal to an English cottage.

Sao Tiago is the chief town on the island being about ten miles from Port Praia. The cliff, on which the latter is built, divides two valleys that lead towards the mountains, the one to the left was by no means unpleasant or destitute of cultivation; I observed the cocoanut, the plantain, the sugar cane, and palm in tolerable luxuriance. The mountains rising from the interior are particularly grand and picturesque. Not far from the beach is a well of tolerable water, but the casks must be floated off to the boat.

It would be unjust to doubt the report of the sergeant respecting the abundance of stock in the country, but Port Praia was almost destitute of the common necessaries of life. Scarcely any poultry was seen and but a few hogs and goats.

In the road we left a southern whaler from Nova Scotia, and a schooner from the American states. The master of the latter informed me, it was his seventh voyage to Cape de Verde Islands, and that in return for dry goods and provisions, he took a cargo chiefly of hides. By the schooner, Captain Bligh sent despatches (by the way of America) of our having reached thus far in safety.

12th

Leaving the island in the night with a fine breeze at northeast, a course was shaped to the southward.

15th

At noon the latitude was observed in 10°..10' north, longitude by direct reckoning 22°..50' west, thermometer 83°, variation of the compass (in the morning) 11°..11' westerly. The ship sailed through a quantity of what the seamen called fish's spawn.* It extended in a line, a few yards broad, as far as the eye could discern east and west having much the resemblance of saw dust on the surface of the water. I have at various times seen this scum, which on being taken on board had the appearance of the small granules forming the spawn of shrimps. Were I to attempt a more particular description, doubtless it would not

---

*   fish's spawn: plankton.

be of a kind whence any certain conclusion might be drawn as to what it really is. Perhaps the seamen are not wrong in considering it to be fish's spawn.

The air now became close and sultry, accompanied with much rain. Brodie stoves were fitted, one in each cockpit, and fires kept in them throughout the day, besides every other precaution being taken to keep the ship dry in her more confined parts. Hoses were fixed to the awnings, by which means a considerable quantity of water was collected, but perhaps it is impossible on board ship to prevent such water being impregnated with the taste of tar.

22nd

In the morning a brig under the national colours of France was spoken with. She was from Le Havre, bound to the African coast. I had never before seen the national flag. On this subject, I shall have occasion to speak, as I go along, but I cannot help remarking that we had been officially instructed to consider it as the flag of France. The commander of the brig promised to report us to the English Admiralty, on his return to Europe.

In the afternoon numbers of porpoises were playing around the ship. The activity and exertion of this fish* is astonishing. It is common to see them leap full six feet above the surface and more than double the distance. On a particular examination of them, it would seem that their horizontal tails considerably aid towards this effect. Many fish leap a great height from the surface, but there is a mode of travelling peculiar to the porpoise. When sailing at the rate of nine or ten miles an hour, it is common to see them in vast numbers taking the same direction, but at more than twice this rate, as if they had some object in view, bounding ten or twelve feet at a time. When rising from the water, they acquire strength and progressive motion from a pressure with their tails on the surface, which is repeated at every leap. To a person not familiar with the sea, I know of scarcely anything more curious than a school of porpoises moving in the manner I have endeavoured to describe. When these fish are seen in a calm, seamen even calculate on the wind coming from the quarter of the compass towards which they are making their progress, an observation which seems idle enough.

Several men of war birds† were about the ship. I was never able to get a close inspection of this bird. It is about the size of a large kite, its wings much out of proportion to the body, being very long, as is the tail, which is forked like a swallow's. The colour except the head, breast and bill, which are white, is dark brown. When in pursuit of prey, its sight is astonishing. At more than twice the height of a ship's masthead, it is common to see them dart perpendicularly and seldom fail catching a fish. An instance this day offered where one having taken a

---

*   this fish: the porpoise is a sea mammal and not to be confused with the dolphin, a
      true fish, that Tobin describes below.
†   men of war birds: frigate birds.

flying fish to a considerable height, it disengaged itself, but by the celerity of the bird, was again caught before it reached the surface of the water.

October 2nd

It was with great satisfaction we saw our commander so much recovered as to be able to read the morning service.

3rd

With a fine breeze at southeast we this day crossed the Equinoctial Line in longitude by direct reckoning* 22°..08' west, by time keepers† 19°..58' west, the thermometer 77°. In the afternoon such as had voyaged only in the northern hemisphere were separately called upon to pay a fine according to their rank, or undergo the ceremony of ablution in a large tub prepared for the occasion, and this I assure you, is highly necessary after the one which previously takes place, as a notched iron hoop for a razor does not effectually remove from the pores of the skin the compound lather with which it has been anointed. The cruel one of ducking overboard was privately prohibited, notwithstanding the day had opened with a most alarming machine suspended through a block at the fore yardarm for this purpose. It was formed of an iron crow, with a collar for the neck of the same metal, and a handspike lashed across for the hitherto uninitiated sufferers to sit on while firmly grasping the crow. They are ducked (as the seamen term it – by the gun) in the briny element some fathoms deep, whence they rise free of the Equinoctial Line. Such was the custom among seamen 'in days of yore', but the plunge from the yardarm has (I believe) been discontinued many years, a less dangerous, though sufficiently filthy ordeal, now serving the purpose of baptism.

The business to your friend was nothing new; he had before entered the southern half of the world, when indeed, more humour and whimsical fancy was displayed than on the present occasion. Our Neptune and his spouse were dull; even the tatler was neither so communicative nor curious as we in general find the softer sex on *terra firma*, but the appearance of both as they ascended the bows and approached the quarter deck, enthroned on a gun carriage, filled some of your young northern navigators with a degree of apprehension nearly equal to that already produced by the ducking chair, still pendant from the yardarm. By far the greater half of the officers and crew were on Neptune's list, who received either in grog or specie, the tribute due from them ere they were passed over to

---

*   direct reckoning: an estimation of the ship's position using astronomical observations and mathematical calculations.

†   time keepers: calculations based on the time differential between two marine chronometers, one set for noon at Greenwich and one set for noon at the current location.

the shaving tub; some, indeed, rather high in office who were able to bribe him well, escaped the iron razor, but all were completely soaked.

Towards sunset all wat'ry hostilities ceased, and the great god, relinquishing the trident, again assumed his station on the forecastle, while Amphilute and her Nereides,* disrobed of their dripping vestments, in jackets and trousers, were soon 'themselves again'.

9th

At noon the latitude was 11°..11' south, longitude by direct reckoning 24°..33' west, thermometer 77°. The wind from the east and southeast, the air so cool and pleasant as to greatly make amends for the close unsettled weather experienced on the north side near the Line.

10th

The boat was sent on board the *Assistant* with some refreshments for our worthy messmate Bond, who, shortly after Captain Bligh being taken ill, had been sent to take charge of her, Mr. Portlock remaining on board the *Providence*. It was not always that we lowered the boat down when we wanted to communicate with our little consort, many a fresh joint being veered astern to her by line. It was now found that we had considerably the advantage of her in sailing making us fearful that, should it be the case on our return from Tahiti we might part company, as the greatest expedition would be necessary in the transportation of the plants, but some alterations Mr. Portlock made in her masts and sails at the Cape of Good Hope increased her rate of sailing to nearly that of the *Providence*.

15th

At noon the latitude 21°..56' south, longitude by direct reckoning 25°..06 west, thermometer 76°. A shark and several dolphins, were taken with hook and line, the latter about three feet in length. I should say nothing of a fish so often described as the dolphin, but that the representations of it, even in the very best prints to books of natural history, are erroneous. Perhaps the accompanying drawing will give you a better idea of its shape and colour than any thing that can come from my pen.† I have never seen them above five feet in length. In the water they appear of a brilliant light blue, but after being taken on board, and in their approaches to death, become so variegated that any effort at description must fail. The back (dorsal) fin extends nearly the whole length of the fish. The two swiftest fish we know of are the dolphin and bonito, yet nothing can be so different in shape. The former is like a vertical wedge, and to use a shipwright's

---

*   Nereides: sea nymphs.
†   See Plate 19.

term, is all run from the head to the tail, while the latter, whose thickness is about two fifths from the head, and is a round full fish, has an entrance nearly as sharp as the run. They are both often quoted as models to build from. In my own mind I have no doubt but the bonito is the fastest of the two, and as to turning or changing its course it has evidently the advantage. In striking at these fish with grains* or harpoon, the bonito, although presenting a broader mark, is by far the most difficult to hit. The albacore has much of the character of the bonito but considerably larger. They are all to be caught with hook and line, and it may be considered a kind of salt water fly fishing, the bait generally being an artificial flying fish towing near the surface. As you are a frequent voyager, I would recommend when you attempt this sport, to use a very long line with a wire snood of at least twelve feet, and with a spar, guy the line over the ship's quarter, so that the bait may tow clear of the wake. The line should be stopped at the end of the spar with a bit of packthread which of course will be broken when a fish takes the bait, but if you wish to be informed without constant watching, you may attach a small bell to the line inside of the packthread. I have entered so much into detail, as I remember you in early days, a keen fisher on the banks of the Avon, before you had scarcely heard of the dolphin, the bonito or the albacore. Of the former indeed, you daily saw a representation at the inn at Southampton which no doubt was as like a dolphin as 'a whale'.

The shark taken had a number of young ones about eighteen inches long in its inside. This I have frequently noticed in the shark and dogfish, but in no other case. The latter, indeed, may be considered as belonging to the shark tribe. The catching of a shark generally occasions some bustle on board, and though I believe sailors to have just as much abhorrence of cruelty as other people, every kind of barbarity is too often exercised on these rapacious fish when taken, probably calculating on as little mercy from the shark, was the case reversed. There is indeed something particularly savage about this monster, but it never fell within my own observation the seizure of a man by them, however much I have been in latitudes where they abound. Nor did I ever meet among my numerous acquaintance, any one person who had seen it. After the case of Brook Watson† and others nearly as well authenticated, I have no right to doubt of its having occurred, but I believe that I am not much in error by supposing the stories we hear of people being destroyed by sharks are, in general, without foundation. Their size, too, perhaps is much overrated. I rather think that I never saw one above twelve feet in length. We read often of their being nearly twice as long. Sailors consider that there are two kinds, the brown and the blue. The latter is frequently seen on the coasts of Europe. There is also the shovel-nosed shark, so called from the formation of the head. With nearly as much avidity as they are

---

*   grains: fishing spears with two or more prongs.
†   Sir Brook Watson, baronet, lost his leg to a shark in Havana harbour in 1749 when he was fourteen years old. He lived until 1807.

caught, all are eaten by seamen whose stomachs seem disciplined to every kind of fare.

30th

Latitude 28°..59' south, longitude 48' east of Greenwich. Albatrosses and pintado (in Spanish painted) birds,* had been about us, from soon after passing the southern tropic. The latter is about the size of a pigeon, webfooted, and in form like a duck, beautifully brown and white spotted on the back, with black head, bills, legs and white breast, but as was said of the dolphin, it were better for you to look at the sketch.† They are only to be seen in the southern hemisphere. By baiting a small hook to a piece of gut or neat horse hair line they may be taken.

The albatross is perhaps the largest of aquatic birds; its colour like the gull (and I believe all sea birds) depends upon age and climate. Some are of a dark brown or grey, some nearly white, and others black and white. On examining one sometime after at Tasmania, it was found to have a joint more in its wing than birds in general. (I rather imagine that the common shearwater, the man of war bird, and a few others have this joint). The feathers, particularly on the neck and breast, are of a thick close texture, and common duck shot had no effect in bringing them down, except under the wings or on the head.

The astonishing length of the wings of the albatross, and weight of the sheep's tails in this part of the world, is what the young voyager hears enough of to raise his curiosity and stagger his belief in his way to 'The Cape'. Of the latter, I shall perhaps speak as we proceed. Of the albatross examined at Tasmania – and it did not in the least differ from those about the Cape – my veracity will not allow the wings, when extended to their utmost limit, to exceed seven feet. Often have I been told of their exceeding twice this length. Nor, have I any right to doubt it. The body of the bird was about the size of that of a goose. The flight of the albatross is rapid and majestic. By the hour I have watched them with immoved wings making their circle high in air, as if weary of skimming o'er the surface of the breaking bellow, watchfully in search of prey.[4] When at the latter tack, their motion is astonishingly rapid, yet so close to the surface that, in the hollow of the intervening wave, (until by a slight motion of the wing, that seems scarcely a hair's breadth from the water, they appear above it) they are shut out from view. These like the pintado birds are only to be met with in southern latitudes. They are caught by baiting a small hook, but a more certain way is to fasten several hooks to the line, and jerking it quickly when they partially settle on the water, catch them by the feet. This method I have heard Captain Bligh describe, and that, in the passage of the *Bounty* near Cape Horn, a great number

---

*   Pintado birds are most likely terns.
†   See Plate 8.

were taken, and being kept in hen coops and crammed – with oatmeal – after a few days became tolerably palatable.

A porpoise was struck with the harpoon but disengaged itself. The rest instantly disappeared. It is a received opinion by seamen that a wounded porpoise ever becomes the prey of the rest. For this fact I cannot pretend to vouch, but certain it is that when one of these fish is wounded, the others instantly disappear. I have seen (you must excuse this egotism) the porpoise in every clime, apparently of the same kind, a circumstance rather remarkable.* In your little museum at home, you have in excellent preservation the skeleton of the head of one, brought to England in the *Providence*. The snout or proboscis of which, in a great measure, resembles the bill of a bird. Probably they have acquired the name of bottlenose, by seamen, from this circumstance. It appears to me that all the whale and porpoise species have a horizontal tail. None of them are ever taken by hook and line.

For several nights there had been a luminous appearance in the sea, particularly where agitated by the progress of the ship. As vast numbers of what are vulgarly called blubbers† were about, it proceeded most probably from them.

November 3rd

A sea-bird called a Cape Hen was seen in the morning. It is about the size of a common fowl, of a brown colour, with a white spot on each wing, being very heavy in its flight. They were afterwards noticed at St. Helena. I have since seen them in the Bay of Biscay.

The ship passed through a quantity of what is called, fish's spawn, some of which was taken on board appearing through a magnifying glass in transparent globules like jelly, of the colour of the water, about the size of a pea. These contained numbers of small yellow specks, but no animation was discoverable. The luminous appearance before mentioned, it can hardly be doubted, proceeds from these and various other marine substances. Indeed, I have seen it confirmed by their being taken on board. It is denied me to describe these to you as accurately as my inclinations lead; much indeed do I lament my inability, but it is a sailor, not a philosopher, who addresses you. I can tell you the colour of a bird, a fish, or an animal, as well as their shape and size; but exactly of what species, or to what genus they belong, I am in the dark.

Of what are nautically called blubbers, there are a great variety in every part of the ocean. Some are as large as a puncheon, others formed like a snake, of colours so brilliant as not to be described, six or seven yards in length. The most common one, in form very similar to the mushroom, when in the water evidently possesses animation, making a regular but very slow course. Others I have seen cut in halves without their being apparently susceptible of pain, no

---

*   There are over thirty species of porpoise.
†   blubbers: jellyfish.

spasm or convulsion taking place. The truly elegant little animal, called the Portuguese man of war, is among the latter number. The whole of these certainly communicate the luminous effect in the sea, so often noticed by navigators. Indeed every fish does it, and a school of dolphins, porpoises or bonitos playing round a ship at night are to be distinguished nearly as plainly as in the day time and often fall by the well directed aim of the grains or harpoon. It should be remarked that many of the blubber species, on coming in contact with the human body, sting and inflame it to a considerable degree of pain.

On the subject of the luminous appearance of the ocean, recollection carries one some years back to a voyage in the course of which it was exhibited in a very strong degree. It had been calm for some days, a great quantity of the small globules before mentioned being around us, when a breeze springing up, increased by night to a strong gale and a following sea, enabling us to make a progress of eight or ten miles an hour, through what might be called a sea of liquid fire to the utmost horizon. The waves rolling after us on either quarter, were particularly grand, nor was the sky without partaking of this sublime effect. A book of common sized print was easily perused by the reflection from the more agitated water at the ships bows.

As we approached the southern cape of Africa, numbers of whales were seen, more indeed than ever fell under my observation, or indeed since, in any part of the world. It is not extravagant to suppose that they find food on the bank extending from this promontory. I am ignorant what the sustenance of the whale consists of, but the fishermen of Bermuda, where the *Thetis* has lately been, say that of a calm night they frequently, when in their boats, hear the whales feeding on sea grass at the bottom.* I cannot here help remarking on the whale fishery at Bermuda, which is carried on by boats a few months in the spring, that the people concerned in it recently requested (such is reported to me) the admiral not to fire the morning and evening gun, as it drove the whales away. If fish do not possess the organs of hearing, this request was unnecessary, or was it the concussion that made them withdraw? We must not quit the whales, without observing that at Bermuda the flesh is frequently eaten, selling at four pence and five pence the pound. It is not inferior to indifferent veal.

6th

Gannets were now seen, a certain indication of being in soundings, or the margin of it. From repeated observation in many parts of the world, I never found the appearance of the gannet deceive in this aspect. The land about Table Bay was soon in sight, the Sugar Loaf – a high pyramidical mountain, bearing east, southeast. The latitude at noon was observed in 33°..56' south.

---

*   Whales do not feed on sea grass, however, some of their communication among themselves sounds like a clicking sound to humans.

In the evening we anchored in Table Bay, in less than five fathoms, mooring with a cable each way, the best bower to the westward and the small to the opposite quarter. The north point of the bay north 28° east, Sugar Loaf south 79° west, steeple in Cape Town south 50° west, about a mile from the wharf. In the bay were several vessels of different nations from India, the American continent, and Europe.

7th

The fort in the morning returned our salute with an equal number of guns, and we began dismantling the two vessels, to refit for the voyage. For the present adieu, I have now got you to this renowned Cape, after the doubling of which, I become licensed to deal in marvellous tales, nor dare a suspicion be thrown on my veracity.

CHAPTER 2ND
November-December 1791

Robben Island.—Captain Hunter.—Southeast gales.—Fiscal.—Place of punishment.—Slave girls.—Slavery.—Oaks.—Company's garden.—Table Mountain.—Boarding houses.—Eating and smoking.—English naval lieutenant.—Dutch landlady.—Penal laws, religion.—Library, hospitals.— Great plenty.—French regiments.—Mynheer La L—s.—Carriages.—Hotten-tots.—Cape story.—A Party up the country to Elsenburg; the Paarl Rock; &c. &c.—Ostriches.—Snake.—Nova Scotia.—Klapmuts.—Stellenbosch.—Distance calculated by time.—Return to Cape Town.—Thermometer.—Variation of the compass.—

Thetis, off Bermuda January 1797

Most of our voyagers find materials for a long chapter in their description of the Cape Town and its environs. It is a beaten track, but I endeavoured to cull something. On approaching the coast about Table Bay, it appears barren and mountainous. To the northward of it about eight miles we passed Robben Island, whose chief inhabitants are convicts from the Cape Town, guarded by a small military force. From this island communication by signal is made to the continent of the approach of vessels. The employment of the slaves is chiefly in working limestone for The Company. The island abounds with quails, and a great variety of the chameleon, of the latter several were to be seen at Cape Town. On either side of Robben Island there is access to Table Bay; the *Providence* entered by the western passage, which it would seem is the best. It is necessary to keep well towards the shore of the continent, by which means you are prepared to meet the strong southeast winds prevalent at this season. During our stay many instance of vessels not being able to secure an anchorage occurred, from their not having taken this precaution. The south and southeast winds rage with such violence that, if a ship does not fetch in, without the sails well reefed and can turn up, she will be driven to sea. The *Waarzaamheid*, Dutch snow,* having on board Captain Hunter and the remainder of the crew of His Majesty's ship, *Sirius*, wrecked in the month of March 1790 on Norfolk Island near New South Wales, was driven over on the east side of the bay, from whence she soon parted her anchors and was forced to sea. Some days after she returned and, by keeping nearer the mainland, reached a secure situation. The sufferings of Captain Hunter needed no addition. I was with him a short hour before his

---

*   snow: a small sailing vessel resembling a brig.

being driven out; he had indeed, almost set his foot on this shore of renovating plenty. An arduous passage of nearly eight months from the land of transportation had in his worn countenance, as well as in those of his shipmates, depicted a claim to rest. It was denied them yet a few days, when, with the assistance of our boats, the vessel was placed in proper safety. Theirs was the return from difficulty and danger. Ours the outset for what might happen.

On leaving the bay and passing on the east side of Robben Island, a good offing is generally secured by a strong southerly wind. During the winter no Dutch ships are allowed to remain in Table Bay, as the north and northwest winds then blow with violence. False Bay at that season is where they are ordered to anchor in. As a proof of the power of the southeast gales, it is a fact that, although a mile from the shore, the sand and small gravel was forced on board and indeed completely whitened the rigging which had been fresh tarred. In the town, while these gusts continue, there is great difficulty in walking about.

There is only one good landing place, which is at a wharf built of wood. Here The Company's hoys* take in and discharge cargoes afloat with ease. On the wharf is a guard house, and no boats, on any account, are suffered to land after a certain hour at night. As well as the military guard, there are officers belonging to the Fiscal whose duty it is to attend the shipping and landing of goods, for which fees, and some not very moderate, are exacted. The appointment of the Fiscal with respect to emolument is said to be even superior to that of the governor, and it was observed to us that they are generally on very good terms. Both the sailor from without and farmer from within, feel the power of the Fiscal, and that they are exciseable. A short distance from the wharf, surrounded by a ditch, is situated the fort, on the town and country side of which is a drawbridge. There is a battery of considerable strength to the northward of the town, and a smaller one near the point, forming the western side of the bay. Were one to judge of the strength of this place by the fortifications, it would seem tenable against a powerful force, but the military are not numerous, or unanimous in favour of the government. It was also said that, notwithstanding the apparent strength of the works, they were by no means well appointed, and a caution to strangers desirous of inspecting them rather confirmed this. Yet during the last war with Great Britain, the Dutch expended fifteen million of guelders towards building and repairing them. There is a militia throughout the settlement, but it was doubted whether, on the appearance of an English fleet, any would be found leaving their farms to resist the invaders. More confidence however seemed to be placed in them by the executive alarm signals being established to a considerable distance up the country.

The town is a little to the northwest of the fort, near which you pass a place of execution enclosed by a wall, but with free admittance for everyone. In

---

* The Company: the Dutch East India Company; hoys: small vessels, usually rigged as sloops (two triangular sails), and employed in carrying passengers and goods, particularly in short distances on the sea-coast.

addition to the gibbet are many cross pieces of wood secured to the ground for breaking criminals on. Humanity shuddered at beholding the marks where some poor wretches had suffered, however guilty they might have been. On a building at one end of the court, is the following inscription

Felex quem facuint aliena pericula cautum*
Anno 1771

From this place of horror, such as thank God is not to be found in our own isle or its colonies† and having before passed a number of despicable little tents inhabited by people of colour who sell liquor, vegetables, ostriches eggs, and other articles to the seamen, a stranger on his first landing forms no very favourable opinion of the town. He will so be agreeably disappointed. It is in general well built, the streets regular, and at right angles with each other, their names being on all of them. Including those up the valley formed by the Table and Devil Mountains, the houses exceed a thousand. The major part are white, with green doors and window-shutters. This partiality of the Dutch for green, is to be seen in all their settlements, and their shipping also partake of it. The houses of the better sort of people are large and commodious, being strongly built of brick and in general two storey high, roofed with durable thatch of reeds. In the middle is a large hall, where the industrious mistress of the mansion usually sits, surrounded by a number of pretty slave girls of various shades, at work keeping them under 'the strict observance of her eye'. They are, to an inconvenience, clean – the houses (not the girls I speak of) – and the most rigid method and punctuality is to be met with in the domestic concerns of their owners, who are as regular as their own town clock.

As I am on slavery, it is impossible to keep from expressing the satisfaction it yielded me, to see this 'bitter draught' administered with more mildness and humanity than I had ever before observed it. I particularly allude to the household domestics of the various families I was in the habit of visiting. Yet was it said that the stretch of power is ofttimes exercised to a cruel degree, but a residence (I may say) of nearly two months at the Cape never gave me an opportunity of asserting it to be the case. In the houses there was an unrestrained manner between the owner and the slave, which, as it did not diminish the power of the former, nor produce inattention and disrespect in the latter, could not but create a pleasing sensation in the mind of the observer. The Cape Town slaves appear cheerful and content; the produce of the soil on which they move, ever ensures them plenty, and there is a degree of emulation in their dress, particularly among the females, almost bordering on coquetry. In an evening they commonly resort to the dancing houses, and the master does not feel his dignity wounded by frequently mixing in the dance, or being the musician to his

---

*   Translation: happy is he whom the danger of others makes cautious.
†   See Chapter 9th for a quite different observation on the British criminal justice
     system.

own slave. Very few slaves had been imported for some years into the colony, nor indeed had been found necessary. The mild temperature of the climate, abundance of nutritious food, and kind treatment had rather increased their population, and scarcely a house was to be seen but what teemed with healthy children of all hues.

In what has been said above, it is not meant indiscriminately to reflect on the proprietors of the human race in our own colonies, nor would it come graciously from one partaking of creole blood. I have seen happiness unclouded, even in the field Negro, who from the 'rising of the sun to the going down of the same', ceaselessly labours to gratify the luxurious palate of the 'whiter man'. In him I have beheld content and gratitude – however hard his lot – for kindness from his master; yet truth, incontrovertible truth, obliges me to declare that, it is not always the case. But to what quarter are we to cast our eyes, and not find, in some instances, power exercised with an iron hand? Let us hope that the recent investigation of this subject has tended to ameliorate the condition of the slaves in the West Indies.* Such cannot but be the cordial wish of every feeling heart.

As to the legality of this heart-rending traffic, or its abolition, custom seems to have sanctioned the former, but for the latter, some little acquaintance with the cultivation of a sugar plantation disposes me to believe that the abolition could not but be attended with the decline of the colonies and consequently a severe loss to the revenue of the mother country. Yet waiving this political consideration, how is the proprietor to be indemnified? This is in common justice due to him. Do this and abolish, if after due consideration, it be deemed proper. Enable the planter to fix his abode in a more genial climate, relinquish all those islands which have proved the Golgotha of so very many of our gallant troops and seamen in giving them a temporary security.[1] Do this, and even more. The British name has ever been conspicuous for humane and generous execution. If the rabble tribe, hitherto employed in tilling the ground for our acquired gratifications, wish to return to their native soil,

> Where the parent shall with rapture run
> To welcome back the long lost son
> And mingle tear with tear
> Let them not wish in vain.
> Launch then the bark, unfurl the impatient sails
> Swell ye kind seas, and blow ye fost'ring gales,
> Oh haste some angel, thro' the realms of air
> To Affric's sons, Britannia's tidings bear.
>
> And now they trace each scene of former love,
> Explore each favour'd haunt, hill vale and grove,
> And soon the well remember'd huts they find,

---

* The first serious Parliamentary debate on abolishing the slave trade took place in 1789.

> Where faithful friends and loves were left behind
> Sudden before her sable lord appears
> Th'enfranchis'd wife, adorned with faithful tears;
> Mothers again their kidnapp'd babes behold
> Sons clasps their sires in slavery grown old.

This would indeed be a work of humanity, but as has before been observed, it would be unjust, without at the same time fully remunerating their owners.

Before quitting the subject, it may be remarked that, during our stay at the Cape, several French vessels, some of large burden, arrived under the national colours, seeming almost to speak 'liberty and freedom', with cargoes of slaves. It was at a period when every heart expanded on witnessing the struggles a great nation was making towards that freedom so well understood in our own happy isle, and without calculating on the possibility of the ensanguined horrors which we know but too well, fill a frightful space in the picture of the French Revolution. Horrors, to which it would seem there is yet no limit. The arrival of these vessels, and with cargoes of the human species, was certainly rather inconsistent with the prevailing French sentiments of 'Liberty and Equality'. They were from the eastern coast of Africa, destined to St. Domingo. The masters all agreed that they were to be purchased at one fourth of the price given on the western coast. Indeed, the master of an English whaler at the Cape assured me that, in the Mozambique Passage a slave had been sold to him for a bottle of brandy, not with an intention of again disposing of him, but being in want of a servant boy, and that he could have purchased many more at nearly the same value. The French are, I believe, the only nation who carry slaves from the east coast of Africa to the sugar colonies.

These slaves differed from those on the Guinea coast in the women all having the upper lip perforated, and in both sexes the wool* being eradicated. They were in a sickly state, and the whole of them infected with a kind of itch or leprosy, nor were the Frenchmen totally free from the disease. Yet in justice to their hospitality it should be noticed that, on some of the officers from the *Providence* visiting these vessels, it was suggested to them that they should not be restricted in any thing their wishes inclined them to on board; our Gallic neighbours probably grudging they had no right to monopolise such a desirable infection.

Oaks have been planted in a few of the streets which, as well as having a pleasant appearance, render the houses near them cool during the sun's heat, which at times is intense. The Batavian taste for water even 'should it cream and mantle' here finds its votaries, scarcely a street being without its ditch, which indeed, is often enough dry. At the upper part of the town are The Company's gardens, and still higher in the valley the country retirements of different gentlemen; some of these houses bear a very romantic appearance. Far beyond, it is bounded by the Table Land, which seems to overhang and threaten the whole

---

*   wool: hair.

settlement, and the Lion's Head, a pyramidical mountain, whence signals to the town are repeated from Robben Island. A little to the southeast of the Table Land is the Devil's Head, and below the Lion's Head, another mountain of a more level form called Theason's Rump. These towering heights, sometimes 'cloud topp'd', varying 'lift their awful form'.

Swell from the vale and midway leave the storm.

If the expression may be allowed, form an amphitheatre for the town. At the upper end of The Company's gardens is a menagerie of some extent. It was but poorly supplied, there being nothing but a few ostriches and some different kinds of deer.

The garden is so truly regular that the eye of an Englishman is distressed by it, while he laments that the ground, as it has the capability,* was not laid out by a countryman of his own. In length it is about a thousand paces, and in breadth a third as much, divided at right angles in walks with hedges of oak, trimmed and kept in the most exact order, by the sides of which run small streams of water bordered by myrtle. Formal as is the garden, the stranger is not a little surprised and pleased after the unfavourable impression received on his approach to this apparently barren coast. There is a shaded walk of about an hundred paces overspread with oak, of singular beauty and retirement. It bears the name of the 'Lovers' Walk' from an unfortunate relaxation of the heart which took place not many years previously to our arrival, and too often recounted at the Cape with cold severity. It was here, unheedful of the future, a gay adventurer, made it his successful study,

To teach a damsel t'was no sin to love.

It was the intention of The Company that their shipping and hospital should be supplied from this garden, but the vegetables in it were so neglected, that few fell to the lot of either. It was said that in the former governor's time the garden boasted a very fine collection of exotic plants. The Company's garden may be said to be the only place of fashionable resort at the Cape, yet was it seldom numerously attended. Of a fine Sunday some pretty female faces were to be seen, but in general its chief visitors were the different strangers at the settlement. Here the governor has a house of much neatness and retirement, with a well arranged flower garden in the centre of which a fountain plays its water to some height.

I am now about to lead you to the summit of the Table Mountain, and if I feel as much wearied as when it was really accomplished, it will be the means of ensuring me a good night's repose. The mountain is only accessible to the pedestrian traveller, but the loose stones over which he is obliged to scramble renders it a laborious undertaking. At about half way it was found very refreshing

---

*   capability: a pun of the name of the famous eighteenth-century garden designer, Lancelot 'Capability' Brown.

to rest near a small fall of water which issued from the fissure of a rock. Here ran infinite variety of beautiful shrubs and plants, (which indeed was the case the whole of our walk) attracted our admiration, and the more so as there appeared scarcely any soil to give them nourishment. Contriving to ascend great industry was exercised in finding excuses to rest, by the extensive prospect this acclivity* affords. In about three hours from leaving the town, the summit was gained, through a chasm in which there was a foot path nearly perpendicular. To our great regret a heavy cloud soon settled on the mountain, but ere being enveloped in it, we were allowed a glimpse of the grand and picturesque view to be seen from this eminence. The shipping in Table Bay appeared 'insignificantly minute'. Yet, as if at a single vault, we could be at the cheerful board of our associates in travel and indeed, there was so much to encounter in retracing our steps downwards that an aerial journey would have been far more desirable. Yet exercise was absolutely necessary, as there was a degree of cold humidity in the cloud which clothed us, hardly supportable. A little boy of the party who had climbed the ragged steep without shoes, stockings, or a single murmur, wept bitterly at the unwelcome visitor, and much did we all rejoice when below it there was a different climate. Fortunately the party had not separated or wandered far, or great would have been the difficulty of finding the narrow passage by which the summit was reached. As far as could be seen the surface of the mountain was nearly level, in some parts swampy and in others of a hard rocky substance, but everywhere well clothed with shrubs and underwood. No animals were seen but a jackal, nor any great variety of the feathered tribe. At the Cape it was said that snipes are frequently to be found in numbers on the swampy part of the Table Land. It was eleven at night before the party reached our boarding house – completely jaded and fatigued.

Some of the officers in a visit to the mountain saw numbers of large baboons; these, the inhabitants informed us, make great depredations on the gardens near the town. Some runaway slaves were dispersed about the mountain, seeming to feel security from their situation, their fires being frequently seen, even at midday.

To the eastward of the town the land is low for a considerable distance, very swampy, and in many parts abounding with dangerous quicksands. This flat country separates Table from False Bay, and over it the southeast winds rage with much violence. In an excursion up the country after passing this part of it, they were no longer felt, but on our return, immediately on entering the plain they again assailed us. You shall have a sketch of this expedition in due time; it was as cheerful and as happy a week as I ever knew, but, as we have descended the Table Land, a few more remarks are due to the town and its inhabitants ere taking leave of them.

The pride of the Cape Dutchman, in whatever situation he moves, is not wounded by taking boarders to his house, many of them indeed gain a livelihood

---

*   acclivity: ascending slope.

by the European and other visitors. Mynheer Horack, who, should you ever reach this promontory, I beg to introduce to your acquaintance as a very worthy man, an indefatigable traveller and a keen sportsman, charged us only six English shillings per day for plenty of everything, and 'good of its kind'; with the use of his servants, both male and female. The former we found useful in attending us about the town and its environs, and I need not tell you who have crossed the Atlantic, how much the assistance of a notable one of the other sex is required, to put in order various articles, sometimes the worse for wear by the tossing and tumbling of a long voyage. Horack's damsels, (being used to boarders from on 'shipboard',) knew this, felt for us, and even anticipated our wants with the charity due to a stranger in a foreign land.

If we did murmur a little – and the Englishman generally does – it was at the thinness of the Cape wine, and the custom handed down to us as almost inimical to our salvation, that of rising with the cloth. To innovate on a Dutchman's domestic concerns would be fruitless, and indeed unpardonable, but as we were allowed to do as 'seemed fitting' in our own chambers, there was generally a case of good claret in one corner with which the English gentlemen regaled themselves. And it was once or twice known to be brought to the general table, even after the removal of the cloth.

Self-denial in eating is not much practised, and the Cape Town inhabitant has hardly finished his meal ere he betakes himself to repose for two or three hours, when he rises to coffee, and to him, the vivifying fumes of tobacco, nor is smoking confined to this part of the day, scarcely an hour passing without the pipe being brought into action. No business, no pleasure, impedes this solace; were any one function of life to be performed without the beloved pipe, doubtless there would be left something yet to wish for. In our walks about the country, even at mid-day, it was not uncommon to meet parties at full gallop whose persons could be scarcely distinguished amid the smoke from their pipes and dust from their horses feet. The pipe is a travelling companion and of course not of that brittle texture used in England.

Content and how enviable – save a little party bickering – seemed to be well understood at the Cape. If the Dutchman eats grossly and is generally enveloped in smoke, he keeps his head cool, and his blood free from the enervating effects of too sedulous an attention to the bottle. Ill health is here seldom produced by this certain means. Mynheer tells you that he is renovated by his pipe and his afternoon's nap, and it would be placing too high an opinion on our own habits and customs to doubt it. The quiet undisturbed fancy he possesses – happily for him – acts much in his favour. He is either a farmer, or a man of trade, and the increase of his funds appears his chief consideration. Yet are some to be met with full of information and research, but in general it is not the case. Ask what are the productions of the Table Land? He was never there, although hanging over his own roof. How far the interior of the country has been explored? 'He does not know, he always resided at the Cape and business never carried him beyond its limits.' At business he is expert and ingenious and quite at home in making a bargain. Yet has he been sometimes taken in even by honest (as we are called) John Bull. There is a story told which, from the novelty and ingenuity of the crime, makes one disposed to lean favourably toward the offender. Several years ago an English naval lieutenant on his passage to Europe from the East Indies found himself so deeply in debt to his Dutch landlord at the Cape that he almost despaired of being able to satisfy him. The hour fast approached for the departure of his ship. Mynheer became clamorous, demanding payment, or threatening a gaol. In vain did the poor debt-contracting lieutenant urge his incapacity without 'doing what would much distress his feelings and be a bar to his future prospects' but, as it was his only resource, and gaining a promise from his creditor not to promulgate the affair until after the sailing of the ship, he blushingly hinted at the sale of his commission,* which he assured him, would bear in England more than twice the value of the debt. The bait took, Mynheer got the commission, and the lieutenant was once more seated among his messmates.

It was not until eight months afterwards that the parchment was returned to the Cape by Mynheer's correspondent in London, informing him of the precise value of naval commissions. This poor man, it was said, sunk considerably in the estimation of his neighbours, for allowing himself to be outwitted by an Englishman. But our countrymen, go where they may, are ever involved in scrapes and difficulties, nor do they always extricate themselves as easily as this lieutenant. Yet the innocent sometimes suffer for the guilty.

It is not half a century since a poor youth, pure and unsinoring,† nearly got his eyes pulled out by the talons of an 'outrageously virtuous' dame of the Cape Town; not knowing for what he suffered. ✶✶✶✶✶ a wicked wag, an officer of the same ship, had wantonly conceived the horrible plan of fixing antlers on the temples‡ of the good spouse of the blue eyed *vrouw* at whose house they lodged. Employed in domestic affairs, she little suspected that these were his wicked designs. Several days passed without his making any progress. His passion now became 'impatient of controll'; what he suffered was 'misery in the extreme', and to gain the 'sought relief' the night was fixed – but all within himself – to effect what he had vainly hoped the language of the eyes would have taught the dame was necessary to his happiness.

The 'host', though a man of general sobriety, was so charged by the hero who intended cornuting** his brows, that, on the breaking up of the evening, he was left on a chair in the arms of sleep and ebriety. The lover had not indulged so copiously, but 'Warm and full of blood Unhappily he stole into her chamber'. The good wife was anxiously waiting the arrival of her lord. Unfortunate ✶✶✶✶✶

---

*   sale of his commission: eighteenth-century British naval commissions, unlike those in the army, could not be bought and sold.
†   unsinoring: without sin.
‡   fixing antlers on the temples: to cuckold, to have sexual relations with another man's wife.
** cornuting: horning or cuckolding.

why with unhallowed intent didst thou aspire to his place? Yet, was all auspicious to his wishes; he had barricaded the outside of the common entrance to 'my Lady's Chamber' and secured, like an able general, a retreat by a small private door contiguous to his own room, in case of an alarm. The darkness of the night favoured the approach of our hero. He was thought the 'good man of the house' was chided and reproved, yet fondly, for his long absence. 'Twas in exchanging an amorous kiss of ductile conciliation – one of those lengthened kisses, which most of the children of love are frail enough to industriously covet – the almost melting dame first gently grasped the tail of her tongue-tied bedfellow. Disastrous and ill-timed discovery. Why ***** dist thou forget, in thy wicked designs, that on the bald pate of our host no tail was to be found?

Hardly when she first took hold of it, could she believe what it was. Her hand glided o'er it, from the end even unto the very setting on of the hair, as with her four fingers and thumb she yet doubting, encircled it – still 'twas the same. She thought it odd. 'Twas a long tail, and else a thick one. One of those kind of tails which in these days of 'croppism' would be thought a bore, such an one as her husband, in his younger days, had suspended from his pole. Still did she doubt. Again she clasped it, closer and closer. Another pressure removed her doubts, for now it came – conviction came – and just in time, that it was an exotic, and not Mynheer's.

Rage here took place in that beating bosom, which but a short moment before, was all pliancy and admission. The tail which had just filled her soft hand, now fell pendulous, while with a spring the lover, in all the agonies of disappointment, was thrown from those joys only to be reaped by her hairless headed husband. The enraged wife hastened to the larger door to alarm the house, while ***** in the dark stole through his private retreat and feigned that sleep all his fellow lodgers really enjoyed.

The door yielded to her vindictive pressure; it opened outwards, at the back of which were placed chairs, tables, and every article of furniture the house afforded, nor must be forgotten, several large brass, highly polished ponderous spitting pots. All tumbling down stairs, in no very 'regular disorder'. The whole mansion was alarmed – even the hero whose eye had dwelt meretriciously on the fair mistress of it. Mynheer only still sacrificed to Morpheus. Each pleaded innocent, nor could the guilty violator be discovered, and until the succeeding morn all was hushed in quiet – but before *****, whose tail was now tucked within his cap, convinced the good lady of the danger in exposing so much beauty to the night air, while barely sheltered by the garment next to her skin.

It was at breakfast that the tail of poor unoffending ***** first caught her eye. As far as she could assimilate what she had felt to her visual organs, the first glimpse convinced her 'twas the tail so chilling to her conjugal expectations. She eyed it 'with neck retorted and oblique regard'. She compared the length – the thickness – the very form and extremity of it. All bespoke it the same tail. Ill placed tail, how didst thou frustrate the achievements of our hero, even when on the verge of all he wished. She was convinced there could be no difference in a tail whether the sun or moon shed their rays on it. 'Twas the same she was positive, and, as 'the woman who deliberates is lost', with all the fury of an injured and disappointed fair one, she seized upon the poor lieutenant, while the daring ravisher silently enjoyed the sufferings of his messmate. Against the assaulted every angry term the female tongue could utter was most copiously dealt out, but as the Batavian language was not among his acquirements, she had recourse to what, in his own country, is called 'club law', and it was with some difficulty, although innocent as a babe, he made his escape, most sorely wounded from this second Lucretia.

With the laws of this colony I am not sufficiently versed to speak accurately but it would seem that the penal ones are exercised with a severity, tending to check the extension of crimes. A place of dreadful execution has been already noticed, and at the point forming the bay, as well as eastward of the town, several gibbets meet the eye with the culprits suspended from them as a sad warning that the law is not to be trespassed with impunity.

Religion is so tolerated that there are many roads for a man to make his choice of, nor does the Frenchman, the German, or the native of our own country, feel heavier penalties than the Dutch. Several places of religious worship open their doors to strangers. The only one I visited was the Lutheran Church, the inside of which exhibited some taste and the essence of cleanliness, while the good pastor, who seemed very much in earnest, exercised his lungs extempore nearly an hour and a half on 'the stretch'. The sexes occupied different sides of the church.

There is a public library and a well arranged hospital. The former, I was given to understand, did not boast many valuable productions.

It would seem that the power of The Company is very enlarged, and as to profit, they have nearly the whole. It is not surprising then that the hardy industrious settlers should eagerly pant for a revolution in the government. After the labour and difficulties of driving their flocks from the distant interior, they dare not affix their own price to them. Their perseverance, which is astonishing, by this coercion receives an insurmountable check. They murmur without reserve, yet still feel the power of the Fiscal. Perhaps there is no spot in the habitable globe so improvable as this promontory, or from its peculiar situation, that ought to be so open to new settlers, but this is only to be effected under the influence and protection of a mild and liberal government, not in the cupidity of a chartered company feeling but for itself. Very different encouragement should be held out, and were it the case, it is not far from extravagant to believe that at no very remote period the ingenious manufacturers would find equal employment with the industrious husbandman. But while the Batavian flag and the same system lord it over this fine extent of territory, such a prospect appears indeed distant. Yet, with all these sad drawbacks, I never saw plenty to so full an extent as in the neighbourhood of the Cape.

In the late war two French regiments formed part of the garrison, and from their intercourse with the inhabitants, the French language became more known than other foreign ones. There was indeed scarcely a genteel person of either sex but what had some acquaintance with it, and never did your friend so sorely feel his ignorance of it, as in this place.

Your father's estimable friend, Mr. Hope, had furnished me with letters of credit and introduction for the Dutch settlements at which we were to touch in the voyage. Among the rest was one for Mynheer La L—s, a gentleman of much importance at Cape Town. Soon after our arrival I waited on him with my credentials. It was unknowingly at the unseasonable hour, that with Mrs. La L—s, Mr. La L—s was – taking his nap – but his daughter, who perhaps had not yet been initiated in this indulgence, a lovely girl about eighteen with blue eyes fully charged with softness, met me at the portal.

There is a disposition in the human frame at the sight of beauty to approximate rather than recede. It has been so since the creation of Eve. And so will it continue. There was nothing haughty or repellent in the fair Batavian. Not a muscle – if muscles they could be called – in her fine full form had that resilient tendency, sometimes seen so chilling to 'the stranger in a foreign land'. Encouraged by a look, I shall long bear about with me, I addressed her in our own language. The language of Botany Bay would have been equally successful. In return she tried one in French and as unprofitably. 'Twas a blank still. Beauteous girl, thought I, are we not both from the same Adam? Were we not cast in a similar mould? Why then this perplexing, the untoward meeting? There is a language travelling in thine eye but too well understood by all, that would subdue the stern resolves of a monk of La Trappe. On presenting Mr. Hope's letter, she smiled at my distress, but it was a smile far removed from rudeness or contempt. 'Twas one of those cheering, ineffable, smiles encouraging to the human heart, and for which I looked as much gratitude as my eyes could convey. What I felt was abundant. A soft hand received what brought us to this embarrassment, and glancing her eye on the superscription she was about to trip upstairs, saying *Il est pour mon père.* But thinking that Mr. and Mrs. La L—s might not have yet consummated the nap they proposed on retiring, charity to their comforts – it was that alone I believe – prompted me to stop their fair daughter from disturbing them. She had only made one step in the road to her papa and mamma with my letter in one hand, when I found the other compressed in both mine. It was rapidly journeying to my lips, or rather my lips to it. In a moment they would have met, but ere that moment arrived, tranquillity was taught us by the approach of Pearce, who, no bankrupt in the Gallic tongue, explained my business to the young lady. So that Mr. and Mrs. La L—s were not disturbed in the enjoyment of their repose.

In the evening I was received with much good breeding by Mr. La L—s, who assured me that his attention should not be wanting to render my stay at the Cape as pleasant as possible, but as our conversation was to be effected by the aid of a third person, it caused a restraint that made my visits less frequent than if we could have done without it. Had I not seen the blue-eyed daughter of the mansion, I should not have felt my ignorance with such severe disappointment. Yet, when at times I carry back my recollection to this African Cape and the short, speechless interview at the staircase foot with this young Batavian, it is not without a pleasurable feeling.

Mr. La L—s lived in good style which is the case with many of the inhabitants; some of them indeed display no small degree of splendour in their equipages, were the carriages not so heavy. The horses are uncommonly beautiful and well matched, eight frequently being attached to the same vehicle and driven at a great rate. Contrary to a received opinion of the impracticability of taming the zebra, I saw four to a carriage, perfectly quiet and tractable. Oxen are chiefly used for labour, eight pair being in common to a wagon dragging wine and other articles from the distant country. Where reins are used, the *septum nasium* is perforated, and the operation being performed on the animal when young, no inconvenience is felt from it. In general the driver guides them by his whip and voice, the latter appearing to be perfectly understood, but where the road is intricate, and in the town, a person attends the leaders. Many of these wagons are under the management of Hottentots in the service of country farmers. A constant intercourse with the Dutch has doubtless in some measure altered the native character of the Hottentots about the town and its neighbourhood. Those who came under my observation were in general of short stature and delicately formed, particularly quick in their motions, with an eye full of cunning. In both sexes the lower part of the face projects considerably, being more pointed than the European. In colour they are brown, but not of that clear tinge to be seen in the native of the South Sea, or even mulatto of the West Indies. Their teeth are good and white, perhaps appearing more so from the dingy colour of the complexion skirting them, for in vain you look for ruby lips. Whether it be hair or wool growing on the head, it would be difficult to pronounce, but certainly it does not flow in lengthy ringlets.

That they are far from cleanly in their habits cannot be denied, and the only habiliment of some is the skin of an ox or sheep, thrown loosely over the shoulders, with a girt of the same sort round the waist. But for the received opinion of their passing the reeking entrails of animals round the different parts of the body, it is not in the power of your friend to confirm it.

There are said to be other peculiarities attached to the Hottentots varying from the rest of the world's inhabitants. It may be so. The peculiarities of the distant tribes I am of course unacquainted with, but for the account given by some exploring anatomists of these unoffending people in the neighbourhood of the town, I feel every disposition to consider them as rather overstretched.* Is it not a Cape story altogether?

Among the females about the town, elegant figures are to be seen, combined with features, notwithstanding the prominency of the lower part of the face, far from unpleasing. I could say more, and that the most perfect symmetry I ever beheld was in the person of an Hottentot girl in a dancing house at the Cape.

---

*   rather overstretched: Hottentot women reputedly had *labia majora* that extended beyond those of women from other parts of the world.

'Tis all, I believe, a ridiculous tale, nor is there that difference in the Hottentot and beauty of our own isle, some travellers have so minutely descanted on. I speak as an observer of nature in its pure unadorned state; far be it from me to dare with unhallowed pen, class them together, or compare the battered flaps of hide which protect these uncivilised, yet good beings from the inclemency of the weather, to the exuberant extramission, finely swelling from the front and rear of our own fashionable damsels. When we arrived in the *Providence* from our voyage, we were not a little puzzled respecting this carneous* appearance of our fair countrywomen, nor without suppressing that frailty had found its way to the British shore from the yielding plains of Tahiti. It was at a time when our troops were mowed down pretty plenteously by the *Sans Culottes* on the continent, rendering the increase of population highly necessary. We therefore gave the fair ones much credit for their patriotic labours; when, to our great surprise, one of them, about sixteen, who we thought very far gone indeed – while she laughed at our simplicity – told us it was nothing but an easy pad. She was a lank unmoist looking thing, with not a curve about her from head to foot, but her good mamma, aided by the milliner and staymaker, had so filled up the many excavations of her frame that nought but a very close approximation indeed could have convinced you but that she was all perfect. Furbelows† and flounces are abominable; yet even the fairest friends we have will not be taught that, the 'garb' which 'sits close' to their fine forms puts fashion – far – in the back ground. But to get on more steady ground.

29th

A party being formed of Guthrie, Mynheer Horack our landlord, the surgeon‡ of our little consort, and your humble servant to visit the country, early in the morning we left Cape Town. Our vehicle was a light covered wagon drawn by eight horses, which were guided by two slaves of the proprietor, one to manage the reins, the other an amazing long whip. For this conveyance the charge was about twenty-eight shillings per day as long we thought proper to keep it, the owner engaging to find provender for the steeds.

Our direction was over the flat country eastward of the town. The greater part of the road is a deep sand which the horses found truly laborious, while it relieved the passengers from the sad jolting which in the more rugged part was particularly felt. A portable dinner being part of the equipment, with good appetites it was partaken of at a small house purposely built by The Company about midway of our day's journey. On this occasion the horses were loosened from the wagon and turned among the shrubs to forage, the drivers having first with a thong fastened one of the forelegs of each to the neck in such a manner as to be useless. It is common to see this done on parties with twenty or thirty

---

*   carneous: flesh-coloured, pale red.
†   furbelows: a contemptuous term for showy ornaments or trimming.
‡   surgeon: Richard Frankland.

horses, no apprehension being entertained of their straggling too far. Towards sunset we reached the house of Mynheer Kestern at Elsenburg, about twenty-five miles from Cape Town. Horack introduced us as his friends, and we were received with an unfeigned welcome by the host, who during our visit behaved with more than a common degree of kindness and attention. Mynheer Kestern's house, and all about it, bespoke plenty, cheerfulness, and content, nor did the first half hour pass without our feeling ourselves 'at home'. Before departing to rest, which the fatigues of the day made very acceptable, it was determined that the next day we should visit the Paarl Rock situated about twelve miles to the northeast of Elsenburg. It must not be forgotten that a sopie or dram was offered to us on going to bed.

30th

Early in the morning, the same vehicle which brought us to this hospitable man, soon conveyed us in about three hours to the village called the Paarl. It consists of about seventy houses, distributed in a regular manner, and well supplied with every convenience. A neat church adds to the beauty of the village. After taking refreshment at a farm house, we began our walk. The sun was oppressively warm, nor had we proceeded far ere Guthrie and another of the party, fearful of not being able to reach the summit, retraced their steps. But as no opportunity might ever offer again, and seeing Horack go on briskly, I did not follow the example of my countrymen, however strong the disposition to it was. We soon crossed a small rivulet which our guide, a black who joined us at the farm house, described as emptying itself into the Atlantic at St. Helena Bay, a long way to the northward of the Cape. It was our good fortune not far from this stream to meet a cool retreat formed by two rocks, leaving a space about ten feet high and eighteen broad. From either entrance the prospect is grand and extensive. Nothing could be more welcome than this shelter, whence after resting an hour, and partaking of some wine, the good farmer had given in charge of his slave, we proceeded. The path here terminated, so that among rocks and underwood, as straight a progress as possible was made to the Paarl. At length the foot of it was reached, but before an ascent could be attempted, it was necessary to pull off our shoes, the surface being so steep and slippery. Arrived at its summit, our labours were fully repaid by the opening of a truly grand and extensive view. Notwithstanding the atmosphere was hazy, the white houses in the valley under the Table Land, full thirty miles distant in a southwest direction, were plainly to be distinguished without the aid of a glass. On the one side, the horizon of the vast Atlantic bounded the view, while on the other, the eye faintly caught the blue surface of the Indian Ocean afar off. To the east and northeast was an extensive plain interspersed with farms and vineyards, bearing every promise of abundance to the various proprietors, sheltered by a ridge of rugged mountains whose heights did not appear accessible to the foot of man.

The Paarl is excavated or it may be said to form two rocks. In a parallel line from the summit of the Paarl to the other rock, the distance is about two hundred yards, but at their bases they nearly join, which is doubtless the case beneath the surface of the ground, and which will be seen at some future period when the soil, by frequent rains, is washed away. Only the Paarl is accessible; it is evidently of granite, a vein of a red colour in squares nearly as regular as brick work, about a foot in breadth, extending in a westerly line across the northern part, but of what depth was not to be ascertained. It is at the base, about half a mile in circumference. Our pencil was missing, but a sketch made from recollection directly on our return to the village must serve,* in addition to what has been said, to give you an idea of these singular rocks, growing as they seem to do out of the surface of the hill. However destitute of soil, the wild aloe peeps from the fissures even on the summit, and many parts in our ascent was clothed with a kind of moss, giving equal relief to the eye and our shoeless feet. Hawks and vultures were flying about the rock. A party of our officers some days before were much amused by the antics of a number of baboons, secure from danger on the opposite rock. A few lizards were seen.

A different route homewards led us to another place of shelter from the intense power of the sun under an arch formed by a single rock resting on each end. As well as at our first retreat, we here saw the names of many travellers to the Paarl. Should fate ever lead you to this distant quarter; you will observe, if not worn away by time, that of your brother among the number. His graver was a pocket knife, the sculpture being blackened by a mixture of gunpowder and water. Not far from this arch, the margin of a cliff gave a delightful bird's eye view of the village. As an Englishman I shall stand acquitted in considering it too regular, with a want of water, to form an interesting landscape. By four o'clock we reached the farm house and after taking a dinner of plenty and hearty welcome, with the subsequent nap, returned to Elsenburg. The road is not so sandy as from Cape Town to Elsenburg, but the face of the country very similar, chiefly a barren heath, with farms interspersed in good cultivation. Scarcely any wood is to be seen, but plantations of the silver, the almond, and other trees, contiguous to these farms. Great numbers of tortoises attracted our attention by their slow creeping motion, apparently heedless of the danger of the wheels passing over them. Yet is it said that such is the strength of their shell, many hundred weight will not crush it. Some of these listless animals were beautifully marked, indeed it is not uncommon to see snuff boxes made of the upper shell. A larger kind of tortoise is to be seen at the Cape, but in less numbers. One was pointed out to us in a yard near the wharf, from the circumstance of its having been there nearly a century. This may or may not be a Cape Story.

December 1st

The next day was appointed for a hunting party, and soon after the sun rose eight of us, with an equal number of fowling pieces, some of them double-barrelled,

---

* See Plate 7.

were taken into an open wagon for that purpose. Wherever there was a possibility of the wagon going with safety, it was driven through 'brake and briar' at no very moderate rate, the plan followed in this country of starting the game from cover, everyone being ready to take his shot. A few deer only were seen, and the whole morning passed without success.

Under the shade of a few small trees, the only ones to be seen for several miles around, we stopped to partake of some good refreshments with which Mynheer Kestern had almost laden the wagon. The horses, as usual, were turned loose to forage, with a foreleg confined, to prevent their straggling. At a spring that supplied us with water, some ostrich feathers were observed, which we conjecture had been left by the birds after washing, but a party of Dutch Boers, who with their families on a journey to the Cape, had stopped on the same business with ourselves, gave us the cheering information that they had shot one in the morning, four other being in company. With great avidity it was instantly determined to look for the rest of the covey, and we had already in idea, each shot 'our bird'. On casting a look around, a brace were discovered grazing on the heath two or three miles distant. The steeds were again harnessed, and charging our guns with ball, the wagon was directed towards the game. Until within about a mile and a half of them, the ostriches continued feeding without any concern, when holding up their long necks to survey their pursuers, they began walking off. A council was now held how to proceed, the result of which was that only three of us should remain in the vehicle, and the rest be posted among the bushes in different directions, with the hope the wagon would turn them within shot of some of the lodged party. The horses were put to their utmost speed for about twenty minutes, but as the birds, though only indulging themselves in a long trot (and frequently stopping to look back on us) soon increased their distance, the chase was relinquished and a signal made to 'close'.

Until I had seen the ostrich in a wild state, I had no conception of its astonishingly rapid movement; yet it appeared that they could have exerted themselves infinitely more. It was noticed that they kept their wings in motion while running, as if to assist their progress. The one killed by the Boers in the morning was shot from on horseback, the party coming suddenly on it. Some of our messmates a short time before were more fortunate than ourselves, having returned with the thigh bone of one of these majestic birds as a trophy of their sportsmanship. This bird they found feeding in high corn where it allowed them to approach within fifty yards, a circumstance considered as very unusual by our host. Whether the ostrich has any enemies among the brute or feathered tribe in these wilds I did not learn, but with its strength and celerity, the danger and difficulty of approaching it must be great.* It may be remarked that their eggs

---

*   Hyena and jackal prey on ostrich chicks and weak or disabled adults; Egyptian vultures will eat their eggs. The adult ostrich can reach the speed of 50 kilometres per hour.

are considered by many at the Cape as a desirable article of food. (Mr. Portlock eating one frequently for breakfast.)

A few deer, all of which escaped our guns, were seen in the evening. At the Cape Town much was said of the abundance of game in the neighbourhood, yet this day above thirty miles were traversed and only a few hares, deer, and partridges seen. It was night ere the wagon reached Elsenburg, the sportsmen in it being completely jolted and disposed for rest.

At our dining place numbers of small birds nests were observed somewhat in the form of a bottle with the neck bent down, hanging to the outer branches of the trees, waving about with every breeze, yet so strongly attached as to be with difficulty disengaged.* They hung over a small pool of water, thus being secure from the attacks of snakes and other reptiles. One of the Boers asserted that the male bird always built the nest, when it underwent the inspection of the female, and if not congenial to her taste, she instantly destroyed it, the male bird with great conjugal perseverance again constructing another, and repeating this until the architecture met her entire approbation. Should you ever quit the state of 'single blessedness' and to be a useful citizen – it is your duty so to do – you may learn to be obediently uxorious from this little African bird. Yet James, 'tis a voyage of doubt and incertitude and should be well considered. Once embarked no port, no retreat is open, should you look as opposite as Greenland and the Southern Pole. Still must you drag the heavy chain along.

Another circumstance attracted our attention. Several of the Boers were busily engaged around a small bush where they said a snake was concealed, and which they knew by noise of a small insect, intimidated by it. The Boers were right, as in a short time the snake was driven out, when the noise instantly ceased. There are said to be a variety of snakes in this country, and that the bite from some is of a deadly poison, but the few that fell under my observation were not at all dreaded by the inhabitants. An opportunity offered the next day of examining a snipe, which did not in the least vary from such as you have seen in Stratford marsh. To 'try back' a little, as we are on a sporting party, to the snake. I remember a few years ago when bathing in a lake near Halifax, a very curious circumstance respecting a snake. One of the party had left his watch on the flat surface of a rock within a yard or two of the water; on returning to clothe himself, a snake was found coiled round the watch seemingly pleased with the situation. Is it not probable that the snake was attracted to the watch by the regular noise of the machinery in it?

After breakfast we walked about the grounds and cellars of our host and some of his neighbours. His gardens were extensive, and in the most exact neatness and order. Some vineyards adjoining were fenced with quinces, of which fruit, almonds and apricots, there were the greatest abundance. Not far from the house was his slaves' gardens, well supplied with various culinary

---

* Weaver birds, most likely village weavers, which build their nest close to human settlements.

articles. He observed that in the previous year, his slaves reaped two thousand sacks of potatoes, the major part of which they sold at the Cape for their own emolument. The country about Elsenburg, and indeed the whole neighbourhood of this promontory, is naturally destitute of trees, but Mynheer Kestern has planted oak, pine and some others which thrive luxuriantly; the silver tree, before mentioned, is of uncommon beauty, its leaves at some distance bearing the hue of that metal. The stables, and indeed all the farming offices of our landlord, were on a very extensive scale; besides about seventy brood mares, two hundred horses, and a number of oxen were kept in constant labour. It is true, the expense of keeping horses in this country, particularly the more rough and laborious kind, is inconsiderable when compared to what it is in Europe, and that of shoeing (except the fore feet of some) is altogether saved, a Dutch farmer holding it unnecessary. The cellars contained a great quantity of various kinds of wine in casks of a very large size, and it was thought necessary by Mynheer Kestern that his visitors should taste of every quality, a polite penalty not particularly acceptable of a forenoon.

After dinner the steeds were mounted to visit a mountain called Klapmuts. Several deer were seen, but not within shot. The horses climbed up as far as they were able, but the acclivity and ruggedness was such that the worst half of the journey was continued on foot. Towards the summit the ascent was more difficult than either to the Paarl or Table Land, but aided by a renovating breeze at this cool hour of the day, no complaints were heard. The view that here presented itself was extensive in every direction, particularly to the west, where the sun was seen to sink behind the purpled Table Land in great splendour, whose level surface formed a fine contrast to the more rugged and unequal mountains of Draakenstein and Hottentots' Holland.

3rd

We this morning visited the much admired village of Stellenbosch a few miles from Elsenburg. On either side the road, it was in most parts highly cultivated with corn and vines. The village, consisting of about fifty houses with a neat church, is in a valley, a fine stream of water passing through it. The inhabitants, as they in truth might, spoke in raptures of the oaks in and around Stellenbosch. A double row ornamented each street and in such a luxuriant state that the whole place was shaded by them. Much to our regret, our leave of absence from Captain Bligh now expired, and which was the more felt as Mynheer Kestern had proposed taking us to his house at St. Helena Bay, which place, though far distant from Cape Town, boasted a more fertile soil than Elsenburg, from whence it is about a journey of three days. It should be remarked that the Cape inhabitant calculates by time, and if you ask the distance of any place you are told so many hours or days. A wagon with eight horses, generally speaking, does not exceed five miles an hour and this is the most common travelling conveyance.

The friendly offer of our landlord to conduct us to St. Helena Bay could not be accepted, but some amends were made for the disappointment by his accompanying us with his family in another wagon to the Cape Town. The caravansary where we dined in our journey out, now answered the same purpose, and we sat down to plenty and good cheer. On entering the isthmus between False and Table Bay, we suddenly met the strong southeast gales, and learnt they had been raging with great violence during our absence, notwithstanding we had experienced the most tranquil weather but a few leagues distant.

The thermometer on board, while the *Providence* remained in Table Bay varied from 62° to 74°, the variation of the compass on board by 24 sets of Azimuths (not by George Tobin) was found to be taking the mean 24°..54'.55" westerly.

CHAPTER 3RD

December 1791–March 1792

Leave Table Bay.—Qualities of the vessels.—Health of the crews.—Cheering.—
Captain Bligh Master with Captain Cook.—Albatrosses &c. &c.—Quaker
birds.—Brodie stoves in cockpits.—Sweetwort.—Island St. Paul.—Seals seen.—
Anchor in Adventure Bay Tasmania.—Wooding and watering parties.—Native
hut.—Coarse pearls.—Trout.—One of the crew of the Assistant missing.—
Maria Islands.—Some account of Adventure Bay.—An apple tree.—Large
bones.—Forest trees.—Fires.—Seeds planted.—Fowls left.—Short interview with
the natives.—Kangaroo.—Birds.—Black Swans.—Gannets.—Fish.—Oysters.—
Leave Adventure Bay.—Rock weed.—Good look out.—Porpoise liver.—Seal.—
Whales.—Pass southward of New Zealand.—Islands seen by Captain Bligh in
the Bounty in 1788.—Crew healthy.—Great attention to it.—Red tailed tropic
birds.—Cockroaches.—Eastern limit reached.—Discover a low island.—No
signs of inhabitants.—Its latitude well fixed.—Such islands truly dangerous to
the navigator.—How formed, general opinion.—Great depth of sea close to
them.—

22nd

It was not until this day that we took leave of the last European settlement with
which the vessels were to have intercourse for nearly a twelvemonth. At this port
of plenty the crews had been liberally supplied with every kind of refreshment,
and it might have been truly said that they were beginning the voyage anew, with
the advantage of being better known to each other. A few passing squalls had
taken place within board as well as without, but by clearing up in time, without
any serious mischief. They happen everywhere, as well on *terra firma*, as on the
quarter deck of a ship.

The qualities of the *Providence*, and her *Assistant* were found equal to what
had been expected, and their crews, many of whom had not sailed beyond the
mouth of the Thames, were now becoming familiar to the cares of a distant
voyage. The good mutton and abundance of vegetables this promontory affords,
gave an equal glow of health to their countenances as when they quitted their
native isle. Yet to this isle did we take a retrospect, nor without the hopes of
returning to it, but the satisfaction we anticipated in visiting more remote ones
banished every sorrowful thought. For myself, James, I began to feel at home in
the charge of a watch, nor without considering my appointment to the
Providence as a very flattering one, particularly as she was the first ship in which I
made my debut as a commissioned officer. In her commander I had to encounter

the quickest sailor's eye, guided by a thorough knowledge of every branch of the profession necessary on such a voyage. He had been master with the persevering Cook in his last voyage in 1776, and, as has been already noticed, commanded the *Bounty* armed ship when the first attempt was made to convey the breadfruit tree to the West Indies. It is easy of belief that on first joining a man of such experience, my own youth and inferiority were rather busy visitors. They were, but we had by this time crossed the Equinoctial and were about doubling the Cape together, and I had courage to believe that my captain was not dissatisfied with me. Of this surely enough, even to you.

Accompanied by our little consort, in the afternoon we left the bay. As we passed them, our cheers were returned by the *Waarzaamheid* and *Swan* sloop; the fort observing the same to our departing salute.

The custom of cheering was once more observed among us than it is now. There is in it something more than commonly affecting. 'Tis saying, we greet you on your safe return, or, may success attend your voyage. Such is the language of the thrice repeated cordial cheer.

24th

We this day lost sight of the African coast. Our Christmas as was passed, perhaps with as much jollity as if on dry land. The place where is noted, which I have been in the habit of doing, and mean to in future. Already it tells what a wanderer your brother has been. What he may be, will depend on the direction of a superior Power.

28th

In the morning a ship was seen standing to the southeast. Our old friends the albatrosses, shearwaters, and silver birds, particularly the latter, were about us in numbers. It is about the size of a pigeon and of the petrel tribe, the plumage of the belly and under part of the wings of a shining white colour. They never came under my observation in any part of the ocean but south of the Cape.

29th

The ship still in sight, apparently a Dutch Indiaman bound to Jakarta that left Table Bay with the *Providence*. Vessels bound to Jakarta or China deem it prudent to stand well to the southward where they generally meet westerly winds. In May 1789 I remember being obliged from easterly winds to reach as far as 42°..30' south where the weather was thick and unpleasant, the thermometer falling to 56°, longitude 34° east, variation of the compass 26° westerly.

January 8th

It being a moderate day Mr. Portlock came on board, giving a flattering account of the behaviour of his little brig during the late boisterous weather. Some sea birds of a light brown colour, similar in their flight to the albatross but not so large, were about us. Our southern seamen called them Quaker birds. The latitude at noon was observed in 37°..30' south, longitude by account 49°..25' east, the thermometer 57°.

17th

The wind continued between the northwest and southwest, generally blowing strong, accompanied by damp unsettled weather, to avoid the bad effects of which became Captain Bligh's study. A good fire was constantly kept in the galley throughout the night and every care and precaution used to keep the ship dry. Brodie stoves were lighted in both cockpits the whole day.

In addition to the many good articles of food given the people, sweetwort* was issued every forenoon. There is no word an English sailor so cordially hates as innovation. When this salutary beverage was first introduced, it was not much relished by them. To set an example the officers brought their mugs on deck, drinking the portion allowed us. In a few days every man in the ship sought it with avidity, and I do assure you that I looked for my pint of wort every forenoon with nearly as much desire as for the same quantity of Tenerife wine after dinner. The latitude was observed in 39°..00' south, longitude by account 75°..33' east, thermometer 65°, variation of the compass 23°..24' westerly on the following day.

A little after noon the island of St. Paul was seen in the north, northeast, three or four leagues distant. The lunar observations and time keepers fix it in (about) 77°..30' east longitude. The bearings and meridian observation, the latitude (about) 38°..50' south. Two islands are noticed in most charts, which in fact is the case. The southern one was seen by the *Providence*. Mortimer, in the brig *Mercury* in 1790, says the northern one bore from the other north, northeast seventeen leagues distant.† Sailing past the south side of St. Paul's at six or seven miles from it, a conical rock was observed off the eastern point. It is said that there is an anchorage round this point, but it can hardly be a secure one. The island is moderately high and about three leagues in circuit, quite destitute of trees, and with scarcely the appearance of verdure in any part. These islands are situated so much in the track of vessels bound by the way of the Cape to Australia, that it would appear prudent to make them for a fresh departure,

---

*   sweetwort: the infusion of malt, before the hops are added in the manufacture of beer.

†   George Mortimer, *Observations and Remarks Made During a Voyage ... in the Brig Mercury*, London, 1791.

1 The Providence, and her attendant, the Assistant

2 Rock, near the Paarl

7 *Near the Paarl Rock, Cape of Good Hope*

8 *Pintado bird, near Cape of Good Hope*

9 *Animal of Adventure Bay in Tasmania*

facing page, from top:
3 *Sucking fish:*
  A Apparently the back
  B Appatently the belly
4 *Flying fish of Sao Tiago, Cape de Verde Islands*
5 *Bonito*
6 *Fish of Adventure Bay, Tasmania*

12 *View from the lowlands to the Northward of Adventure Bay, Tasmania*

13 *Point Venus, Island of Tahiti*

previous pages: 10 *Wooding place, Adventure Bay, Tasmania*
11 *In Adventure Bay, Tasmania*

14 *The observatory &c. &c., Point Venus, Tahiti*

15 *Near the mouth of the Ha'apaiano'o River, Island of Tahiti*

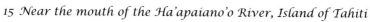

following page: 16 Canoes of Tahiti

particularly where the whole dependence is placed on the 'dead reckoning'.* The island, St. Paul, is sufficiently high to be seen, even in the night, nor from the nature of its shores, are hidden dangers to be expected. Several seals were seen in the course of the day. It never fell under my observation meeting these animals but in the neighbourhood of land.

February 3rd

The sun rose fiery and full of threats. At noon it blew a strong gale from the northwest. The latitude by account 41°..43' south, longitude by account 126°..35', the thermometer 62°, variation of the compass in the afternoon 4°..29' westerly. Rock weed was seen.

5th

Wind from the westward. Latitude observed 43°..46' south, longitude per account 133°..18' east, thermometer 60°, variation of the compass 00°..14' easterly.

8th

At daylight the coast of Tasmania was seen from east by north to north, northwest, 4 or 5 leagues distant. At noon the latitude was observed in 43°..46' south when the South Cape bore north 34° easterly 4 or 5 miles distant. Eddystone and Swilly Islands south 65° easterly 6 or 7 miles, thermometer 63°.

9th

In the morning both vessels were safely anchored in Adventure Bay in nine fathoms. After mooring, Penguin Island bore north 64° easterly. Cape Frederick Henry north 25° easterly, distant from the nearest shore about a half a mile.

The land about Southwest Cape is hilly and more free from wood than to the eastward. From the inequality of the line of coast, it is more than probable secure anchorages may be found, but this, from her distance, was not determined by the *Providence*. The surf in general broke high, but in some places it appeared practicable for boats to land.

Shortly after rounding Fluted Cape, a high bluff land clothed with trees to the summit, except where it terminates toward the sea in a perpendicular rock appearing like closely connected columns, we passed Penguin Island which forms the eastern part of Adventure Bay. This small island is close to the mainland, and

---

* dead reckoning: navigation without the aid of astronomical instruments with calculation using the speed of the ship from point to point.

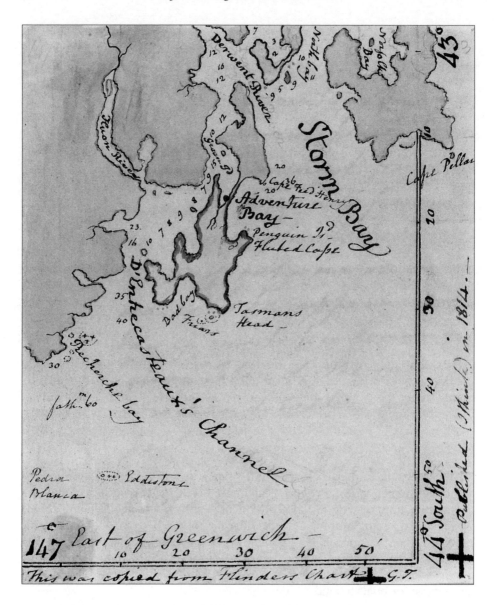

Map 5 Storm Bay

at most times, it is easy to walk across among the rocks above water. The soil on the island is good, producing plenty of grass.

The watering and wooding parties were now formed, the former under the direction of poor Guthrie, the latter falling to your humble servant. The recollection of some happy days passed with my late friend on this uncultivated shore gives birth to the most pleasing sensations, but they are embittered in the melancholy truth that he is now – no more. Our posts were about half a mile apart, but we always met at the hour of dinner in a hut of the natives contiguous to a stream at which we watered most part of the time. Though we did not 'fare sumptuously every day', it was with hearty uncontaminated appetites, the chief viands being from the destruction of our fowling pieces and the produce of the sea shore. Close to the wigwam abundance of small trout were taken with hook and line, so that there was no apprehension of famine. A parrot, or a sea gull was indeed sometimes thrown into the iron pot, and relished with great *goût* as if either had been a woodcock. But there was always a standing dish of mussels, and however an opposite opinion prevails, no bad effects ever arose from eating them. It was to the *ci-devant* tenants of our mansion we were indebted for feasting on them without apprehension, numbers of the shells, the remnant of their meals, being scattered about. Self-preservation is most probably as strong in the native of Tasmania as in the most refined European, and it was the sight of these shells which first gave us courage to try them. It is remarkable of the Adventure Bay mussels that they contain, in general, numbers of a small coarse kind of pearl.

You must not doubt what has been said about trout fishing in this distant spot. They rose with more eagerness than was ever the case with us, at Guy's Hole, Dowse's Hatches, or even Bowles's Broad, but not one reached a quarter of a pound weight so that there was no sport, as at your grandfather's, in playing them.

21st

Several parties were sent in the morning to beat the woods in search of one of the *Assistant*'s people* who had deserted her boat. Throughout the previous night a light had been kept at the masthead and guns fired at intervals, supposing he had lost himself. After some time he was discovered by Pearce, concealed in such a manner as left no doubt, it was his intention for the vessels to proceed without him. He assigned as a reason for his absence, being unjustly accused of theft, which determined his taking this desperate step. The poor wretch must in all probability have soon perished, not having the smallest portion of food with him, or anything to produce a fire with. When taken, he declared he preferred the risk of starving in this distant country, or meeting its natives, to remaining on

---

*   The man involved, Bennet, was a gentleman volunteer who had signed on to the *Assistant* as an able seaman.

board under such an accusation. Charity would encourage us to believe him innocent. The thermometer 60½°. In the evening it being calm, the vessels were towed farther out.

22nd

We weighed in the morning and stood along shore to the northward with the hope of discovering the entrance of Frederick Henry Bay, which bay was easily seen from the hills near our anchorage, but without our being able to decide the access to it. After in vain for several miles, looking for an entrance on the eastern side, the vessels were hauled off shore, the south point of the Maria Islands bearing east two or three leagues distant, Cape Frederick Henry west, southwest about as far. Our soundings while coasting to the northward, Maria Islands, 24 to 29 fathoms.

The Maria Islands appeared more free from wood than the mainland. Smoke being seen proved their being inhabited. It is to be regretted that the channel between them and Tasmania has not been correctly surveyed.[1] In the short distance the *Providence* stood to the northward of Adventure Bay, little was effected. Should a ship remain any considerable time in the above bay, her boats might be advantageously employed for this purpose, taking care to arm the crews, as we are almost wholly ignorant of the habits and disposition of the natives.

In pressing the vessels to weather Cape Pillar, the south part of the Maria Islands, the *Assistant* carried away her foreyard, which occasioned our again anchoring in Adventure Bay to repair the damage.

23rd

Before weighing, a good meridian observation gave the latitude in 43°..22'.15" south, when Penguin Island bore north 85° east 2½ mile. Cape Frederick Henry north 24° east, and the east part of the table land, a long way distant, the summit of which was of a light colour, or covered with snow, north 18° west. This appearance of snow had not been noticed before.

Adventure Bay may certainly be considered as a convenient place for vessels bound to the Pacific Ocean to touch at for wood and water. It is only exposed to the winds from the northeast quarter, but Maria Islands being in that direction, at the distance of only six or seven leagues, no very heavy sea is to be apprehended. The east part of the bay is most free from surf and there, and on Penguin Island, the only good grass is to be procured. Wood and water are to be found in almost every part.

From Penguin Island to a low isthmus, not half a mile in breadth, dividing Adventure from Frederick Henry Bay, is six or seven miles to the northward, the coast taking a winding direction, in some parts sandy, in others craggy and nearly impassable. Excepting some low land in the south part of the bay (behind which at about the distance of half a mile is a brackish lagoon) and the isthmus before mentioned, the country is hilly and richly clothed with wood. Some of the trees are of great height and magnitude. One not far from the beach measured twenty-nine feet in circumference. These large trees are all the same kind, and do not branch off till at more than half their height. The bark is of a very light colour. It bears a long narrow leaf and the ground was plenteously strewed with the fruit, or seed, something in the form of a button but not edible.* The wood being tough and close grained, in some degree like American hickory, it probably might answer for building. For masts and yards the carpenter deemed it too heavy. There are a variety of other trees, one was observed of the fir kind, the wood of a deep mahogany colour.† The fern tree was among the number. The soil in general is light and sandy, but on the slope of some of the hills, a fine dark mould, which is also the case on Penguin Island. In these spots the trees are not so numerous, and they are free from underwood.

On the east part of the bay there was one of several apple trees remaining which were planted by Captain Bligh in 1788 when the *Bounty* touched at Adventure Bay; it was in a healthy state but had not much increased in size, the others probably had been consumed by fire, no traces of them being discoverable.

Most of the valleys small streams find a passage to the bay. The largest where Guthrie was encamped (Resolution River) was not more than ten or twelve feet in breadth. Its source was not ascertained, but that of a small tributary stream was found gushing from a rock. Numbers of small trout were in all of them.

The wigwam where we messed on the banks of the Resolution has been noticed, but without a description. It was eight feet wide, and half as much in height at the entrance, which extended nearly across, being constructed with branches of trees stuck in the ground and fastened at the smaller ends with coarse grass; over these rafters, pieces of bark from the large tree were placed in the manner of tiles or shingles. Wretched as such a habitation may appear, it sheltered us from many a 'pelting of the pitiless storm' and hot ray of the sun. It had not been long deserted, the remains of native cookery being still fresh. Mussels have been before mentioned, the bones of animals were also strewed about, which were conjectured to be those of the kangaroo. In another hut the vertebrae ones of some large fish or animal were found; these from their magnitude were probably of the whale or grampus.‡ Some hard white stone wrapped up carefully in soft bark made us suspect they were materials by which the natives produced fire, but our efforts to effect it with them were fruitless.**

---

*   A gum tree.
†   A type of cedar tree.
‡   grampus: one of various kinds of blowing, spouting, blunt-headed delphinoid cetaceans.
** Tasmanian aborigines may not have been able to produce fire artificially, but rather preserved it with fire sticks when it occurred naturally.

An observation or two may here be hazarded on what has been advanced by some visitors to this country, that its wretched inhabitants take up their residence in the trunks of trees, hollowed out with fire for that purpose.* I certainly met with burnt trees in our walks, the tracks of the natives, as well as in the mountains where no vestige appeared of their ever having been, but it is difficult to believe that the most barbarous savage would allow indolence so much to operate on him as to live in a hole not capable of containing more than two or three, and those not with ease, when in a short hour, from its simplicity, he could erect a comparatively comfortable habitation. Rather would it seem that where the trees have the appearance spoken of, fires have been kindled for the temporary purpose of cooking. Indeed, in our shooting parties the trunks of the trees against which our parrots had been grilled, exhibited on the succeeding day one of these supposed habitations. Yet, this leaves us at a loss how to account for those in the higher grounds, where there is no appearance of human foot having reached. But many sapient heads have been puzzled about a less knotty point than this. Perhaps at a former period the hills were more resorted to.

Near a stream on the south part of the bay Captain Bligh planted some water cress seed, with an inscription on a tree near, to point out the spot. Some quince, strawberry, fig and pomegranate plants, were also left. A fine cock with two hens were turned into the woods; he seemed to exult in his consequence and freedom, but we lamented the probability of their being destroyed by the natives. Captain Cook left a boar and sow in the year 1777, but there was no appearance of an increase from them. On sending for our goats to Penguin Island, where they had been to browse during our stay, a she one was missing. At low water she had most likely found her way over the rocks to the mainland.

Though smoke was frequently seen no distance to the northward, but one slight view was gained of the natives. Some of the officers came suddenly on a party of about twenty, but except one young man who remained a few minutes, they instantly decamped. In the short interview with this man he was persuaded to take some bread, but his terror was so great that he soon followed his countrymen. Close where they were discovered was the skeleton of a new wigwam with two kangaroo skins in it, and some short spears, sharp at one end and hardened by fire. Hasty as was the view of these wretched savages, it did not appear that either sex were quite naked, the skin of an animal being thrown loosely over the shoulders, but seemingly more to protect them from the weather than from any sense of decency. The beards of the men were not in any degree removed. In the group was a child at its mother's breast. These are the few particulars collected respecting them. Under the hope of a more satisfactory interview, the skins were left in the wigwam, but in this we were much disappointed. No kind of boat or canoe was observed about the coast.

---

* Some evidence indicates that the Tasmanian aborigines did occasionally live in hollowed out tree trucks and caves.

The only animals seen were the kangaroo, and a kind of sloth, about the size of a roasting pig, with a proboscis two or three inches in length. On the back were short quills like those of the porcupine.* This animal was roasted, and found of a delicate flavour. The kangaroos were so rapid in their motions, they escaped all our guns.

Of birds, these are a great variety, both land and aquatic. Among the former several kind of parrots and hawks, some of the first, full as large as the macaw. A parrot in a wild state was quite a novelty, nor until these was 'ocular demonstration of it' could I suppose their flight was so rapid. I speak particularly of a small kind, of which there are abundance in these woods. When convocated on a high tree a 'confusion of tongues' frequently attracted our attention. A few of the smaller birds are singularly beautiful in their plumage and not without a pleasing note. They are particularly shy of the approach of man, from which it is fair to infer that they form a part of the sustenance of the natives. Partridges were reported to have been seen by some of the officers, but they did not come within my own observation. Nor, (though some are introduced in the drawings)† am I able to say more respecting black swans. In the lagoon were wild ducks, and on the shores of the bay, gulls, gannets, and a variety of sand plover.

The gannet in pursuit of its prey I have observed frequently in this bay, and with astonishment at its wonderfully clear sight and celerity so fatal to the finny tribe. When striking at a fish from an amazing height, this bird descends with such force as to be wholly immersed for nearly a minute ere rising with its prey to the surface, which having swallowed, it again ranges aloft with a watchful eye in pursuit of more. It would seem that the gannet is common on most coasts not near the tropics. One of my messmates here tells a story of a wag who was with him in the *Hind*, respecting one of these birds which he had procured from the Isle of Bas, near the mouth of the Firth of Forth. The gannet is beautifully marked yellow on the head; this induced him to dub it a Golden Phoenix, and meeting with a curious admirer of ornithology, he with much reluctance was persuaded to part with it for a crown. The purchaser of the Golden Phoenix, wishing much to know the qualities of his bird, requested to know if it could walk quick? 'If your honour will but try', he replied, 'see how soon you will be satisfied, he can walk as well as I, and fly much better.' The bird took no time for exhibiting the first qualification, but trusting to its wings was not long in finding a way from Leith to the Isle Bas, leaving the collector poorer by five shillings, which was soon spent among the *Hind*'s boat's crew, nor without their joyfully boasting how they had gulled the landsman.

The seine was frequently hauled, and at times with considerable success. The fish taken were chiefly Spanish mackerel, besides many others unknown to us. One kind the seamen called elephant fish from their having a long snout like that animal. With hook and line a very delicate sort of rock cod were caught in the

---

* This animal is most likely an echidna, a form of ant-eater.
† See Plate 12.

bay, and it is probable that the large kind of cod would be found in deeper water as the latitude does not vary much[2] from that of some of the fishing banks on the coast of Newfoundland and Nova Scotia. The same observation perhaps applies to salmon, but while the *Providence* was at Tasmania, it was not ascertained. The dog fish were so numerous as to be very troublesome to the lines. Several seals were seen.

The wooding party killed snakes of different kinds, but without ascertaining whether their bite was poisonous or not, nor was it judged prudent to make any personal experiments on such a question. A large kind of lizard seeming to partake somewhat of the West India iguana was killed; its length about a foot, but very thick in proportion and bearing a disgusting appearance.

The sea coast abounded with a variety of shell fish, most of which are eaten by the natives. In Frederick Henry Bay are some fine oyster banks, perfectly dry at low tide. A very beautiful large kind of limpet, to seamen known by the name of ear shell, was found adhering to the rocks under water. The shells of lobsters were strewed about, contiguous to where fires had been kindled.

Where the rocks did not admit of walking along the shore the natives, a little distance in the woods, had beaten a tolerable path, but many large trees having fallen across it, our progress was but slow, nor was it unfrequent that they served as bridges fifty or sixty feet in length, and eight or ten high on which our feet found but a slippery foundation. In no part did these paths take a direction to the interior, from which circumstance it may be concluded that the natives dwell near the sea shore; indeed, in confirmation, it may be remarked that all the wigwams were but a short distance from the bay.

23rd

We now took leave of Tasmania, shaping a course to pass southward of New Zealand.

28th

Rock weed was seen and various kind of sea fowl, indeed the latter had been daily observed after leaving Adventure Bay. The latitude at noon was 47°..27' south, longitude by account 159°..45' east, thermometer 57°. It was now Captain Bligh's custom every evening to reduce the sail so as to be able to haul by the wind in case of any sudden alarm. As well as in the day time, a man was constantly looking out all night at the foretop masthead.

March 1st

Continued to see rock weed. A porpoise was struck with the harpoon. Some of the liver was fried. Prejudice certainly intruded not a little, or it might have passed for that of a hog.

2nd

A seal was seen in the morning and much rock weed. Whales and porpoises were playing around the ship. The wind continued from the westward. At noon the latitude was observed in 49°..32' south, longitude by account 168°..47' east, which made us from the South Cape of New Zealand south 17° east thirty-five leagues distant, the thermometer 55°. As rock weed has been noticed, I cannot help remarking that it never came within my knowledge to observe it, but in the neighbourhood of land, and the same of tangle weed. The appearance of either certainly ought to teach a seaman the necessity of a good lookout. Indeed, except what is generally called gulf weed, (from it being supposed to come from the Gulf of Florida) I never met any kind, at a considerable distance from the shore.

4th

Wind from the west, southwest sharp squalls and thick gloomy weather as the day opened. It veered to the south by east, a very cold air accompanying it. At noon it was again from the southwest quarter. Soon after the vessels were hauled to the northeast; and very good look out kept for some rocky islands discovered by Captain Bligh on the *Bounty* in September 1788.

6th

The weather was squally, wind from the south, southwest and southwest. A hail storm early in the morning lowered the quick silver in the thermometer to 45°. Latitude at noon 47°..03' south, longitude by account 173°..21' west.

23th*

The wind and weather continued variable though a sensible difference was felt in the temperature of the air, the thermometer at noon being 61°, latitude 36°..42' south, longitude by account 142°..34' west. Scarcely an albatross or any of the aquatic birds of a colder region were to be observed, and the people as they approached the tropic, were seen about the deck in their summer dress. Health, that invaluable blessing, still voyaged with them, which could not but be attributed, under the guidance of Providence, to the persevering care and assiduity of their commander. The crew being at three watches was not among the least of their comforts, as it ensured them that repose so absolutely necessary in a voyage where frequently, more than a common degree of health and exertion was required. It is by foresight and preparation for 'the occasion' that difficulties are to be surmounted.

---

*   Having crossed the International Date Line sailing eastward, all dates will now be marked as one day earlier than Tobin indicates in his manuscript.

If I descend to a detail of the common food of the common sailor, it is from a conviction, gained by experience on this voyage, that too much attention cannot be paid to it. It has been observed that the vessels had been supplied by the government with every article deemed conducive to the health of seamen. In the application of them, according to the weather and other circumstances, every degree of attention was paid. Sauerkraut was issued every forenoon, which was cooked various ways, but perhaps the best is by parboiling, and then using it as a salad. As an anti-scorbutic it has ever been allowed to have great efficacy. Borecole, a preparation of dried cabbage, was, among many, in high estimation. On days where neither beef nor pork are allowed, a quantity of this article and portable soup* were added to the peas for dinner, making by no means a despicable dish. For breakfast, the crew had generally a warm mess of gruel, rendered more nutritious by mixing borecole with it. Spruce beer and grog, in many parts of the voyage were issued alternately. The first is readily made at sea, as well as conveniently carried. It was brewed chiefly in warm weather. To one pot of the essence, were added two gallons of molasses, and one pound of hops. This made a puncheon, which was sufficient for the daily expenditure. Vinegar was served weekly.

As well as to the aliment, every degree of attention was paid to cleanliness and comfort of the crew. This duty appertained to the officer of the morning watch, whose report that every part of the ship was clean and dry for the inspection of the captain was made in the forenoon. In the day time fires were constantly kept in both cockpits,[3] with funnels leading through the cable tiers, and in wet or damp weather, the galley fire was not extinguished throughout the night. To keep the ship clean and wholesome in the more confined parts below, water was let into the well every evening and pumped out again. The cables, sails, slops† and other stores were frequently got up on deck to air.

Much of the sickness on board ship proceeds from the men who have the watch on deck, sleeping about in damp exposed situations, and it is to be lamented that more care is not in general taken to prevent it. From a hot, confined hammock a sailor finds his way up the hatchway ladder and whether the dew falls heavy or not, he little heeds, as after answering his muster, the first plank serves him to stretch his length and repose on, until a sail is hoisted or taken in, when he again seeks it. Any attempts to convince him how prejudicial it is to his health is fruitless, nor can it be prevented but by imposing some penalty. Even in our small crew it was not conquered for a considerable time. The English tar is generally as careless of his health in prosperity as of his person in the trying hour of danger. He wants nursing and though he may sometimes murmur, is not always found ungrateful for it. On arriving in the warm latitudes the great coats were always put carefully away, to be used in more severe ones.

---

*   portable soup: a dehydrated beef soup.
†   slops: clothing.

31st

We had not quite reached the southeast tradewind yet was the air so warm, that the awnings were fitted. Tropic birds,* varying from those of the Indian or Atlantic Ocean, were about us. The tail feathers are in form like those of the common tropic bird, but the colour a bright crimson, only two in number, being considerably longer than the body of the bird.

Other visitors tempted by the change of climate from their lurking places, gave us considerable trouble. The ship swarmed with cockroaches. To destroy them the beams and carlings were frequently washed with boiling water. Many methods are practised to get rid of these troublesome and destructive insects, but hot water thrown with force into their hiding holes seems the most effectual; yet to arrive at it altogether is impracticable. The increase of the cockroaches is astonishing; by exposing the egg in a phial to the sun, after detaching it from the female, above sixty young ones were counted on the shell bursting.

April 1st

Wind from the southeast quarter, and weather fine. From leaving the Cape of Good Hope the men had been constantly trained to the use of small arms and were now so perfect, little doubt was entertained of their being steady in case of an attack from any hostile Indians.

A course was now shaped, so as to get into the latitude of Tahiti, some degrees to the eastward of it. The most eastern limit the ship reached, was 137°..30' west.†

4th

In the forenoon a low island was discovered in the west, southwest, which was passed at two or three miles distance.‡ The latitude at noon was observed in 21°..39' south, longitude by account 143°..05' west by account, the thermometer 77¾°, when off the southwest point a ridge of breakers extended about half a mile. It did not appear practicable for boats to land on any part of the island seen by the *Providence*. From the masthead it was easy to determine that the island was a low belt of land encircling a lagoon, three or four miles across. No entrance could be seen, though in many parts the sea washed nearly over. From the light coloured water, it is most likely of but little depth. The soil appeared sandy, but not destitute of trees, among them a few of the cocoanut. On the beach were several large detached dark rocks. No hut or canoe was observed, or anything to

---

*   tropic birds: phaetons.

†   137°..30' west: Tobin's journal shows 222°..15' east (138° west) by account as their turning point.

‡   Tematang in the Tuamotus Islands. It was first named Bligh's Lagoon.

indicate the island being inhabited. A little after noon, made sail to the northwest quarter.

Discovering this island so near noon, enabled Captain Bligh to fix its situation very correctly. When it is considered, the great number of these low lagoon islands with which the Pacific Ocean is studded, it appears almost a miracle that ships should escape them. Nothing indeed, but the greatest vigilance aided by prompt execution, can prevent it. The lead,* which by the navigator in most parts of the ocean is in some measure depended on, is here useless. Here, he cannot, when night closes on him, feel his way, many of these islands have not a single tree on them,[4] nor aught to give warning to the anxious voyager, but the white foam or roaring of the breakers.

Many opinions have been indulged respecting the origin of these curious spots, starting as they seem from the bottom of the deep. Such opinions may serve to amuse, yet do they leave conviction far behind. It has been said that they owe their rise to the accumulation of coral at the bottom, which in time reaching the surface, becomes a resting place for birds, whose dung cementing with it forms a contexture of a vegetating quality. This is by no means impossible, or that the seeds of plants should be deposited by the same means. The cocoanut, indeed, does not require the aid of birds, as after remaining a considerable time in the sea, it readily takes root. It is in fact a tree that delights in its roots being washed by the salt water. The finest groves of this excellent and useful tree, are always to be found close to the beach.

The foregoing conjecture respecting the formation of these coral islands does not appear very extravagant. What is the progress in the growth of coral I am ignorant, but as I have seen it growing in the most beautiful forms nearly fifty feet from the bottom, there does not appear any reason why, in course of time, it should not reach a much greater height. Certain it is that, within a short distance of the margin of most coral banks, a great depth of water is to be found, and increasing the distance a little no bottom will be gained with a common sounding line.

----

*   the lead: a piece of lead attached to a long, marked line to indicate water depth.

CHAPTER 4TH

April 1792

*Draw near Tahiti.—The doctor humanely employed.—Pass Mataiea.—
Intercourse with the natives.—Arrive at Tahiti.—The Matilda whaler.—Jenny
of Bristol.—War at Tahiti.—Establish a post near Point Venus.—Visit Pare.—
Young Tu.—Sailing canoes.—Sharks.—Poeno and Tapiru.—Mother and
daughter.—Ari'paea's love of spirits.—Tattooing.—A theft.—Botanists.—
Pomare's first visit.—Vaiareti and Ari'paea.—Abundance of flies.—A white
native.—Kava root.—Chiefs from Moorea.—Heiva dance.—Make a party up
Matavai River.—Offering to atua.—Shaddock trees.—Nelson, the botanist with
Captain Bligh in the Bounty.—Cascade called Peeir.— Delightful spot.—
Fishing.—Mahau visits the ship, the taio of Guthrie.—The botanists collecting
plants rapidly.—'Itia intoxicated.—&c. &c.*

Thetis, off Bermuda February 1797

April 6th

As we approached Tahiti, it was among our amusements to prepare and assort
the various adventures which we brought out to trade with its inhabitants, nor
without anticipating at the sight of every ten penny nail a favour from some chief
or princess.[1] The charity of these good people had been so warmly described by
the interesting pen of Dr. Hawkesworth* that, not a doubt arose, but all our
wishes would be gratified. Can it then be a wonder that, after a long voyage from
the wilds of Tasmania, we chid† the tardy hours until a more genial spot
presented itself. Latitude observed 19°..02' south, longitude by account 147°..24'
west.

In the afternoon, with but little distinction, the whole body corporate passed
through the hands of our worthy associate, Ned Harwood, and never did the
doctor take a pinch – of snuff, with more solemnity, or handle a subject,‡ with
less risible countenance.

---

* John Hawkesworth, *An Account of the Voyages Undertaken ... for Making Discoveries
   in the Southern Hemisphere*, London, 1773.
† chide or chid: scold, rebuke, find fault with.
‡ Bligh had the doctor examine all the men, including the officers, for venereal
   disease before landing on Tahiti.

It was ever his nature to be gentle, and memory tells me there were moments, and but moments, when I paid him in a different coin.* Yet never, but that it recoiled on me with double force.

It was his duty now, to examine – the affairs of men – with a scrutinising eye. In his report, to 'nothing extenuate, or set down aught in malice'. The report was favourable, and such as to acquit the crew of the *Providence* of a fresh importation of misery to this still cheerful Island. If two subjects could not strictly 'pass muster', we will not doubt, from their situation in the ship, that a sense of benevolence restrained them from error.

7th

After divine service Captain Bligh read some regulations to the officers and ship's company for encouraging an amicable intercourse with various natives with whom we might have intercourse during the voyage. He particularly enjoined us on no account to promulgate the unfortunate death of Cook.[2]

At noon the latitude was observed in 17°..55' south, longitude by account 149°..44' west, when the centre of the island, Mataiea (which had been seen some hours), bore west ½ south about 7 leagues distant, thermometer 80¾°. By four in the afternoon, while passing the north side at about the distance of a mile, three canoes were observed paddling with great exertion to overtake us; the vessels were in consequence brought to the wind. With the hearty confidence of an unoffending people they soon jumped on board and bartered some breadfruit and cocoanuts for nails and other articles. One among our visitors who called himself an *ari'i* or chief, and who, from having taken copiously of an intoxicating beverage called *kava* was quite riotous, entertained us in no small degree. He was dressed in a European shirt, of which he was not a little vain, and gave us to understand it was procured from a ship (*pahi*) that had recently visited the island. We afterwards were informed that it was from the *Matilda* whaler he had got his finery.

The vessels drifted fast from the land, which about sunset occasioned the departure of our visitors who did not wait the canoes coming along side, but jumping overboard with their English goods in one hand, with the other they swam to them. This little island, not above a league in circuit, is one of the most beautiful spots that can be conceived, being in most parts well clothed with a variety of trees, the breadfruit, plantain, and cocoanut, being among the number. The very summit is nearly destitute of verdure for a small space where there is a chasm apparently by some convulsion of nature; probably it is the seat of a volcano. There were several courses from this part of the island to the sea, similar to what are to be seen in most mountainous countries from the effects of heavy

---

*   paid him in a different coin: if an officer or other crew member wanted treatment for venereal disease – usually in the form of mercury – his pay was debted for the treatment.

rain. The habitations of natives, like those of Tahiti, are near the sea. The vessels kept under easy sail throughout the night, in the course of which there was heavy rain.

8th

At daylight we were gratified with a sight of the long wished for island, but at too remote a distance to distinguish, even with our glasses, more than its blue mountains. When about eight miles from Point Venus, the most northern part of the island, our expectations were more than realised in the many delightful views opening in succession as the vessels passed a short league from the shore. The heavy showers of the preceding night had given additional verdure to the lower grounds, while they served to form numberless white cataracts, serpentining amid the foliage on the distant mountains. The beach was tumultuously crowded with natives from their huts, scattered under the umbrage of the luxuriant breadfruit or towering cocoanut, whose leafy plumes waved towards the opposite horizon, on every projecting point of the isle, from the ceaseless pressure of the eastern breeze. Numberless canoes were in motion within an angry reef that seemed to girt the island, yielding security to these pigmy vessels. And on the reef itself, where in a few spots the sea did not force a passage, the natives of both sexes were industriously employed, in procuring shell and other fish; yet not without indulging a respite from their daily avocation in viewing the *Providence* and *Assistant* as they passed.

By noon we were safely anchored in Matavai Bay, after a passage from Spithead of thirty-six weeks. The ship moored in nine fathom water about half a mile from the beach, our consort not far distant. The bearings when moored: The end of the reef north 9°..30' west, Point Venus north 30° east, the heads of Taharaa east end south 3°, west end south 25° west.[3]

Our surprise was great when entering the bay at seeing a whale boat pulling towards the ship. On the crew coming on board we were informed that she was one of four boats which had left the ship *Matilda* of London, Captain Weatherhead, a southern whaler, wrecked a short time before on a low key in the latitude of 22° south, longitude 139°..30' west. On finding it impossible to save the ship, the crew were divided in the boats and steered for Tahiti, which they all reached the ninth day, a distance of nearly seven hundred miles, though one parted company on the first night. The second mate with two seamen left Tahiti a few days before our arrival with a quadrant and compass, under the desperate hope of reaching Sydney in New South Wales 3,300 miles distant, intending to stop for supplies at the Tonga Islands and New Caledonia. To this hour, I have never been able to learn how this ill-judged attempt terminated. With every comfort, it might be said, every luxury within their reach, to trust themselves to the mercy of the waves and power of Indians, in an open boat through a tract of ocean but imperfectly known, could only argue that hardihood and indifference of danger inseparable from British seamen. Yet, is it impossible not to warmly admire the spirit and enterprise of such men.

On the day these daring men took (we have to fear) a last farewell of their shipmates, the *Jenny*, a small vessel belonging to Mr. Teast of Bristol left the island for the northwest coast of America on the fur trade, taking Captain Weatherhead as a passenger. The remainder of the crew perhaps acted wisely in remaining at Tahiti.

The crew of the whaler reported that the adjoining districts of Matavai and Pare, in the neighbourhood of the ship, were in a state of hostility. When the boats of the *Matilda* landed, the greater part of what they contained, particularly four muskets, the ships papers, and a small sum of money, got into the Matavaians possession. The people of Pare laid claim to these articles intending, as they said, to restore them to the first English vessel that arrived, but the Matavaians not thinking proper to comply with the demand, war was declared against them. No hostile operations took place while the *Jenny* remained at the island. Some of the *Matilda*'s crew joined the Matavaians, to which may be attributed in a great measure the cause of the quarrel, as doubtless a positive demand from the royal party of Pare, in conjunction with the whole of the crew, would have been complied with. Their antagonists, headed by Poeno and Tapiru, considered the profession of returning the money and arms to the first ship as an artful scheme to get them in their own possession.

Before the vessels were scarcely at anchor, canoes laden with hogs and various fruits were about us in vast numbers, the natives bartering these articles for iron and other wares. Hatchets were in the greatest demand.

Several chiefs came on board, and in the afternoon we were honoured with a visit from 'Itia, the queen, from whom it was understood that Pomare, the king regent, was at Moorea, an island in sight to the westward. 'Itia, as well as all the visitors, expressed unfeigned joy and satisfaction at meeting their old friend Captain Bligh (*Brihe*) and agreeably to the custom of the island, brought a present of cloth, hogs, and fruit, the former being wrapped around him by Her Majesty. The beauty of her countenance, and the elegance of her figure had felt the ravages of time, but there was in her deportment a complacency and good humour sensibly interesting.

As the sun declined, the canoes returned on shore leaving by far the most desirable part of their freight among our crew, which after the trying self-denial of a long voyage, shut out from the dearest solace life affords, could not but be truly acceptable. 'Itia was among the number, attended by her favourite *tavini* (servant) Mideedee,* the poor fellow who afterwards unfortunately embarked in the *Providence*, in search of distant wonders. The natives in the course of the day

---

*   Oliver uses the word, *teu teu*, for servant, but the dictionary uses, *tavini*. The modern Tahitian for a cook is *tu tu*, which may come from the older term. The name Mideedee is rendered as Hitihiti by Oliver, but his description of that person does not quite fit this individual because Tobin later says his name is the contemporary term for child, which was mideedee.

had been dexterous enough to make my pocket lighter by the handkerchief. With our other visitors came an incredible number of flies.

9th

The natives in their canoes were about us by early dawn and the stock of hogs and fruit increased rapidly. For a *foey* (a flat piece of iron made for the purpose in England, and which the natives fasten to a handle and use as an adze) a moderate-sized hog was procured.

Many chiefs (*ari'is*) visited the ship, and we all began to establish our individual friends. 'Itia examined all the cabins, seemingly quite 'at home' and well acquainted with a ship. I exhibited my stock in trade, and everything I conceived would gratify her, when on presenting her with a few ornaments, she offered to become my *taio*, or friend, which distinguished honour I most readily accepted. As the dinner hour arrived, she sat down at table with us, used her knife and fork not awkwardly and drank many bumpers of Tenerife with great good will. In the evening she presented me with a large hog and two pieces of the island cloth, when we underwent the ceremony of Tahitian friendship. The smaller piece, which was of a thick texture about a yard wide and three in length, in the centre of which there was a hole, I was instructed to put my head through, the ends falling before and behind leaving the arms at freedom. This done, the other piece, above a dozen yards in length, was wrapped round my waist until I became so swaddled as to be nearly immoveable. We then kissed, joined noses, and exchanged names. Her Majesty in return received a present from my store of everything she desired, seemingly quite rejoiced with the treaty. Most of the mess soon established their *taios*, going through nearly a similar ceremony.

The royal party this day applied to Captain Bligh for his assistance against Poeno and Tapiru, who in consequence sent Mr. Norris, surgeon of the *Matilda*, the friend of one of these chiefs, to demand the English property. Mr. Norris passed through the hostile parties without molestation, the whole amounting to about thirteen hundred. They had been engaged with their slings, which they use with great dexterity, but neither side had lost any men. A few muskets were among them. Poeno and Tapiru gave assurance to the surgeon that the articles should be delivered up in a day or two, with which report he returned on board.

10th

Canoes were along side to trade as on the preceding day, bringing hogs and fruit in abundance. Most of the seamen had now established their *taios*, and the cook this day underwent the same ceremony that his captain had done before, but with a native in a more subordinate situation. In the afternoon the Pareans, from which district we had only been visited, were hurried on shore by their chiefs to battle. A little before sunset they were seen returning in great numbers armed with spears and slings; a few among them wore *taumi*, or war mat to protect the breast. The Matavaians had one man killed by a musket, and several wounded with stones.

Old Ha'amanemane, a priest, the *taio* of Pearce, now came on board in a state of great agitation, expressing much dissatisfaction that the royal party was not assisted by King George's people, who they considered as their allies, urging that hostilities were undertaken solely on his account. The old man raged violently, but was pacified in some measure by Captain Bligh assuring him that the Matavaians should not pass the heads of Taharaa (One Tree Hill), a cliff of some extent dividing the two districts.

11th

A native this day was discovered stealing some articles of dress from the *Assistant*. Being the first offence he was pardoned; yet on the same evening he was detected hanging on her cable, waiting the darkness of the night to make a second attempt at theft. On being discovered he swam for the shore and his dexterity was such in diving that had not Mideedee, who was in our boat pursuing him, jumped overboard, he would have effected his escape. On being brought to the ship he was put in irons.

The queen did not sleep on board, having taken leave of us to bring Pomare, the king regent, from Moorea. In the evening we were informed that the Matavaians had retreated to the mountains.

13th

Captain Bligh this morning in company with Ari'paea, next brother to Pomare, went on shore to fix on a spot for an officers' party. This he did, not far from Point Venus, at the back of which the Matavai River emptied itself into the sea. Ari'paea undertook to clear the ground and erect a large shed for the plants, as well as two small houses for the officers and men on duty at the post. The surgeon of the *Matilda* again went to demand the arms.

Soon after breakfast I was sent by Captain Bligh in the cutter to Pare, to bring up the mate of the *Matilda*, who was living in that district. I carried with me a present from the captain to the young King Tu, the son of Pomare, who had taken the late name of his father. Soon after reaching Pare, the youth made his appearance carried on one of his *tavini*'s shoulders, the style in which he ever travelled. He seemed about twelve years of age; his countenance free and open, yet with much curiosity painted in it. The ornaments of dress did not much incommode the young monarch, having nothing but a wrapper of fine white cloth around his loins. On signifying that there were presents from Captain Bligh, I was instructed to give them to his attendants, and afterwards learnt that the custom is strictly observed, it being considered derogatory to his dignity to soil his fingers with anything until reaching his own house. During the whole of this interview, Tu examined with searching looks our different dresses and was particularly pleased with the sleeve buttons of the petty officer. I had scarcely anything about me to offer him but a knife (*tipi*) which was received by one of his suite while the man on whose shoulders the king rested withdrew several paces. On returning, he begged my acceptance of a hog (*pua'a*) but as the mate had now joined, which was the chief object of my mission, and being anxious to lose no time in reaching the ship, I took leave, promising to return to Pare ere long. There was a vast crowd about the boat who waited no solicitation to assist in launching her from the shore.

A number of sailing canoes arrived in the afternoon at Pare from Moorea. These canoes carry a very lofty narrow sail of matting, and in smooth water are able to beat to windward, and yet the natives never attempt to lose sight of the island but with a fair wind. So that from Raiatea, Huahine and the other Society Islands, a voyage to Tahiti is never undertaken with the usual trade wind, which is also as adverse to a canoe reaching Mataiea from Tahiti. Accidents frequently happen, and canoes have been driven to sea nor more heard of. Ari'paea stated that a short time previously to the arrival of the *Providence*, his canoe overturned coming from Tetiaroa, a low island in sight to the northward, and after remaining several hours in the water with his wife and *tavinis*, they were saved by another canoe. Like the common canoes, they are fitted with an outrigger on one side, the double ones, indeed, do not require this security being fastened to each other from the gunwales, about their own breadth asunder. The natives have a singular, yet very simple way of clearing them of water when leaky or from other causes. It is common to see them leap overboard, and by motion of quickly moving the canoe backward and forward, force the water over at each end. It surprised us on these occasions, to observe the little apprehension entertained of sharks. Yet are the natives sensible it is a fish of prey. It had the desirable effect of giving the crew such confidence that the major part bathed along side every evening, which in many tropical countries would have filled them with fears. Only one shark was taken along side during our stay, but from the vast number of their teeth used by the natives in their different ornaments, it would seem that they are not a scarce fish. The shark is call *ma'o*; another kind named by seamen shovel-nosed shark, *ma'o-taupo'o*, the latter part signifying the bonnet worn by the women. These, as well as every kind of fish are eaten in a raw state. It was impossible not to feel disgust, however gratifying the sight of beauty, in beholding a lovely girl mutilating with the most delicately formed fingers, the inside of a large bonito, while feasting on it with the keenest satisfaction. When not eaten this way, after being wrapped in a plantain leaf, it is baked in an oven formed underground with heated stones in the same way as the hogs are cooked. And here it may be in truth observed that the European method of baking is very inferior to it. Sometimes fish are dried in the sun for keeping, but we thought them very insipid.

By the return of Mr. Norris it was learnt that Poeno had quitted the Matavaian district for Ha'apaiano'o a few miles to the east of it, whose inhabitants had given him protection. He received Mr. Norris with real kindness, but refused in the most determined manner parting with the arms, at the same time promising solemnly that the money should be speedily returned, urging as an excuse for not sending it before that it had been conveyed to a distant part of the island. If his enemies, he said, would deliver to Captain Bligh all the arms in their possession, he would readily do the same. Without which, nothing should induce him to leave himself in a defenceless state, as in such an event after the departure of the ships, his district would become a prey to the Pareans, which he had no dread of, while he had firearms to oppose. In case of an attack from the English, it was his intention to fall back to a narrow pass in the mountains where we should never take him alive. Tapiru, the colleague of this enterprising chief, had received a wound in the late battle and was importunate with the surgeon to bring him a speedy cure. The whole of their ammunition did not exceed forty balled cartridges.

In the evening a scene presented itself the most repugnant possible to human nature, a father and mother bargaining for the untasted charms of their child, and it was difficult to discover, which expressed the greatest delight, the parents or their daughter at her being engaged to yield her virgin treasure for a few foreign ornaments, for such were considered a couple of shirts and three or four strings of beads. *Maita'i piriaro* (good shirt) was often heard from the lips of these damsels when particularly interested in pleasing their English visitors. The teenless* fair one, if the expression may be used to a lovely face, partaking more of the olive than either the lily or carnation, received the tempting bait, which the mother took from her with eager joy, leaving her on board 'nothing loth' without that remorse – it is yet to be hoped – which would attend the most depraved European in a transaction of such a nature.

This was not the only instance of the kind that had occurred since our arrival, and it is an indisputable truth that the Tahitian considers it as but a mark of confidence and attention, the offer of a moiety of his wife, and the entire of his sister or daughter to him, with whom he has entered on terms of taioship. Of the turpitude of such an action among ourselves there can be but one opinion. Of its effects on these less rigid people, there is no reason to believe them inimical to order or the most cordial harmony. Never does it take place but with the most hearty and unreserved concurrence of all parties. You may call it indifference if you please, and doubtless to the jealous monopolising European it cannot but appear so. For your friend 'He'd rather be a toad and live upon the vapour of a dungeon than keep a corner in the thing he loves, for other uses.'

The pliant Tahitian argues differently. Yet even there, where the fond swain seldom breathes his warm wishes unheeded, the chilling repulsive denial is sometimes heard. Happily for them, such instances are rare.

The instructed daughters of chastity in our colder regions, no doubt, in their own strength, look with pity and contempt on the infirmity of these poor islanders. True, from their infancy they are taught that this alone will pave their

*   teenless: carefree, happy (teen: affliction, woe).

way to heaven. This jewel inviolate, every discordant passion may riot without impeachment or control. The children of these southern isles know no such doctrine, nor are they the less happy for it. If frail, yet do they largely teem with charity and benevolence. Then condemn them not too harshly, for, with all the frothy aid of systematic instruction, yet do our own fair fall, and deep indeed, for such is the prejudice of an unfeeling world – that the once fond mother who sedulously watched their infant years, and sisters who shared the warm confidence of their bosoms – must know them no more. 'Tis a heart-rending truth. Better then, perhaps, do the thoughtless South Sea islanders act, in looking with a benevolent eye, on what mankind has from the 'beginning' and will to the 'end' err in, even should civilised institutions – which is hardly possible – become more severe, and a still greater restraint be imposed on the laws of all powerful nature.

Ari'paea came on board in the evening after having with a number of natives been working at our encampment. With the greater part of the chiefs, he had acquired a violent attachment to spiritous liquors (*Kava no Pretaney*). Towards night he became quite intoxicated and in high spirits, talking much of his honour and consequence and made many promises to his *taio*, Bond. The wind was from the westward in the morning, giving more than a usual degree of warmth to the atmosphere. The thermometer at noon was $87\frac{1}{2}°$.

The operation of tattooing was this day performed by a native on one of the seamen. The marking instruments are of various breadths, from a quarter of an inch to two, formed of fish bone with teeth like a comb. This is fastened to an handle, forming an adze. After being dipped in a black composition, it is applied to the part intended to be marked and struck sharply with a small wooden spatula. The blows produce blood, as well as considerable pain and subsequent inflammation, but this ceases ere long, while the ornaments, which are various, remain indelible. It is frequently necessary to repeat the operation, from the acute pain endured, when applied to the more susceptible parts of the body. There are many marks adopted by particular classes. The *Ariois* have generally a large spot under the left breast. About the time of entering their teens, the young girls become fit subjects for the tattooing instruments, the swell of the hip and its environs, being chosen for the field of operation. This is sometimes done in curved lines, and at other in a broad one of two or three inches, which on a clear nankeen* coloured skin has a lively effect, giving great relief to the eye. Some prefer the Vandyke fashion, diverging o'er the smooth surface of their more fleshy part, forming a star of nearly half a foot in diameter.

No girl at any of our fashionable finishing seminaries in the neighbourhood of Queen or Bloomsbury Squares, when she takes leave of her tucker,† feels warmer hopes than do these damsels when they submit to this short lived pain.

---

*   nankeen: a yellow or pale buff colour.
†   tucker: a piece of lace or the like, worn by women within or around the top of the bodice in the seventeenth and eighteenth centuries.

The deeper the wounds, the greater the triumph, the more their boast, nor is persuasion at all required to gain an exhibition of these proud stains.

The sight was interesting and novel. Their contempt of pain at so early an age, we could not but admire, yet not more than their complacency in anticipating our most critical researches. The operation is sometimes performed with such severity as to raise the skin considerably, nor were subjects wanting, on whom the rays of light were not necessary, to prove their being tattooed, a *basso-relievo* being very evident to another of the senses.

As whim and notoriety seem, my dear James, to be the 'order of the day' among you, it has surprised me much that some of our dashing demireps* have not come forward – backward might have been said – completely tattooed. If on the embrowned skin of the Tahitian fair one it proves so interesting, how heavenly would it appear in contrast with the snowy whiteness of the ignoble part of our own lovely countrywomen. And then the luxury, with what trembling timidity, would the gazing operator, lost in admiration, apply the instruments. In the evening there was the usual trade wind.

15th

A party under the command of Guthrie landed this day and took possession of our post near Point Venus. Pearce, with his marines, served to give it quite a military appearance. I am not writing for the world, it is true, but I cannot resist bearing, even to you, my humble testimony to the unremitting attention and good conduct of Pearce and his small party from Chatham. Indeed, in essential points of service this truly valuable corps have rarely been found remiss.

The thief this morning, when we were busy, contrived to throw himself overboard without disengaging the irons. By very prompt exertion he was saved from drowning. His countrymen reporting him insane (*maa maa*), he was sent on shore.

Messieurs Wiles and Smith, the botanists, were by this time making considerable progress in the collection of breadfruit and other plants, which were deposited in the shed before mentioned as built for the purpose. About the time there was a cessation of hostilities, but Poeno and Tapiru still kept aloof with a small party.

Pomare paid us his first visit today, but without any form or ceremony. He was accompanied by his father, Teu, a venerable old man apparently about seventy, very grey and infirm, and whose skin was much affected from drinking of *kava*. In the dress of Teu and his son, there was no difference from the other chiefs, but the canoe in which they came was covered with an awning of canes and network. 'Itia was of the party and her sister, Vaiareti, a younger and more handsome wife. My *taio* brought me a hog, some fruit, and a quantity of cloth, the latter being wrapped round me as when we became friends.

---

*   demireps: women of doubtful reputation or chastity.

In honour of the regent's visit some guns were fired which rather alarmed him, nor did he quit the side of Vaiareti, the whole cannonade. 'Itia now complained of hunger, nor was she many minutes in devouring full two pounds of pork, with as much brandy and water as would have staggered any seaman in the ship. Pomare and his two wives slept on board. Poor 'Itia seemed neglected for those charms still in bloom of her younger sister and was seldom allowed to share her lord's bed.

16th

Facts are all I deal in; you, who have more leisure and research, may reason on them as 'seems wise'. It was my destiny this morning to stumble on Ari'paea, brother of the king regent, in an unequivocal situation with Vaiareti. It was by accident, be assured, as it has ever been my maxim – and ever shall – not to interfere with the private avocations of anyone. Nor, should I have entered the six foot cabin of my friend Guthrie – at least without knocking – had I in the slightest degree suspected it had been converted into a rendezvous for gallantry. The discovery, however, served to convince me that the royal family were as incontinent as those in a more subordinate sphere. An enjoinment of secrecy took place, not only from the parties, but, strange to tell, from 'Itia, the neglected and almost repudiated 'Itia. But I am disposed to suspect that she had her weak moments, and that Pomare was the dupe of both. The very high-bred, hackneyed dames of quality of our own island might here take a lesson of courtly indifference.

Dining with Captain Bligh I found Pomare of the party, who never contaminates his hands with the touch of food, but is crammed like a turkey by one of his attendants, nor is it possible to conceive anything more ludicrous than this operation. He received several glasses of wine from me, which I was instructed to pour down his eager throat as he sat with his hands totally unemployed. Pomare appeared about five and forty, as well as his brother's, his skin was darker than that of most of the natives, nor was it much tattooed. In height he was above six feet, and of a strong muscular frame, but an awkward stoop, with a vacant unmeaning countenance, in which indolence and good nature were the leading features. Certainly it must be confessed that Vaiareti evinced taste, although at the extreme of constancy, in preferring Ari'paea, who was a most interesting figure, and bore the character of a great warrior, while that of the regent was quite the reverse.

Pomare had but little external distinction paid him, nor was it uncommon for the *tavinis* to converse jocularly with him and sit in his presence. The women, it is true, were not allowed to eat in his company, indeed the sexes, among all classes at Tahiti, separate when at their meals. It was, however, dispensed with on board the *Providence*, 'Itia and Vaiareti constantly joining at our dinner table with the chiefs.

Many of the Matavaians having withdrawn from the district, their antagonists availed themselves of it to plunder the houses of the few article left in them.

17th

Visiting the post this morning, my messmates seemed comfortably settled, except being dreadfully tormented by flies which are very numerous at the island. I did not hear of any mosquitoes, which is rather singular in a tropical country.

The botanists were busily employed in bringing in plants and forming a little garden. Young Tu was about the post all day, but never dismounted his *tavinis'* shoulders, who alternately relieved each other of their princely burden. Pearce had given him a scarlet jacket, of which he was not a little vain, making him in return a present of some cloth, fruit and a hog. His young majesty without much ceremony asked for everything that particularly pleased him, and had all his requests been complied with, some of us would have been left *Sans Culottes*. Of his privileges he seemed to an inconvenience tenacious; it rained heavily the major part of the day, yet he did not condescend to enter any habitation, taking shelter under the umbrage of a breadfruit tree, and we were informed that he never on any account entered any house but his own. He had the happy facility of pronouncing many English words, particularly those expressive of his wants.

In the young king's retinue was a native of colour disgustingly white. Similar instances have been met with in many Indian countries. He was of a weak frame of body, and by no means equal to his countrymen in figure. The Tahitians have dark penetrating hazel eyes, but those of this poor wretch, who seemed to have been ushered into the world imperfect, were of a light grey colour, and so weak that it was with difficulty he kept them open. His hair and eyebrows, though equally strong with the other natives, were of a white flaxen colour. His skin was sorely blistered by the sun which encouraged the flies to incessantly torment him. The sight of this man perplexed our seamen considerably, nor was it without much persuasion they were convinced he was not a European settled on the island.

I remember being once with you, where a person of a similar description from the African coast was exhibited as a phenomenon. We only went to see. It is for those who search deeply into physical causes to aim at explaining – what they will still be in the dark about – as much as you or me.

Strolling not an hundred yards from the post the Matavai River came suddenly on my view, on the banks of which clear and beautiful stream, the breadfruit, cocoanut, and *avee* were growing in the most luxuriant state, amid which it was mortifying to see most of the houses deserted and many totally destroyed by the war. In crossing the river, which was on the shoulders of a native, there was a friendly conflict among them for this post of kindness and attention. To have refrained from dispersing the few beads (*poes*) in my pockets, among this more than willing group, would have argued a heart callous to every grateful sensation.

18th

Numbers of chiefs were on board early in the morning, their *tavinis* bringing a quantity of *kava* root for their recreation. As the whole process of manufacturing the liquor took place on board, I was particular in observing it. The root, fresh from the ground, the earth not being washed off, is first masticated by the *tavinis* for about two hours, the juice expressed from it being discharged by the mouth into a wooden tray. At this time it becomes of a consistence similar to the cud of an ox, the remains of the root being with it. Milk from the cocoanut is now added and well beat up together. There yet remains to eradicate the coarse and stringy parts, which is effected by rinsing a bunch of grass which collects it, leaving the *kava* a liquid of the colour of muddy water. It is now portioned into cocoanut shells for drinking, and no sooner swallowed than everyone eats immoderately of breadfruit, plantains, or *mahee*, a preparation of the first by fermentation.

'Itia drank nearly a pint of this deleterious beverage, but it seemed that the effect, and not the pleasure while drinking it, was alone cultivated, as no child ever evinced more disgust at a dose of rhubarb than Her Majesty and the whole party did as it passed their lips. It soon spreads its baneful influence on the human frame. In ten minutes my *taio*, scarcely able to support herself, begged permission to recline her tottering limbs on a bed, which was no sooner reached, than she unavoidably sunk into a profound sleep for several hours. Another of their courtly party came reeling into the ward-room with all the symptoms of epilepsy or affection of St. Vitus's dance; this man it was also found necessary to support to another couch. Yet so violently is the attachment of these people to *kava* that it is among the few plants cultivated in the lower grounds, and however averse the Tahitian is to exertion, he thinks his labour well repaid by bringing from the distant mountains this pernicious root, where it grows in abundance. Like many other opiates, it is succeeded by the most enervating effects to the whole body, and when taken to excess, affects the skin with a rough scaly appearance.

Guthrie and myself, however disgusting the preparation, were willing to follow the example of our visitors. About half an hour after taking a large tea cup full, which was but a moderate dose, its narcotic effects were very perceptible, a pleasurable giddiness succeeding, which soon terminated in an undisturbed sleep of about three hours. The small quantity taken was probably the reason why I suffered but little after awaking, a slight uneasiness over the temples, which subsided in about an hour, only taking place, but so sweet is the sleep promoted by *kava*, that were it now within reach of your friend, it would be sought with avidity, even with the certainty of a subsequent headache, on shattered frame, sometimes experienced by taking too copiously of *kava no Pretaney* (English *kava*). My messmate experienced similar effects with myself.

It is not within my recollection whether the *kava* plant was taken on board the *Providence* at Tahiti, but it certainly never reached the West Indies. The root from its powerful nature might probably be of use in medicine. It would appear, from an account in some old voyages, that it was known in these seas nearly two centuries ago. Schouten in 1616 at Horn Island in latitude 14°..16' south says, 'After this, they prepared for solemn banquet, and in order to do it began to make ready their liquor, which they did in this slovenly manner. There came into the presence a company of fellows with a good quantity of Cana (which is the herb of which they make their drink) each of which, having crammed in a mouthful of it, they began to chew together; having chewed it awhile, they put it out of their mouths into a large wooden trough and poured water upon it, and fell to stirring and squeezing it, and having pressed out all the goodness, they presented it to the two Kings.'

19th

Several chiefs from Moorea visited the ship, Pomare being very assiduous in pointing out her different parts. Although a dull man, he gained much in our esteem by his uncommon good nature. I again met him at Captain Bligh's table, where 'Itia and Vaiareti joined the party and ate in his presence, notwithstanding a forbearance of it was strictly observed on shore. His younger wife shared the honour of his bed on board.

About sunset the girls collected on the quarterdeck to dance the *heiva* – as usual. No solicitation was required, as they took great delight in this amusement. The party on these occasions consisted, generally, of from ten to twenty. The chief study of the performers seemed to be in keeping exact time with their feet and hands, clapping the latter together with great regularity and a sharp noise; at the same time repeating short sentences with an arch look, chiefly the scandal of the day, where our names, as well as those of our island friends, were frequently introduced. The dances were of short continuance, but often repeated, the performers exhibiting their pliant well-formed limbs in the most sportive postures. At times, full of the most encouraging invitation, when suddenly, as if anger or neglect gave birth to it, the coy repulsive movement succeeded – but of short duration – as, at the winding up of the dance, every look, every motion, solicited the warm admiration of the gazing spectators. And may the good and cheerful girls, long dance the *heiva*, unconscious that among us, it would be deemed full of danger to the morals of our refined damsels. 'Tis the custom of our favoured isle, and in doing it, you are as free from turpitude as the city miss, who, under the strict observance of her mamma's eye, stiffly paces at Lord Mayor's ball the laboured minuet, or rustic red-cheeked lass, who, in the hoyden* revel, receives the eager pressure of her partner's lips with more than half met joy.

---

*   hoyden: a rude or ill-bred girl.

21st

Having made a party in the hope of reaching the source of the Matavai, we left the post at early dawn. Its direction for a short distance was parallel with the beach, then from the east about a quarter of a mile, when it again took a northern course from the mountains.

About a mile and an half from the post, after passing the low land which in most parts girts the island, we entered a valley about half a mile across, the hills rising gently on each side richly clothed above half way to their summits with breadfruit, cocoanut, *avees*, *eratta* (a large kind of chestnut) and many other trees whose names were unknown to us. The soil was here very rich. We passed many houses, but in general they were injured and deserted in consequence of the war. The valley, however, was not destitute of people, and, as is ever the case with the European traveller at this island, our party increased as we went along.

Advancing up the stream, breadfruit and cocoanuts became scarce, and the valley more confined. After walking about three miles, having crossed the river several times on the natives' shoulders, we came to some inhabited houses, contiguous to which was an offering to the *atua* (or god) on account of the war. The oblation consisted of twelve hogs placed on four stools, three on each, about five feet from the ground. Near them was a square pavement of about twelve feet, and one high, with twenty long stones standing upright on it, ornamented at their tops, about two feet high, with the common bonnet (*taupo'o*) worn by the women. Ignorance of the language denied our getting any information, but that everything was sacred to *atua*, and that the offering was for his protection in the war. The hogs were in a dreadful putrid state, giving the air of this part of the valley by no means a fragrance. A little higher up, three very fine shaddock trees attracted our notice, two of them teeming with fruit. The natives estimate* this fruit but lightly, though they call it *Uru no pretaney* (English breadfruit) They were brought from the Tonga Islands.

These trees were planted in 1777 by the late Mr. Nelson, who was with Captain Cook in his last voyage. An old man, whose habitation received shade from them, spoke with affection and the warmest gratitude of our countryman, and with unfeigned sorrow lamented his death when informed of it. Here, we sufficiently understood one another's language; little indeed was there to explain. Nelson died at Timor in 1789. The country soon became more wild and picturesque. In many places the current being impeded by huge rocks, where it did find a passage, was very rapid. Breadfruit and cocoanuts were no more to be seen, but there were plantains the whole of our walk, and the soil, where free from rocks, productive. On either side many beautiful cataracts from a great height suddenly caught the eye, yet not without a warning as we approached, by their roar in forcing a passage among the woody cliffs to the stream below. At this distance no more habitations were observed.

---

*   estimate: esteem.

Our guides now became urgent for returning, but though every foot became more difficult, we were not willing to leave undetermined the object of our pursuit; another inducement also, the hope of reaching a cascade called Peeir by the natives, made us journey on. Extending our rugged walk about two miles, we were indeed rewarded for our labour. It is formed by a perpendicular basaltic rock of above an hundred feet, extending at its base, on the right bank of the river, more than two hundred. The margin above projects a few feet, the water falling in a broad sheet without meeting resistance until it reaches some detached rocks, whence by several channels a still, deep pool receives it. The pillars are closely connected, but in many parts broken. Similar rocks were observed in the course of our walk. The drawing of the Peeir was from recollection on returning to the post,* perhaps the pillars may not be critically correct, but the general appearance is all that is attempted. The weather had been dry for some days previously to our excursion up the Matavai; doubtless after rain the fall acquires an additional degree of beauty and grandeur.

Above the Peeir the river became very confined. In some places it was a clear deep pool, while in others it rushed amid the rocks with great force and rapidity. Our island friends had by this time quitted us in numbers, being reduced to about a third of the party gleaned in the valley. The day advanced so fast, we were under the necessity of returning, much chagrined at not having reached the source. A rock in the mid-stream served as a resting place, where we sat down to refresh ourselves with cocoanut milk, of which fruit some had been brought from the lower grounds. There could not be a more delightfully retired spot. Every surrounding object disposed the mind to quiet contemplation. On the one side a lofty mountain rich clothed with various trees to the summit, whose branches nearly reaching a stupendous bald cliff opposed to it, overhanging the river full of threats, scarcely allowed a glimpse of the blue canopy of heaven; yet through the playful foliage was a faint view of the purpled summit of the isle (Orohena) far above the fleeting clouds along its side. The tropic bird, the shearwater, and other sea fowl, as if weary of their wat'ry element, were ranging high in the air above these craggy steeps, in whose recesses they rear their young. Here no animal, no reptile with envenomed fang, as in most tropical countries, is to be found checking the ardent researches of the traveller. Not even the soaring rapacious kite, the trembling dread of the smaller feathered tribe, was here ever seen.[4]

From so interesting a spot, it was not that we returned to the boisterous scenes of nautic employment without reluctance. It was night ere we reached our encampment, not a little fatigued, yet highly gratified with the excursion.

In many parts of the river the natives were procuring small fish by making a dam across it with stones where it was shallow. To this dam the fish were driven by people coming down the stream and beating it with bushes, interstices† being

---

*   See Plate 17.
†   interstices: intervening spaces.

made to which baskets were applied. It is hardly credible what numbers are taken in this simple way. Others were caught near the bottom by introducing a small 'landing net' under them.

22nd

Mahau, the *taio* of Guthrie, visited the ship this morning. This chief, a native of the island of Raiatea, was above six feet three inches in height, with a handsome countenance and very robust figure. A recent discovery proved him to be as incontinent as his neighbours; but the sister of Pomare was always remarkable for her gaiety,* and is mentioned by Captain Cook as excelling in the *heiva*. Nor indeed had she forgotten it, frequently mingling in the dance with the younger damsels on the quarterdeck of the *Providence*. As the Tahitians do us the honour of imitating some of our manners, no little pains were taken to please her, in the assurance that our English ladies never felt old, that being grandmothers rendered them more lovely in the eyes of our chiefs, and that five and forty was the criterion of beauty, while the warm blood mantled but in vain on the vermeil† cheek of neglected sixteen. Where, James, did our countrymen acquire this strange, this unseemly propensity? Is fashion, as in the cut of our coats, to influence us in an election where nature should alone guide? Surely, such ought not to be.

In the evening the marines were exercised with which the natives, who had assembled in vast numbers, were highly satisfied.

Breadfruit and other plants were rapidly collecting, and Messieurs Wiles and Smith soon expected to complete their numbers.

Tu about this time built a small house not far from the post, intending to spend some days at Matavai. Ari'paea with his wife, Vahine Metua, and her sister were on board most of the day; the latter, Ari'paea presented to his *taio*, nor would the laws of hospitality admit of his refusing the boon of this generous chief. Vahine Metua was fed by one of her *tavinis*, but we were informed, only for a certain period, in consequence of the recent death of a relation. In her ear she wore a lock of the hair of the deceased, her own being cut in ridges as a mark of sorrow.

Every day served to convince us the more of the violent attachment of these people to intoxicating liquors, as well as to their own *kava*; 'Itia this evening on the parade was past utterance, and it was necessary to support her from falling.

23th

In the afternoon I accompanied our worthy doctor in a walk to the eastward of the river. Our notice was soon drawn to a double canoe hauled up on the beach

---

*   Oliver gives the name of Pomare's sister as Auo.
†   vermeil: vermillion.

near to which was Tu's house. Here, for the first time, I saw him sit down. Being desirous of examining the canoe, as we approached it the young monarch evinced much displeasure, his attendants repeating *atua, atua* (the god, the god): not wishing to give any offence we proceeded no farther, but it sufficed to observe that on one of the prows there was a roasted hog with the head of another besides breadfruit, plantains and sugar canes. The other prow supported a large bundle about five feet in length covered with red European cloth. Several bunches of feathers were hung to different parts of the canoe, and on its fore part was erected a stage three feet in height, supported by a railing on which was a long box in the form of a coffin covered with a canopy of reeds and network. It was understood that this box was to protect the *atua*, (who was wrapped up in the red cloth) in bad weather. The canoe had recently arrived, decorated in this manner from Pare, Tu coming in her. On the beach were two island drums ornamented with European cloth. The provisions were for the *atua*'s consumption. Tu's house was nearly full of the different finery with which he had been presented by officers of the various vessels that had visited Tahiti.

April–May 1792

Visit Pare.—Coral rocks.—Tarro.—Pomare's large house.—Climbing cocoanut trees.—Terano.—Fishing.—Dine with Tarro.—Fare tupapa'us, with a corpse.—Meat, how baked.—Bamboo forks.—Salt water for sauce.—One Tree Hill.—Girls dancing the heiva.—Talk of peace.—Great desire of the natives for shot and powder.—Strong liquors.—Mr. Whyte robbed.—Dine with several chiefs in the cabin.—Vaiareti, Pomare's younger wife.—Visit Ha'apaiano'o with the surgeon.—Upset in a canoe.—The root taro.—Secession of the sea.—Visit Tapiru.—His character.—Ha'apaiano'o River.—Visit Vaetua.—Stone marae.—Vaetua's wife Tai Aiva.—Taurumi, the operation of.—Native fishing for mullet.—Excursion up Matavai River.—Mother of the king regent visits the ship.—Maid of honour.—Native punished for thefts.—Plaited human hair.—Tamow.—Statutes at Large.—Vahine Metua jealous.—Noise of pigs.—Pomare fed.—Arioi Society.—Sheets stolen.—Pomare's attendants.—Virgin.—Drummer punished.—Kids wanted.—Attend watering party.—&c. &c.

Thetis, coast of America February 1797

24th

A small party this morning was made to visit the district of Pare and the country westward of it. On reaching the harbour, which we did in a canoe, the sea was as smooth as glass, affording us the gratification of a submarine view of the coral rocks on either side of its deep but narrow entrance, branching in the most singular forms, among which a variety of highly coloured fish were gliding about in search of food.[1] Soon after landing our party was increased by the surgeon of the *Assistant*, with his *taio*, Tarro, who ordered a hog to be baked for dinner against our return. For five or six miles our walk was by the windings of the coast, a reef encircling it the whole way from a quarter to three quarters of a mile distant, through which at about mid-way, there is an opening to Taawney Bay. On the west part of this bay was a very large house belonging to Pomare at this time inhabited by an old Raiatean chief, who received us with real hospitality, instantly sending his *tavinis* to a neighbouring tree for cocoanuts to refresh us.

The natives climb these trees with an agility and confidence really surprising. They first fasten to their feet a piece of soft rope made of grass, about three feet in length, which being doubled extends nearly as much. After embracing the tree, they tress with their feet this band, which prevents them from slipping, and thus alternately shifting their hands and feet, in a short minute reach the fruit which is frequently nearly an hundred feet from the ground. Nor is the manner in which the fruit from this height is preserved from injury in the fall, less to be admired. This is effected by a sudden twist of the hand, giving it a spiral motion while descending through the air, by which means it falls on the point without bursting, which otherwise would be the case. They do not always succeed in the attempt, and when the fruit falls on its side a loss of milk is generally the consequence. You are well acquainted with the cocoanut and will be the more surprised in being told that it is not uncommon to see these islanders taking off the husk with their teeth without any difficulty.

As this was the largest house I saw on the island, it made me particular in getting the dimensions. The length was sixty-two yards, and the extreme breadth fifteen, supported at the ridge by nine pillars about sixteen feet high, and at the eaves by seventy-two, half of that height. Except at one end for about ten yards, where it was enclosed by bamboo railing, the whole extent was open to the free current of air; the roof was a strong thatch of the *wharra* tree (wild pine).* Waiting some time with the old Raiatean, our walk was continued to the house of Torano, an elderly lady related to the royal family, and who was frequent in her visits to the ship. On presenting her a knife (*tipi*) she was very thankful. The sun became so oppressively warm as we walked along the beach that it obliged us to return. The tide had fallen, and it is almost incredible the number of people, chiefly women and children, that were employed along the shore and on the reefs in procuring shell and other fish by various means. There was one boy with a stick about ten feet in length, at the end of which was a fine line, which being passed through a small hole, acted as a noose. This he applied to the small recesses of the coral rocks, snaring the fish as they passed in and out with great success. The stick he guided with his right hand, attending the line with his left. Not anything that the sea produces is rejected by the Tahitian; even the sea egg† is eaten; greedily in the raw state.

Torano's house again served as a resting place, where we found a mat spread on the grass under a breadfruit tree with the usual refreshments. Being engaged to dine with Tarro, the old lady's friendly offer of slaughtering a hog was not accepted. She in fact ordered her *tavinis* to put one in requisition, which Tarro communicated barely in time to save it.

The route homewards differed by its being through the plain. The intense heat of the sun, with the progress of a flood tide had brought the fishers among the shady breadfruit from their labours, and the same number of these cheerful people were still seen. Several streams from the mountains served to refresh every part of this plenteous plain. Some *maraes* or burying places, as well as *fare tupapa'us*, where the dead are for a time placed until ultimately deposited in the former, attracted our notice. These were scattered all over the district, no particular part being allotted for them. One, considerably more splendid than the

---

*   *wharra* (wild pine): screw pine.
†   sea egg: sea urchin.

rest, you will see a drawing of.* It was a square of fifteen feet by twelve, and nearly five in height. Inside this enclosure of reeds, which was decorated with bunches of the *wharra* (wild pine), was a stage about six feet from the ground, supported by wooden pillars. Boards were fixed on this stage, the corpse being laid on them, covered with the country cloth, red as well as white. From the stage, rails on each side supported a canopy of reeds, covered with black and white cloth, richly ornamented with tassels of cock's feathers. The back and sides of the canopy were hung with white cloth. Under the stage a large sleeping mat was folded with much care, and in the front of the enclosure a quantity of white cloth lay on the ground, near to which a square of about eighteen feet was covered with fresh grass in the manner of the floors in some of the chief's houses. The mat, we were told, was for the deceased to sleep on when it was necessary. A few yards from the *fare tupapa'u*, different kinds of food were placed on a small table, which was to be frequently replenished.

A small *marae* was near at hand, consisting of a pavement nearly thirty feet square and about two high, with nothing remarkable about it, but the bust of a man carved in stone, the only instance I saw of sculpture among these people. Cocoanuts and plantains were growing among the stones of the *marae*.

It was the corpse of the child of an *ari'i*. The mother was present while we were peeping into the contents of the tomb, more amused with our curiosity, than concerned for what gave occasion to it, laughing heartily, the whole time.

Soon after reaching Tarro's house, a fine hog smoking from the oven made its appearance. It can hardly be necessary for you to be informed that the Tahitians bake their meat by first digging a hole in the ground, in which are placed stones heated for the purpose in a fire close at hand. The animal being wrapped in several folds of plantain, or other large leaves, is laid on these stones, when more, equally hot, are placed above, and the whole well covered with earth, the air being totally excluded. In less than three hours a large hog is in this manner admirably baked, superior indeed by far than could be effected in the most finished European oven. Plantains and other fruit are frequently placed inside of the animal baking.

Tarro's dinner was served up with as much taste as his island utensils would admit. He did not forget to point out having prepared a table cloth in the English style, and he had employed his own and his *tavinis* time during our walk in making forks of bamboo, supposing it would please.

Here, have we a lesson for the frothy unmeaning courtier who would smilingly persuade us, he anticipates our every comfort. While, perhaps in the same breath, he wishes us at – the devil. Tarro did it in the honesty of his soul.

As a substitute for salt, a cocoanut shell of the pure Pacific Ocean was placed by each guest, nor without being found very palatable after a little use. After taking a hearty and most welcome meal, and with *kava no Pretaney* drinking the health of King George, a custom generally followed on such occasions by the

---

*   See Plate 20.

chiefs, we bid our host a good evening. During the whole visit Tarro's house was surrounded by natives, striving who could be foremost in rendering us any service.

The distance from Pare to the post was about two miles. A cliff called generally by us 'One Tree Hill' is the boundary line of the two districts. After passing this spot, we met a large party of girls dancing the *heiva*, who on joining, redoubled their exertions to please, nor could we in return resist distributing a few beads (*poes*) left in our pockets, among these nimble damsels. They were on their road to get a lodging on board the *Providence* or *Assistant*, and having a little leisure, ere the hammocks were piped down, travelled in this cheerful manner. It was common indeed, to see them when on a journey from one district to another, dancing merrily along the whole way, nor without the hope of meeting some of our countrymen who were always solicited for some trifle or other with such an artless smile, it could not but be complied with.

About this time Poeno, with many of the Matavaians, returned and began erecting houses on the spots where the old ones had been demolished by their enemies. Peace was much talked of, a meeting of the chiefs having taken place at Pare to consider of it.

Walking up the river with my gun many natives attended, and it is impossible to describe the pleasure they evinced at seeing a swallow shot flying. So great is the estimation these people place on all kinds of firearms and ammunition that a dozen of them were anxiously employed in picking up the few shot that fell on the ground in charging my gun, and but a few days before one of the chiefs offered the sergeant of marines some curiosities in great demand, for four balled cartridges.

The traffic at first so acceptable to these altered people now bears little value when compared with weapons of any kind, and there is but too much reason to dread the sad consequences of vessels, particularly trading ones, touching at this and the neighbouring isles. For a dozen muskets and a good proportion of ammunition a large vessel could procure an abundant supply of provisions. Strong liquors are also sought with avidity. These among too many others are acquired evils at Tahiti, unknown happily, until introduced by the visits of civilised nations. What does the future promise? Does the avaricious trader much heed what misery his destructive articles produce among untutored Indians? He wants refreshments and supplies to enable him to prosecute, in this distant quarter of the globe, his greedy scheme of gain. And if gunpowder, or pernicious enervating brandy, should be demanded in preference to the useful axe, or ornamental bead, will they not be given without reflecting on the consequences?

Until this day, the natives only interrupted us by kindness in our excursions, but Mr. Whyte, one of the surgeon's mates wandering too far without a guide, was plundered of his handkerchief by a man whom he met in the woods. The thief displayed some address and ingenuity having offered his friendly services to conduct our countryman to the hills, while his shoulders bore him safely over many a stream, until far from the busy 'haunts of man', when, being by far the strongest of the two, he without ceremony rifled the doctor's pockets, nor did he leave instructions which was the shortest way back to the post.[2]

With Pomare, Ari'paea, 'Itia and Vaiareti, I had the honour of dining at Captain Bligh's table today. The king regent had scarcely finished his meal when he betook himself to toy with the false Vaiareti who, heedless of our presence, was reclining her finely turned limbs, not too much enveloped in drapery, on the cabin floor.

There was a disparity in years of Pomare and Vaiareti, which at Tahiti is by no means uncommon. It has before been observed that His Majesty is of the numerous fraternity of cuckolds, but like many among ourselves, seemed not aware of what he was robbed, or else, was indifferent about it. Yet did he dote on his younger wife, who with an art, inseparable from her sex, managed this amorous infirmity to her own benefit and amusement.

The whole day Ari'paea was very indignant in consequence of several articles having been stolen from our shipmates at the post, giving every assurance that strict search would be made to discover the thief.

29th

Early in the morning Harwood and myself quitted the ship for the post, with an intention of walking to Ha'apaiano'o, five or six miles eastward of Point Venus, first calling on board the *Assistant* for a gentleman who was to be of the party. The canoe in which we were going on shore was a single one, very small, and heavily freighted, nor was it long before she overturned, sousing us all completely. Had not our good doctor effected a fast grip on the outrigger, where he clung magnanimously, the 'number of our mess' would have been reduced, and the world have lost a truly estimable character, as he could no more swim than one of his own coins. To the rest, it was rather a ludicrous affair, as a boat from our consort soon landed us in safety. This disaster did not frustrate the excursion, and getting our clothes dried at the post, we proceeded with two confidential natives.

We soon passed a quantity of taro, a kind of yam or *eddoe*, with which the island abounds, it being issued daily to our crew as one of the substitutes for bread. This root delights in a moist soil: in many places it was in a luxuriant state nearly half a foot in the water. Some pains had been bestowed in enclosing it against the destruction of their hogs.

The surf along the beach broke high, though sheltered by a reef, an opening in which appeared about two miles from Point Venus, as well as others, as we walked eastward. The path along shore was nearly obstructed when about four miles from the post, by a high cliff forming the western boundary of Ha'apaiano'o. As well as their language would admit, our guides described that when Captain Wallis visited the Island in 1767, there was no travelling, even at low water, at the foot of these cliffs and that there had been a gradual secession of the sea on the most parts of the island.

Tapiru had taken up his residence in this district, to whom we paid a visit, being received with much civility, yet with a reserve that seemed to arise from an apprehension our views might be hostile to his party. He was surrounded by Matavaians and his own family, apparently prepared for an attack.

The whole conduct of this chief evinced a spirit of enterprise and dignity of character superior to anyone I had yet seen. Most of his front teeth were missing from the blow of a stone in defending what he deemed his right, and he had still an unhealed wound in his knee from the same weapon. In our conversation pistols were mentioned, which certainly caught his attention, while it animated a countenance in which suspicion could not but be perceived that he still doubted his visitors. This it was our study to remove, when he anxiously requested to see them. Thinking he would be gratified I fired at a mark, which more from accident than skill, took place exactly, gaining me so much applause that I had prudence not to risk losing it by a second attempt. Being our host, we said nothing, from a point of delicacy, of the *Matilda*'s muskets, but were afterwards informed that he kept them under his sleeping mat.

The usual refreshments of fruit and cocoanut milk being taken, the walk was continued about two miles further eastward, when the river presented itself, after our having crossed several smaller streams. The mouth of the Ha'apaiano'o is above an hundred yards across, its bed being formed of large dark pebbles. The view up the stream is singularly grand and picturesque, but it was rendered imperfect this day by the distant mountains being enveloped in clouds. A sketch I made will give you a faint idea, – and but a faint one – of this beautiful landscape.* The usual mode of crossing the rivers, on the natives shoulders', placed us on the eastern bank, but after heavy rains, this is not to be effected but in canoes.

Vaetua, the *taio* of Harwood, who had a house in this district, received us cordially, instantly ordering the slaughter of a hog (*pua'a*) but as time would not admit of the whole being baked, a limb was cut off and put in the oven. As usual we were surrounded by men, women and children from all parts of the plain who, without any deference to the mansion of a prince of the blood, soon completely filled it.

While the joint was baking, we strolled up the stream to a place sacred to the *atua* (god) in a large enclosed square of railing. Near to it was a stone *marae*, (burying place) and, as at the *fare tupapa'u* in Pare, a small table with different kind of provisions. All information was denied us by our ignorance of the language, except that everything was sacred to *atua*, even a musical instrument formed of a large conch shell with a bamboo pipe to it. Apropos, there is one of them in our collection at home.

The shoulder was served up on our return, and cleanliness, if not elegance, was as conspicuous as at the most fashionably appointed table in Europe. Leaves, fresh from the tree, served for a table cloth, the appetite had been assisted by

---

*   See Plate 15.

exercise, and we had the cheering looks of our host – when awake – with those of his pretty wife Tai Aiva – the Belle of the Isle – to crown the whole.

Vaetua during our walk had taken a moderate portion of *kava*, and we found him reclining on the lap of his wife, much disposed to sleep, nor was it long before the somnific effects of the *kava*, aided by the operations of *taurumi* (in which Tai Aiva and the *tavinis* were employed), fixed him in a sound nap for an hour or two.

After fatigue, I have experienced the most delightful relief from this custom (*taurumi*) of rubbing and compressing the different parts of the body, and so sensible are the natives of its salutary effects that we never entered a house after a long walk but that it was offered to be administered, which I can assure you was ever eagerly embraced by your friend. Pomare was generally encouraged in his afternoon nap by the operation *taurumi*, nor was it uncommon to see it persevered in, after the drowsy god had taken possession of His Majesty. Taking a friendly leave, we returned towards the post.

Tai Aiva crossed the Ha'apaiano'o in simple nudity, unconscious of her hitherto hidden charms. For the translucency of the stream but ill served, however in some places deep, to envelop them.

Tapiru's served as a resting place, where everything was prepared for our refreshment. It was flood tide, and many of the natives were fishing for mullet with rod and line in the same manner the fly is used for trout.

May 2nd

Mr. Frankland, surgeon of the *Assistant*, accompanied me early in the morning to explore the mountains towards Orohena as far as the day would allow. In our way through the plain three natives attached themselves to us. The hills above the plain rose gradually in ridges, being generally clothed with fern, but nearly destitute of trees. The soil did not appear good, but higher up it improved. A path was soon reached taking the direction we wanted.

About four miles from the post, in a southern direction, having passed the middle hills before mentioned, the country became more woody, as we continued along a ridge separating Matavai River from a smaller one eastward of it. The path was so narrow, our march was by Indian file. On either side was a valley some hundred yards beneath, in many places the descent nearly perpendicular. Two of the natives here bade us farewell, but the one, on whom we placed confidence as a guide, journeyed on with spirit.

On the departure of his countrymen, a small piece of baked hog, a single cocoanut, and a small pocket flask of brandy, was all our provender, and though surrounded with trees, none offered any fruit that was eatable. The air was oppressively warm, and our limbs felt wearied in clambering these steeps. One now before us was so discouraging that it was with pleasure the almost lost path was observed to take a direction down its eastern side. Here were great forests of wild plantain trees, but not in fruit. We were, however, agreeably surprised in meeting water in the hollows of the rocks. Of this we drank perhaps incautiously, rested awhile and followed the path which brought us to the other side of the mountain, but only to present still higher rising to the view. Here they shut out the river to the eastward, but the natives beating of cloth lower down its banks was still heard.

On a bird's eye view of the Matavai from this spot there was a village of about a dozen houses on a spot of cleared land near the base of Orohena. To this village the *Ariois* resorted at particular periods to indulge uninterruptedly in unbounded licentiousness.

As, for want of time, it was found impracticable to further ascend the mountains, the guide promised to conduct us to the *Arioi* village, giving an assurance that after surmounting a high steep in front, a path led directly to it.

It was about noon, and a refreshing breeze, hitherto attending us, began to decline. Our limbs courted rest, and on looking at the guide, the cocoanut was missing. All these drawbacks staggered our resolution, and it was determined, instead of proceeding higher, to strike directly through the woods for the Matavai.

As nearly as could be estimated from the rate of travelling, we were at this time about seven miles in a direct line from Point Venus, and five from Orohena, but it appeared impracticable to ascend the summit by the northern side.

On looking about ere we descended, on all sides but the north, where the ocean and the small island of Tetiaroa formed the limit, we were surrounded by mountains richly clothed with wood to their very tops. Our elevation was so great that the eye circumnavigated Tetiaroa, from whence to the visible horizon, was several leagues, and it was plain to determine, like many of the South Sea islands, that it was encircled by a reef. The *Providence* and *Assistant*, at anchor in Matavai Bay, though so much nearer, could only be distinguished as two specks on the blue surface of the water.[3]

Our grand object was to reach the river, but for ten yards before us there was no answering, the woods were so very close. The guide, however, pushed on cheerfully, and by vaulting from tree to stone, and from stone to tree, with the variety of sliding on a part which the climate did not require to be heavily covered, trusting frequently to unfaithful twigs, and mouldering rocks, we found ourselves about an hundred yards lower.

While the Tahitian continued in view, all went on well. Yet could we not conceal that our situation was not cordially relished, and we found too late that to inveigle us into it was a plan for the purpose of robbing us with impunity. Taking advantage of some thick underwood in front, he scampered off with the agility of a monkey, nor more to be seen.

The ingenuity of our fellow traveller was great. I had my pistols with me, which to satisfy his curiosity had been frequently discharged in the course of our walk, and in return for this attention he very politely offered to carry them for the English chief, who as simply granted it. Besides the pistols, he had both our jackets, and, direful to relate, the bit of pork for which our stomachs now yearned. The brandy bottle was still left, with which we sat down on a projecting stump without a casting vote as to our proceedings. After a short debate, the same course was continued, not without execrating the Tahitian, and our own simplicity, until we came suddenly on the margin of a precipice, the bottom of which could not be seen from trees. However laborious the task, it brought us to the necessity of again ascending, which short as was the distance, took nearly two hours to effect.

Journeying homewards by the old path it felt light in comparison, however much we were fatigued, but the want of water was indeed felt, nor did a frequent application of the brandy bottle give relief to your friend, though it had the wished for effect with his companion. At length reaching the water among the rocks, we almost deluged our parched frames, and to our great joy found the lost cocoanut, which was swallowed with avidity. A simple lunch of the wild plantain was here seen, but after the trouble cutting down the tree, the fruit was so strong and coarse as not to be eatable. Ginger and turmeric were growing in abundance; the latter indeed is to be met in most parts of the island and is used by the natives as a yellow dye.

The moon assisted us to the post late in the evening after having lost our way several times. Nor was the good supper and *kava no pretaney*, prepared for us by our shipmates, at all unwelcome; yet could we have dispensed with the laughter occasioned by our disasters.

Though we did not reach Orohena, it was ascertained that the Matavai was supplied by numberless falls of water from this mountain, which serpentining amid the woods had a picturesque appearance. Many fern trees, some above twenty feet in height, were in great beauty on the mountains; *kava* was also observed, appearing to thrive best in a high situation.

3th

Purea-Tepupaia, mother of the king regent, this morning paid her first visit to Captain Bligh. The old lady was so very corpulent it was necessary to hoist her on board in a chair. She no sooner reached the cabin, than a very curious scene took place. To express her happiness at meeting Captain Bligh, she threw herself on the floor weeping bitterly in loud lamentations. Her whole suite soon caught the sad infection, and it was a full hour before this woeful ceremony closed; when the queen dowager and her court regained their wonted cheerfulness, visiting our different cabins, where they asked for beads and other articles.

On her receiving a present from one of my messmates, she graciously begged his temporary acceptance of one of her 'maids of honour'. He was ever well bred, and incapable of giving offence, so that, however his philosophic disposition resisted it, the power was denied him of refusing the friendly offer of Purea-Tetupaia.

The queen dowager appeared above sixty, yet with as fine a set of teeth as can be imagined. The teeth indeed of these people are in general desirably white and regular. Perhaps the latter quality is occasioned by their mouths being larger than most Europeans, which I am disposed to believe arises from the custom of extending and distorting it when dancing the *heiva*. The quantity of vegetable diet used, no doubt preserved their colour, while it gives a purity to the breath rarely to be met with where too much animal food is taken into the stomach. After meals they seldom fail thoroughly washing their mouths.

In the evening Purea-Tetupaia was lowered into her canoe and went on shore – her suite being reduced by the aforesaid maid of honour – which no doubt was it to reach the ears of many bearing the same rank in our red book,* a degree of indignation would be felt at the frailty of the Tahitian court.

A scarcity of cocoanuts was observed about this time in the public stock, and other provisions were brought in but slowly. The eager demand for shells, ornaments and other curiosities, however publicly discouraged, occasioned this scarcity. Some petty thefts were committed by the natives, on board, as well as at the post, to check which Captain Bligh caused one man taken in the act of stealing a handkerchief to be punished. After receiving a dozen lashes, which he seemed to heed but little, he jumped over board and swam on shore with perfect indifference.

Nothing was yet heard respecting the *Matilda*'s money. It had most probably been dispersed about the island, as one of the officers had recently purchased two dollars for a knife from a native whom he met in the woods.

The Matavaian district was now rapidly increasing with its old inhabitants, and many new houses were erected. Tapiru, however, still kept at Ha'apaiano'o with the arms.

4th

The whole court remained on board nearly the whole day. It might indeed have been said, from the length and frequency of their visits, that they were our own family.

My *taio* brought me a present of plaited human hair, about the thickness of a double thread. It is worn by the women as an ornament round the head in the manner of a turban, and called *tamow*.† The superior sort of dancing girls generally decorate themselves with it.

This was the only present brought to me by 'Itia for a considerable time, which occasioned our being rather on cool terms. She had reproved me for not being more bountiful, which in some measure was a true charge, but as I wanted some articles difficult to be procured in the neighbourhood of Matavai. I still thought it politic to withhold any gifts until she brought them, at the same time making as great a display of my riches as possible, which had the desired effect of soon placing me in possession of a war mat (*taumi*) and some other curiosities.

---

*   red book: most likely this is *Collin's Peerage*.
†   *tamow*: Tobin's term for these objects.

To get such kind of articles there was no little difficulty, from the eagerness with which we sought them, and from the introduction of European implements having rendered many of them nearly useless, the stone-adzes in particular, nor have I a doubt but that nine tenths of those brought home in the *Providence* were purposely made for sale. Though very profitable to them, the natives laughed at the avidity with which we coveted all their household and other goods. Yet have they at Tahiti their collectors, and their cabinets of European curiosities, and you will hardly credit it, that old Ha'amanemane, the high priest, was in possession of a volume of the *Statutes at Large*, which he had procured from a vessel that had touched at the island, on which he placed as much value as some among us do, on a brass oto,* a petrified periwinkle, or even (as you and I once heard a showman say) a 'stuffed baboon from the mines of Golconda'.

In the evening, many of the natives were fishing with rod, and nearly up to their shoulders in the water, to the left one a small basket is attached to put the fish in, of which numbers were taken daily this way. A small seine managed by two men was also in use but with less success.

5th

Ari'paea was on board at early day bringing the pistols that had been stolen in the mountains. He said that his brother, Vaetua, intercepted the thief at Ha'apaiano'o when making his way to Teahupoo, the windward peninsula of the island. It was more than probable the pistols had been carried to Ari'paea, but that the apprehension of Captain Bligh's displeasure, in the event of a discovery, had induced him to return them, and that the story of the thief being taken by his brother was a fabrication, the more so, as in some recent transactions Ari'paea's veracity had been doubted. I could not, however, help making some acknowledgement for his exertions, which he at first declined, but a little persuasion soon conquered this delicacy. He was loud in condemning the thief calling him a bad man (*ino tane*).

Metua Vahine, his wife, felt amazingly jealous of him, and spoke this day in angry but affectionate terms of his incontinence. It was that meretricious 'queen' Vaiareti, who tempted Ari'paea to wander from his own home. Of this I had ocular demonstration, yet did it seem charitable to aim at persuading this neglected wife that her fears were groundless, but it was in vain, the 'green eyed monster' had taken too strong a hold.

In return for a present, 'Itia sent me an amazing large hog, with a quantity of fruit, and a promise of cloth. The music of these cloven footed animals was no little annoyance to the nerves of your humble servant. To prevent irregularity, trade was only allowed to take place on one side of the ship, and this, unfortunately, was where my six foot apartment was situated. So that, from the 'rising of the sun 'till the going down of the same' did the ceaseless lamentations

---

* oto: ear.

of these poor half-strangled grunters din my ears, nor without an apprehension of their finding a passage through the port in their struggles, while dragging up the side from the canoes.

Pua's (a hog) – (*vahine*, a woman, must not be forgotten) – seems to be one of the first words our countrymen understand. It is indeed the staple commodity of the island, and what I verily believe these good people think, brings us among them. Both indeed, have been said – and perhaps with great truth – to be of a very delicate flavour. Yet so affectionate were the terms some within the sides of the *Providence* had been on with the latter of these good articles, they were sorely lamenting they had not confined their researches to the former. This day I had again the honour of being a spectator to the cramming of Pomare.

Our host, Tarro, paid a visit to my cabin and had his hair powdered, which he always made a practice of doing when on board. Tarro is of the *Arioi* Society, of which you have heard a great deal. I readily confess myself unacquainted with its customs; indeed, with scarcely any knowledge of the language, I am precluded speaking confidently of any of their mysterious ceremonies. What has fallen under my own eye it is no arrogance to repeat, but giving an elaborate account merely from conversation with an Indian whose tongue I do not understand, had better be withheld. In one circumstance, that of the *Arioi* frequently destroying their children the moment of their birth, all accounts agreed, nor could we at all persuade them of the inhumanity of it. It was good (*maita'i*) they said, and the custom of the island. And the same of the horrid practice of sacrificing their countrymen on various occasions.

Three or four of such oblations to their gods were made during our stay, but without any of us being present on the occasion. It is said that the most worthless in society are fixed on, and however horrible the custom, from ignorance and superstition, some consideration and humanity is observed in the manner of their death, being knocked privately on the head without the least apprehension being entertained of it. The corpse of one of these poor wretches recently killed was shown me. It was in a long basket made of cocoanut leaves, in shape resembling a hammock and suspended in the same way to the lateral branch of a tree but a full mile from any *marae* or place of religious observance.

6th

A message came from Tapiru importing that, if Captain Bligh would send for the *Matilda's* money, it should be given up. Mr. Norris in consequence, and some of her crew, proceeded to Ha'apaiano'o with instructions to first secure the money and then request the arms. The messenger acquainted us that Tapiru had retreated to the Ha'apaiano'o mountains, an attempt having been made by Vaetua to secure him.

7th

While at dinner in the ward-room a native took the opportunity of stealing my sheets through the port. Mideedee, who was upon deck, observing a canoe paddling on shore with unusual exertion inspecting, suspecting something wrong, pursued and overtook her just as she reached the beach. The thief offered to share the booty, but this worthy islander was not to be corrupted, and being the most powerful man, brought the sheets back.

8th

Mr. Norris returned with the major part of the money. The remainder, Tapiru informed him, was a long way distant in possession of another person.

This persevering chief was found a long way up the Ha'apaiano'o, surrounded by about an hundred of his faithful Matavaians. It was in vain, he said, to expect the muskets, as with his life he would only yield them; he repeated as he had before that, in case of an attack, he would retreat to a narrow pass in the mountains and defend it until his ammunition was expended. He reprobated in contemptuous terms the pusillanimous conduct of his brother who had deserted him and was at Matavai with the females of his family who, notwithstanding the quarrel, had remained unmolested by the Pareans. It appeared that one of Tapiru's party had treacherously deserted, giving Vaetua intelligence of his retreat who, under shelter of a dark night, made the unsuccessful attempt before mentioned. His five 'stand of arms' were constantly kept under his bed; that is, his sleeping mat.

9th

Early in the morning I was awakened by my *taio* who, according to her promise, had brought me a war mat (*taumi*). In the afternoon Pomare begged permission to take a nap on my bed. He had once before enjoyed the privilege, but unfortunately left two of his attendants behind, which my bed maker (the officers in the *Providence* that it might not weaken the crew had no established servants) found in solemn march upon the pillow, and to use his own expression, swore they came from the head of His Majesty by 'their colour'. Captain Bligh though truly friendly to the chiefs, kept them in such excellent order that they never took any liberties with him, by which means he enjoyed some degree of retirement. However fraught with danger, it was not in my power to refuse Pomare the boon he asked.

Such were the fears of a trembling unmellowed damsel as the sun sunk behind the distant hills and the hour of dedition* approached that, unequal to the contest, she leaped into the briny element and reached the plain, undeprived of that – she was urged on board – to lose. Thine own friends, my good girl,

---

*   dedition: surrender.

with an *Ari'i no pretaney* (an English chief) had formed a compact against thee. Hadst those come free and uncontrolled, like many others who sought the *Providence* for English finery, I might have felt for the disappointment of him, who with meretricious longing coveted thy unsapped charms.

10th

Preparations were making at this time by Ari'paea and other chiefs for an expedition to Papara on the southwest part of the island. The chiefs of this district were in possession of a few firearms, and an attempt to get them by stratagem was to be made by Ari'paea, by his going round laden with presents that no suspicion might be entertained of his intentions. Of this he made no mystery to his English friends, attaching no dishonour to such a proceeding.

The drummer was this day punished, in the presence of a number of the islanders, for forgetting in his amours that he was under the care of our messmate, the doctor. The beater of parchment perhaps thought retaliation no crime and that as the Tahitian fair ones had given him a warm token of remembrance, he had a right to return it 'in kind'. But whether he reasoned so or not, the dozen he received was properly and justly inflicted. With that tenderness inseparable from them, the natives pitied his sufferings, but acknowledged that he deserved punishment.

In the evening there was a more crowded *heiva* than usual. Among the strange customs of the island may be mentioned that of the names of things and persons being frequently altered, and which has occasioned great perplexity in the accounts given at different periods of these people.

The dances (*heivas*) about this time were called *hoopaowpa*, some person of consequence having taken the former name. Ari'paea had changed his name to Aboobo (tomorrow).* The king regent, Pomare, when Captain Bligh was at the island in the *Bounty* in 1789, bore the name of Tinah, and at a former period it was Tu. And here it may be remarked that the engraving of him in Captain Cook's second voyage is an uncommon strong resemblance, however the lapse of time may have altered his features. Hitherto the young 'king' has been known by the name of Tu, his father's former one. In future visits to the island, it is probable we may find it changed. His grandfather, Otue, in 1773, was called E-Happai.

My pen is frequently obliged to touch on subjects which the purity of him who guides it would rather avoid, yet, this would be withholding from you some simple facts strongly indicative of the manners of these islanders. Among other good things required for the passage home were some kids. Assistance from the shore was necessary on the occasion as our Nannettes were living in a state of celibacy. If a congregation of the Tahitian fair did not withdraw from the consummation of their nuptials, habit must acquit them of indelicacy. There are

---

*   *hoopaowpa* and Aboobo are the words Tobin uses.

scenes which the English maiden has been taught to close her eyelids on, the uninstructed *poti'i api* (virgin) of this isle views with indifference. Yet, if she is familiar with *that*, doubtless as well concealed from her, she owes not her knowledge to aught but simple nature. *That*, which is acquired under the broad shelter of art, or affected mystery, belongs not to the Tahitian.

There was a fresh trade wind outside the Dolphin Reef, though it continued calm all day in Matavai Bay. The departure of the chiefs for Papara gave us considerable relief; it is true, nothing could be more cheerful and amiable than their demeanour, but the ship was so constantly crowded with them that little rest was allowed us.

In the morning a woman came on board with her child, whose unfortunate father was a mutineer in the *Bounty*, and had been taken by Captain Edwards of the *Pandora* with many others, about a twelve month before. There were on the island three or four children of this description, besides one belonging to Brown, a man left by Captain Cox of the *Mercury* brig in 1790. Brown it seems left Tahiti in the *Pandora*.

The mother of the child[4] was sensible of the fate that awaited the unhappy mutineer, yet without expressing much sorrow on the occasion, so little does serious reflection intrude on their thoughtless disposition. A Tahitian may be tenderly affected for a short period, but it would appear that no circumstance whatever is capable of fixing a lasting impression on the mind.

As the children of the mutineers have been mentioned, an enquiry naturally follows, why, after the many visits to the island, more children are not to be seen partaking of European blood. It is certainly a fact that until recently, not a single instance has been noticed from the time of Messieurs Wallis and Bougainville in 1767 and 1768. The fathers of the children brought to the *Providence* resided on the island above a twelve month and were individually attached to the mothers, which may account for the children being born; and yet no proof, I believe, has reached us of the females, under any circumstances, using means to promote abortion. The *Arioi* Society, it is known, destroy their children instantly on their birth without the least reproach or stigma attending it. This may have been the case with the children of the casual visitors to the island, from the conviction of the mothers that they were left fatherless on the departure of the ship to which such fathers belonged; whereas it most likely was not calculated on by such women as had connected themselves with the mutineers of the *Bounty*. Indeed, had the mothers felt any disposition to destroy the children of the latter, no European father – it is to be believed – could have consented to it.

In going to an island key in the evening to the eastward, vast numbers of natives were on it collecting sea eggs and different shell fish for food.

Having the engravings to Captain Cook's voyage on board, they were shown to Pomare, but the sea horses* on the coast of Kamchatka was what alone interested him. He had some days before seen some curious articles only to be

---

*   sea horses: walrus.

purchased at the Chinese market, but he was not satisfied until his younger wife, Vaiareti, was allowed a similar inspection, which to quiet his importunity, was granted.

About midnight we were alarmed by a noise in the water occasioned by a native who had stolen the sheets from off our premier Bond. Two muskets were fired over him, in the hope he would return, but such was his enterprise and activity in the water, he effected his escape, notwithstanding three boats were in pursuit.

A native who had been troublesome and thrown stones at the watering party was punished with three dozen lashes with the entire approbation of the chiefs. He seemed little concerned, either as the pain or disgrace of the punishment.

Vast numbers of cavallies* were taken in the seine, some above twenty pounds weight. The south part of the bay was found to be the most productive for fishing, close to the eastward of the heads of Taharaa (or One Tree Hill), particularly after rain.

19th

In consequence of the insult offered a few days before, I was sent this morning in the watering boat, a duty which had hitherto been conducted by a petty officer. The natives were perfectly civil and peaceable. Owing to some heavy rain that had recently fallen, the banks of the Matavai were overflowing, and the sandy isthmus separating[5] it from the east part of the bay, not above sixty yards across, through which the sea had perforated so as to render the water brackish at the usual filling place, obliging us to go farther up the stream with our casks.

'Itia returned from the Papara expedition with the common present of a quantity of cloth. The major part of the chiefs still remained there, with the hope of getting the fire arms.

The supply of hogs was very confined, so that we were under the necessity of sending to Pare and purchasing for the daily expenditure, a hatchet being required for a moderated sized one. Yet was the island teeming with them.

---

*   cavallies: a kind of horse mackerel.

CHAPTER 6TH

May–July 1792

Visit the marae at Pare.— Curiosities.—Corpse of Maua Roa.—Houses, different ones.—Scissors.—Carved figures, etee.—Marae.—Transparency of the sea.—Visit Ha'apaiano'o, a war canoe.—Tai Aiva's breakfast.—Tapiru dines with us at Vaetua's.—'Itia neglected by her husband, Pomare.—Pomare much intoxicated.—Vaiareti enjoying the rain.—Grievous ceremony.—Mideedee.— Our king's birthday.—Paper balloons.—Excursion to Tautira.—Wild ducks, perch on trees.—Birds.—Pomare not a warrior.—Breadfruit scarce.— Cocoanuts.—Second excursion to Tautira.—Scurf on the skin from drinking kava.—Island Tetiaroa.—Began watering.—Articles from the wreck of the Matilda.—Plants embarked.—Sorrow of the natives.—Party embark from the post.—Ship unmoored.—Crowded with natives.—Anchor weighed.—Chiefs sleep on board.—Parting.—Leave the island.—&c. &c.

Thetis, coast of America March 1797

20th

Harwood was kind enough this day to accompany me on a visit to the *marae* at Pare. Our pockets were filled with different articles to exchange for anything curious which might be met with. It was soon circulated through the plain that two *ari'is* from the ship were in search of curiosities. The natives ever laughed at the avidity with which such collections were made and to show their contempt some brought a stone, another a feather and so on, being highly delighted with the tricks they were playing on us. One fellow really deserved much credit as a sharper. I had bargained for four of the beautiful little blue parakeets called *veneys*, with a promise to call for them on returning. In about an hour after; he came lamenting that two had escaped from the cage. As I did not doubt his veracity, he received the whole price, which was no sooner done than a boy brought two more and sold them; but we soon discovered by the looks of those around that the whole was a scheme to get double pay for the birds.

Understanding it was in the neighbourhood, we visited the exposed corpse of the late chief Maua Roa. We were informed that he had been dead about four moons,* and that every evening the body was placed under a shed. The corpse was in a sitting posture – on a stage about four feet high, but different from the common *fare tupapa'u*. Except a bandage of white cloth over the middle, and

---

*   Maua Roa died in January 1792.

another round the temples, the body was in a naked state. It was more tattooed than any I had seen on the island, the legs and the thighs being marked so as to leave no remains of the natural colour of the skin. The arms were in circular ridges from the shoulder to the wrist, and under the left breast was the broad mark of the *Arioi* Society. The stage was decorated with a quantity of striped red and white cloth, a rail at the back of which supporting the body from falling, being hung with the same. The whole of this, and the shed, was enclosed in a bamboo fence of about eighteen feet by six, partly open at one side for the attendants on the corpse to enter by. It was the only body I saw exposed in this manner. Several inferior *fare tupapa'us* were in the neighbourhood, nor would it seem that any particular spots are appropriated for them, which is the more remarkable in so cleanly a people, as the stench from them is very offensive; yet the inhabited houses were quite contiguous to many, without any annoyance being felt, or apprehension of disorders being generated by the putridity of the air around. It is customary, when a corpse is exposed this way, to first remove the intestines. Maua Roa was related to the royal family. His widow, Mari'ia, was living.

Not far from this spot, the pillars of a large house were standing, the roof having been removed. Much labour must have been bestowed in constructing these supporters, and it was with pleasure we observed that the proprietor to prevent their decay had covered them carefully with coarse matting.

The houses are of various kinds, some being enclosed from the eaves all round with a railing of bamboo, having a door on one side. Others are left entirely open, supported by three rows of pillars like the long one before mentioned. The leaf of the *wharra* tree, a species of palmetto, is generally used as a thatch, being very durable. None of them are floored but the chiefs' houses have generally a carpet of cut grass, laid regularly, which as it decays, is supplied by fresh. The furniture consists of a sleeping mat, a small wooden pillow for the head, and sometimes a larger of the same form to sit on. These are made in a neat manner, chiefly from a hard wood of a mahogany colour, and previously to the introduction of European tools, must have been a work of much time and labour, as the legs are carved from the solid block.

Gourds are in use to contain water, and the cocoanut shell to drink it from. Besides a few other cooking utensils, little else is to be seen in a Tahitian mansion. All these are kept remarkably neat and clean; indeed, about Matavai and Pare, there were few who had not European boxes or chests to keep their valuables in. Anything foreign bears some estimation. You have been told of a volume of the *Statutes at Large* being in old Ha'amanemane's (the high priest) possession, and this I believe nothing could induce him to part with; he even kept the book concealed, dreading it might be taken from him.

Scissors were much prized, with which the natives were constantly amusing themselves cutting their hair in various forms. Some of the women were not ignorant of the use of the needle, and linen was so plentiful among them that there was a great demand for soap. It was said that one of our noncommissioned officers, a pleasant good tempered fellow, had been so bountiful to his female friends that his wardrobe from three dozen shirts was, on the departure of the ship, reduced to three single ones. The mention of soap calls to my recollection that we all had Tahitian washerwomen, whose bills were paid in beads, spike nails, and other commodities.

As well as the houses already mentioned, there are small portable ones scarcely able to contain two persons, for embarking on the double canoes; and young Tu had a small one erected on pillars in the water, some distance from the beach in Pare harbour.

In our walk we saw several of the carved figures called *etee*. The most remarkable one was about twenty feet in height consisting of sixteen figures, the base being of the female sex, about three; the others decreasing gradually according to the size of the tree. They are carved without the tree being cut down, and it must be a tedious undertaking. The *etee* was observed in various parts of the island, distant from as well as contiguous to *maraes* and *fare tupapa'u*; the distortion of the mouth as when dancing the *heiva*, seemed to be imitated, and in some of the male figures the distinguishing mark of the sex was most preposterously evident, affording no small degree of giggling to some Tahitian damsels, who retreated not from their god of gardens.

As we approached the *marae*, the eastern breeze wafted to us no very odorous perfume from numbers of hogs that had been sacrificed as an oblation to the deity. These were on a stage about forty feet in length, supported by three rows of pillars eight feet high, long rushes nearly reaching the ground from each side of it. Close to the stage were two tables, on one of which was a single hog. Those on the stage amounted to about fifteen. The *marae* was a pavement about a foot high, sixty-four long and forty-two broad, at one end, indeed, it was raised – four or five feet, like two steps – which part was decorated with carved wooden figures, some of them representing *heiva* dancers, birds, and lizards. A few upright stones were fixed in different parts of the pavement, three or four feet high, and breadfruit and cocoanut trees were growing among them. A human skull, and one of a hog, were hanging to some carved figures near the *marae*, and another skull was brought to us which our guides said was kept with great care at this place, it being that of Thompson, one of the mutineers in the *Bounty*.

A case for the *atua* nearly similar to the one seen on Tu's canoe at Matavai was near, supported on a platform, about six feet high, by nine pillars. Close to it was an uninhabited house, but for what purpose we did not learn.

As well as the pavement already mentioned, there was, on the eastern point of Pare harbour, not an hundred yards distant, a large pile of stones in the form of the base of a pyramid, regularly placed in four storeys. Many carved figures in wood, similar to those on the pavement, were here placed upright, and the *toa* was growing luxuriantly among the coral rocks, though its roots were washed by the ocean. The windward side of this projecting coral point was sheltered by a wall, inside of which were several human skeletons lying in different directions.

But I am wearying you with descriptions, perhaps more tedious than clear, and will therefore refer you to the attempts of my pencil.*

In our way home, a quarrel having taken place at Matavai, we found two of the natives fighting. The weaker man had a fast grip of the other's hair, nor could he be disengaged the whole conflict. Kicking and every advantage was taken, and one gave the other such proofs of the sharpness and strength of his teeth that the blood gushed out amain.† It did not continue long, but the wounded man brought a handful of hair from the head of his antagonist ere he 'gave in'. The women of the combatants were weeping and lamenting bitterly in loud shrieks the whole time.

21st

With the exception of Tu, Ari'paea and Ha'amanemane, the party returned from Papara, not having succeeded in their stratagem of getting the arms.

The watering party was not in the least molested today. The fellow, so recently punished, was about us, exhibiting even with humour, the marks of its effects to his companions.

22nd

Among our visitors was old Mari'ia, widow of the exposed dead chief at Pare (Maua Roa), and women in abundance. My cabin was soon crowded, where beads were distributed to many of them. 'Itia was highly gratified on my presenting her some English cloth, promising largely in return.

Pomare, with other chiefs, having in the evening to pass One Tree Hill and it being extremely dark, had sent their *tavinis* to prepare fires at different parts of the road; these had communicated with a quantity of high reeds, causing a brilliant illumination over the whole bay. It was the only instance during our stay of the chiefs being assisted this way in their journeys; indeed, travelling by night rarely happens, nor is a Tahitian often seen out of his house after the day has closed.

23rd

We were again alarmed at night by a thief near the ship, yet notwithstanding the shore party were posted along the beach, and the boats in pursuit, his activity in the water was so great he effected his escape. But they are so early habituated to this element, and remain so long under its surface, that our pursuits on such occasions were always tedious and frequently in vain. When nearly within grasp they dive, nor is it possible to tell in what direction they will rise. Most likely you

---

*   See Plate 25.

†   amain: in or with full force.

have been shooting, or rather shooting at loons and divers on some of the 'American waters', if so, you may form a tolerable idea of a Tahitian in the sea.

From the gangway of the *Providence*, I have frequently seen children eight or nine years of age leap into the sea for beads fifteen or twenty feet below the surface, scarcely ever failing to rise with the reward of their exertions. Their vision under water must be astonishingly clear, as when the smallest beads have been thrown into it, several yards asunder, after securing some, they have returned with the same success to others in a different direction. Doubtless the sea among these islands (which indeed is the case in most tropical latitudes) being so very translucid, greatly aids the distinguishing of objects in it.

While speaking of the agility of these people in the water, it is impossible to help reflecting how little the qualification of even swimming is cultivated in our own country. To sailors and soldiers it is particularly useful and should be encouraged by every means. Yet even among the former, who may be said to live on the deep, how small the proportion of those who can swim.

25th

In the morning Guthrie and myself left the post for Ha'apaiano'o to examine a war canoe, of which, great praise had been given by Pomare. As usual in all our walks, several natives joined us, and it was with difficulty we prevented the party being too crowded.

A spot was pointed out to us where one of the recent battles had been fought, and many of the trees exhibited deep marks from the stones of slings. These weapons in the hands of a resolute people would occasion sad destruction. The Tahitians use them with great skill, but their timidity, which seems excessive, prevents any warfare being carried on with energy.

In our way we called on Vaetua, who instantly ordered a hog to be prepared for the oven. Tai Aiva, his wife, was breakfasting on fish barely warmed, according to the custom of the island, alone in a small shed about fifty yards from the house.

Vaetua, next brother to Ari'paea, appeared about seven and twenty. His countenance was handsome, and figure elegant, both of which had been much injured by an unrestrained use of *kava*. As a warrior he was esteemed the best in the island and had killed Mahine, a chief of Moorea. It is true, the manner of his death gave nothing heroic to the conqueror, as he was seized by several *tavinis*, while Vaetua beat out his brains with a stone. Much confidence however seemed to be placed in this prince by the state, but he appeared a complete voluptuary and from the account given us, his indulgencies were so various, it was difficult to believe them true at Tahiti.

He was among the few who entertained jealousy of his wife's conduct. Tai Aiva was considered as the Belle of the Island, as well by the English, as her own countrymen, and the temptations to seduce her from the 'right path' were various, and often repeated – but in vain. Ruffled or unruffled, she was still the same cold, repellent fair one. Had Tai Aiva been more yielding, the wardrobe of many an English chief would have been expended, and this kindly isle far the richer in various sorts of foreign drapery. Little credit was given her by her own sex, this sturdy denial being alone attributed to the dread she entertained of offending her lord, to whom she was very inferior in blood. In this surely there was some merit due to her. Let us at the same time soften the guilt of others, whose husbands and relatives rather promoted than suppressed a more complying conduct.

The Ha'apaiano'o was crossed several times, as usual on men's shoulders, before we reached the shed under which the canoe was building. Its dimensions were as follows vizt:

Extreme length	70 feet
Extreme breadth at about one third of the stern	3¾
Height at the stern	17
Height at the head	11¾

Like the common canoes it was formed of a number of pieces sewed together, the seams being payed over with a black composition not very unlike pitch. On the head and stern was the rude figure of a man. It had seven knees, or timbers of a single piece of wood. About the sides, head and stern, were carved figures of turtle and lizards, and on the fore part was placed an *afata no atua*, the wooden case, which has been before mentioned, to shelter the deity in. It also serves him as a sleeping place. I never saw a canoe decorated for any religious occasion without an *afata no atua* being affixed to it.

In a shed near at hand was a piece of carved work twenty feet in length, to be erected as an ornament on the stern, and a conical helmet formed of bamboo, decorated with cock's feathers, to be occasionally worn by the priests. The canoe was a full quarter of a mile from the Ha'apaiano'o, yet when finished; was to be carried to it by the means of poles on men's shoulders. We were informed that it was small when compared to some in the Society Islands. Mahau told us that at Raiatea, he had one that employed several men to steer it. This one on the stocks, and another smaller at Pare, were all we heard of in the neighbourhood of the ship. How different the state of the Tahitian Navy, when Captain Cook described the armament at Pare in 1774.

Tapiru, who was at his stronghold some distance up the river, learning we were in the neighbourhood, soon paid us a visit, and what seemed rather inexplicable, accompanied us to the house of his enemy, Vaetua. The two chiefs hardly noticed each other, but this coolness did not prevent Tapiru assisting us to demolish the hog of his antagonist with a good appetite, while he informed us that the greater part of the furniture we were using had been taken from him in the late attack. We could only conjecture that our presence was a protection to Tapiru. Yet, could Vaetua have made him prisoner on his return from accompanying us part of the way to Matavai, had such been the object.

The hog was served up whole with baked breadfruit and plantains. Milk from the cocoanut was our beverage, and salt water the sauce to our meat. From having frequently used it as a substitute for salt, so easily are our prejudices surmounted, I found it equally palatable.

Pahraihea, a chief of Ha'apaiano'o, behaved with much kindness, insisting we should not return to the ship without a live hog, and our friend, Tapiru, loaded our attendants with a variety of fruits.

26th

Ari'paea returned this day from his unsuccessful expedition to Papara. Pomare and his wives dined on board, during which a native arrived from an eastern district with an invitation from its chief to Captain Bligh. As a token of friendship, he brought the branch of a particular tree, to the end of which the captain fastened a red feather as an acknowledgement.

'Itia's feelings were put to the test at dinner by our commander expressing his surprise that she thought so little of the illness of one of her children left at Papara. She, for a few minutes, wept bitterly, exhibiting every symptom of unfeigned grief, when drying her eyes, laughter soon succeeded, and the child no more intruded on her thoughtless disposition. It was the same with Vaiareti a few days before on being offended with a favourite *tavini*. Her tears flowed copiously, when, in almost the same moment, she was romping about the cabin like a hoyden. The besotted partiality of Pomare to this silly woman was as extraordinary as his total neglect of poor 'Itia. To variety, and her being several years younger, it could alone be attributed, for in manners and disposition, she was every way inferior. What should we think in England – indifferent as our manners seem to be approaching – of two sisters living under the same roof with a man in the most cordial harmony, the elder one utterly repudiated for the scarcely ripened charms of the younger? Nay, this very neglected sister was fully acquainted how false the favourite was to their lord's bed. Yet with the most yielding unconcern concealed it from him. This is being even more cool than what we hear of our philosophic enemies composing the 'great nation', whose morals, God avert from our own little island. We want them not.

In the afternoon the king regent had taken such an immoderate dose of *kava*, in addition to the captain's wine, as to become so unmanageable, it required several men to confine him. He exhibited every symptom of a violent epileptic fit.

It rained excessively part of the day, but on clearing up, a bright gleam of sun produced one of the most beautiful landscapes conceivable, every hill and tree being enlivened by the showers.

The Tahitian seldom loses an opportunity of bathing in fresh water. Vaiareti, in the middle of the rain, surprised our frail nerves by suddenly emerging from the cabin in a state of nudity. She was a wicked jade, and we should all have been much more pleased had it been Tai Aiva or Warrianow. After getting thoroughly soaked, and playing numberless tricks and sportive gambols to a congregation that – of course – increased on such an occasion, she as suddenly disappeared to enrobe herself in the cabin, but not without leaving us in admiration and wonder at the ingenuity with which she disposed of her pliant and beautifully moulded limbs; yet seemingly accidental and unstudied, while they scarcely presented a shade of what she aimed at concealing.

'Itia took leave of us for a few days, having heard of the death of her child in its passage from Papara to Pare. She seemed scarcely affected on the occasion, yet some of the officers saw her afterwards at Pare in all the 'mockery of woe'. She was preparing for the grievous ceremony when the party met her. In exhibiting a sharks tooth wrapped round with cloth, the sharp point being bare, it was with a smile on her countenance. The time at length arriving for lamentation, she began and continued wounding her head, the blood flowing about her in streams. The period of sorrow over, she resumed her wonted cheerfulness.

28th

A reply of poor Mideedee to Captain Bligh at dinner gained him much credit. The captain was gently reproving him for something that had been neglected. He urged forgetfulness as an excuse. And how came that Mideedee? *Aita i papu ia'u* (I do not understand) said he to our commander, nor how you came to forget the sky rockets you promised us. Mideedee's retort was so just that Captain Bligh assured him he should soon have the fireworks.

June 3rd

In honour of our royal master's birthday, the two vessels were dressed with flags, and we all appeared more than usually grand in our apparel. Salutes were fired, as well as at the post, a great concourse of natives attending the cannonade, with which they were highly gratified. This loyalty, when so remote from our native isle, gained us the unqualified approbation of these good people, nor without their participating in it most cordially as our allies.

With several chiefs I took the birthday dinner at our post with my late valuable friend, the whole royal family, except the gay, the jovial Vaetua, were the captain's guests on board. Vaetua soon became warm and vociferous in praise of the *Ari'i tane no pretaney Keen Yore* (King George) and our country, but yielding at length to the powerful influence of our Tenerife wine, he sunk into the arms of sleep and ebriety. The day passed cheerfully, nor in drawing a comparison between civilised Europe and this happy isle, did the scale incline much in favour of the former.

In the evening a variety of fireworks were exhibited for the gratification of the natives, as well as two paper balloons which had been prepared for the occasion. One of them succeeded beyond my expectations, taking a direction towards Moorea, nor did we lose sight of it for nearly a quarter of an hour. These balloons were (I believe) the first ever displayed at the island, and I cannot but confess that

I felt some degree of mortification at the natives not expressing stronger marks of surprise and satisfaction; with the rockets they were infinitely more pleased. Perhaps, having no stationer's shop on the island, I felt sore at not being able to get a fresh supply of silver paper. Of rockets, there were more in store.[1]

5th

Captain Bligh early in the morning sent me to Tautira, a district seven or eight miles westward of the ship, to procure provisions, the supply (particularly of breadfruit) having decreased considerably. I first landed at Point Venus, before day break, for Pomare who was to accompany me and use his influence in the district. His Majesty did not think proper to embark without first having his breakfast, which consisted of about three pounds of baked fish, nor was it without much difficulty that I persuaded him to quit the false Vaiareti. Poor neglected 'Itia was reposing on a couch hard by.

He was very facetious the whole way down, undertaking to pilot the boat between the coral reefs into Tautira, and imitating our manner of conning. On first landing, he ordered the slaughter of a hog for dinner, and then proceeded in search of plantains, without much ceremony to the proprietors of such as fell in our way. Indeed, had not this prompt measure been taken, we should have returned to the ship empty, not a simple bunch being voluntarily brought to him. Walking about two miles westward; the boat followed the windings of the coast as near as a coral bank would admit. Here the country was even more populous than at Matavai, or Pare. The plain was not so broad, but the small rising hills near the coast were abundantly clothed with breadfruit, *avee*, *eratta* (a large kind of chestnut) and various other trees, the houses being distributed among them in a picturesque manner. A *fare tupapa'u* was here pointed out to us, where the corpse of one of the mutineers' children had lain, previously to its being buried.

Monah, an old chief who frequently visited the *Providence*, resided in this district and had prepared refreshments of various fruits for us. At the extent of our walk Pomare made a seizure of more plantains; after which we were carried above a quarter of a mile on mens' shoulders, over the coral bank to the boat and embarked for our first landing place, where we found the hog smoking from the oven; nor was it long, with the assistance of the boat's crew and good appetites, ere most of it was demolished.

In general the chiefs did not partake of meals with their guests. So it was this day with Pomare who, retiring about an hundred paces to the shade of a breadfruit tree, took his meal alone, first bathing in an adjoining stream, a practice seldom omitted, and which is truly indicative of the cleanliness of these people. His dinner was of fish which, in our way from Matavai, he had taken out of a canoe, the fisherman not at all appearing dissatisfied with the regal theft.

About three miles westward of where our dinner was taken, a small island nearly joins the mainland, but there appeared to be sufficient water for canoes to pass. Many flocks of wild ducks were here seen. It may be remarked that the wild duck of Tahiti, although web footed, commonly perches on trees.

A bird called *otatarrey* was here shot, being about the size of a skylark and very similar in plumage. In the morning and evening, particularly after rain, it has a note nearly approaching to that of the thrush. In some ponds up the stream a small kind of moorhen was observed, *omawmow*. The birds of this island are not of great variety, and it is a curious fact that there are none of the hawk species. Of herons there are two kinds, the one of a dark lead colour the natives bear a superstitious reverence towards, being always displeased at our shooting them. Parrot, or *ah ah*, the green dove, and small blue parakeet (*veney*), are both brilliant in their plumage. They were brought to us in great numbers without being the least injured; but by what way they are taken, I cannot say. One fellow who had made himself useful about the post, I employed to get some. He was absent in the mountains three days, returning with about two dozen, not at all injured or disfigured. Great pains were taken to bring them to England, but with scarcely any success. On quitting the island I had above forty, apparently in high health, but a few months occasioned a mortality of the whole, both doves and parakeets. One pair of the latter, if I recollect right, reached Lady Banks, which the gunner* had by uncommon attention saved. These little birds are about the size of a common house sparrow; they have all the character of the largest parrot, except that of the imitation of speech. The colour is a beautiful dark blue, with a white throat, and yellow bill and legs.

There are of sea fowl, shearwaters, tropic birds, noddies, and a small kind of gull with some others. In bad weather, which was rare, the small black petrel (Mother Cary's Chicken) was occasionally seen in the bay. Sand larks, red shanks, and two or three kind of curlews frequent the shores and coral bank.

A light western wind accompanied the boat nearly to Pare, where we met the fresh sea breeze. Our course had been along the reef at about thirty yards' distance, the bottom of coral being visible nearly the whole way, although of considerable depth.

Pomare slept quietly by my side until he was alarmed from his afternoon's nap by my firing at a curlew, which produced a conversation on firearms (*pupuhi*). He had some time before accused me of being afraid (*mata'u*) for not suffering him to navigate the boat inside the reef. It appeared a good opportunity to retort on him, but this he did not at all feel, making no secret of his want of courage; saying it was not necessary for a king to go into battle, and concluded by asking if 'Keen Yore' (King George) ever did. On being answered in the negative, he seemed more than usually pleased exclaiming *maita'i* (good), but he could not be persuaded that it was not from want of personal courage in our *ari'i tane*.

The effect of early habits is particularly strong in the different characters of the Tahitian royal family. Pomare, from being taught that a king should not appear in battle, is the most pusillanimous man possible without feeling the least stigma attached to it, while Ari'paea and Vaetua arrogate no small degree of

---

*   the gunner: John England.

consequence to themselves as warriors and are deemed the bulwarks of the state. There was another brother who seldom visited the *Providence* of the name of Te Pau whose person was very inferior to the rest and, we were told, equally deficient in understanding. Most probably young Tu has already been instructed in attending to his personal security. At a very early period the *ari'i tane* meets the regard and reverence of his people. Before France by its revolutionising system had reached the sanguinary disorder now to be found there, no Frenchman ever spoke of the '*Grand Monarque*' with more heartfelt pride and exultation than every individual of this island does of the *ari'i tane*. No wonder then that they use every care and precaution for his safety. His parents, and his parents' parents ever approach him with the most submissive respect. These have I seen, while humanity revolted at the sight, uncover themselves and bow before the royal stripling, by early habit taught to view the tottering palsied limbs of his grandsire thus nakedly degraded and exposed, without the slightest emotion of pity or compassion. Such is custom.

Breadfruit was now so scarce that it was with difficulty Pomare procured any for our repast, yet the trees around were teeming with young fruit of the approaching season. It would appear that the natives are supplied nearly throughout the year with this valuable fruit, as it was now making rapid progress towards maturity and a few of the preceding season still on the tree. The rest had been cropped and made into a kind of paste called *mahee*, which keeps a considerable time. It is not with confidence that I speak respecting the seasons of the breadfruit (*uru*), it being collected from the chiefs, who stated that the island is not above a month without it, which takes place about the middle of the year.

They enumerated nearly thirty kinds, yet differing but little in taste, or indeed in the appearance of the tree, except that the leaves are more or less indented at their edges. I am denied giving a botanical description of this nutritious fruit, indeed, you must ere this have seen the tree in our colonies, however in an early state. I shall only observe that, of all vegetable substitutes for bread, it appears the most promising yet discovered.

Means may be found, perhaps to granulate it, but this we were not able to effect in the *Providence*. Baked whole, in the ground oven, was found to be the best way of cooking it. I do not know when I experienced more gratification than, during a recent visit to New Providence in the Bahamas, on seeing a fine breadfruit tree nearly twenty feet high in Mr. Forbes' garden, which but a few years ago was embarked on board the *Providence* at Tahiti, when not as many inches. At Bermuda a few have been tried without success. Of the fate of some left at St. Helena in 1792, I am altogether ignorant, but should fear that the soil was not favourable to them.*

---

* According to Bligh's letter to the Admiralty secretary, he only left half a dozen healthy breadfruit on St Helena. Modern studies of plant life there do not list breadfruit.

The earliest account I have seen of the breadfruit is in the voyage of Mendana de Neyra in 1595, from Peru to settle the Solomon Isles. The editor says –

> Mendana de Neyra discovered the same year the islands he called Marquesas where a tree is described to yield a certain fruit which comes to be like the head of a boy, whose colour when ripe is a clear green, and extremely green when unripe; the outside appears with cross rays like the pineapple; the figure is not quite round, it is somewhat narrower at the point than at the foot, from hence grows a core which reaches to the middle, and from this core a web. It has no stone or kernel, nor anything useless except the outside, and it is thin; the rest is one mass, with little juice when ripe, and less when green. Much were eaten in every way. It is so delicious that they called it blanc manger. It was found to be wholesome and very nourishing. The leaves of it are large and very jagged in the manner of the papays.

The above description is doubtless meant for the breadfruit, and I have given you this extract as well as a former one respecting the *kava* (*cana*) merely to point out that the chief sustenance of the natives of the South Sea islands, as well as their favourite intoxicating beverage, did not differ two centuries ago from the present hour.

18th

'Itia this day sent me a hog and some breadfruit, the latter being a great rarity. Boiled plantains and a kind of yam (*taro*) were issued as a substitute to the crew. Not an ounce of European bread had been expended since our arrival, and so familiar had our palates become to the vegetable kind as not at all to feel the deprivation of the 'king's own'. The supply of yams was never bountiful, and of but an inferior quality; sweet potatoes were still more difficult to be procured. *Taro* was generally in plenty, and cocoanuts were ever brought to us in amazing numbers. It was calculated that the daily expenditure of these fruit, on board the *Providence*, her consort, and at the post, amounted to above a thousand, the milk from them being our common beverage. In our own colonies the cocoanut is not considered as by any means wholesome, but the conviction of its salutary effects on our people at Tahiti disposes me to doubt the truth of such an opinion.

25th

Early in the morning, Captain Bligh sent me to Tautira in search of a native who had stolen a bag of linen from the post. Pomare accompanied me to assist on the occasion. A few days before a fellow had been discovered concealed under one of the boats, who notwithstanding, effected his escape after being fired at by the sentinel. The traces of his having been wounded were visible a considerable way among the rushes. The Matavaians disclaimed his being of their district, saying he belonged to Tautira. There was therefore a probability of hearing of him also in our excursion.

Mr. Portlock left Matavai before us for Teahupoo, the next district south of Tautira, to bring up one of the *Matilda*'s boats, which had been left there by some of the crew. We landed with the cutter to the west of a small island at the most distant part of Tautira, in a cove where there was twelve or fourteen feet of water close to the shore. Notwithstanding, till this convenient spot presented itself, the boat could not approach within an hundred yards of the beach for the coral banks. A small stream separating Tautira and Teahupoo runs into this cove.

Leaving a petty officer with the boat, Pomare, myself and a few of the crew continued our route about three miles, following the windings of the shore, which here took a southerly direction, when we reached the house of the person suspected by the Matavaians, but found he had received intimation of the pursuit and absconded. On our entering the house, a young plantain tree was placed at the feet of Pomare as an acknowledgement of friendship. The women declaring that the man was innocent and had absented himself entirely from fear.

After representing the injustice of the act, by saying that the English were never guilty of stealing from the natives, we took our leave, but not without a threat that if the linen was not returned, Captain Bligh would send a party to the district and destroy the houses. This, they said, were they guilty, would be right, but still pleaded innocent, condemning the thief in loud an angry terms.

Pomare exerted himself but little on the occasion which, after so long a journey from Matavai, rather displeased me. This was the second expedition I had made with him on business, and it served to confirm one in an opinion I had formed of his indolence and want of authority. His brother, Ari'paea, ever settled any disputes we had with the natives in a more prompt and satisfactory manner. The *tavinis* had prepared two baked hogs for our dinner, but the king regent, after bathing in fresh water, took his meal, as usual, alone.

In the afternoon Mr. Portlock returned with the *Matilda*'s boat, bringing with him some chiefs from Teahupoo, one of whom was marked to a very great degree with the scurf attendant on too great an indulgence in *kava*. Every part of his body was covered with a rough scaly skin, his eyes seemed wild and wandering, and, although a fine young man under thirty, every limb was sadly enervated. Notwithstanding the rapid and dreadful harm this baneful beverage makes on the human frame, by abstinence it wears off, the skin becomes smooth, and the bodily powers regain their pristine vigour.

The voluptuary of Tahiti, like the shattered unhinged debauchee of our civilised metropolis, when every indulgence sickens on the sense, withdraws to a spot where by self-denial his health is restored. The small island of Tetiaroa, but a few leagues northward of Point Venus, abounding chiefly with fish and cocoanuts, is his Margate or Tunbridge and is frequently resorted to on such occasions.

July 2nd

As the time approached for our departure, we began watering the ship from Matavai River. It has been observed that her capacity for stowage was very considerable, which was indispensable, as we had a long and arduous passage to make by Torres Straits to Timor before this necessary article could be replenished. The plants, it must be remembered, would require no small portion; every cask was therefore filled, which completed the stock to above an hundred tons.

3rd

Some of the *Matilda*'s crew who had been at Teahupoo on the eastern peninsula reported having seen a cask and some other floating articles that had been on board when the ship was wrecked.

7th

The major part of the royal family dined on board, all of them but Pomare, who seldom put aside his native dress for European finery, appearing in sumptuous apparel. 'Itias dress was truly ridiculous, being a crimson coat with gold button holes, brought purposely from England by Captain Bligh as a present for her husband. Vaiareti differed from her sister in wearing blue. One had a sheet wrapped round her waist, and the other a tall cloth. Ari'paea exhibited himself in a captain's uniform coat which had been given to him by Captain Edwards of the *Pandora*.

They supped and slept on board. Their whole conversation was now, with great feeling, on our departure. We were told that the ceremony of wounding the head with a shark's tooth would take place, and *rahi ta'i* (much crying).

Being employed at the watering place, 'Itia learning it, with her usual kindness and consideration, sent every refreshment the island afforded, and if with the assistance of our seamen, a large baked hog was not demolished, I was abundantly gratified in filling the bellies of several of her *tavinis*, young and old partaking of her 'barbeque'. The remainder of the week was employed in preparations for sea; provisions reached us in abundance.

13th

More than half of the plants were this day embarked, and in the most healthy state, the natives assisting to convey them to the boats, yet not without heavy hearts at the thoughts of our departure. It was unsettled weather on the following day, which prevented the remainder being brought on board, but until night, the two vessels were attended by canoes laden with various supplies. Hogs were so numerous that many could not be received for want of room to accommodate them. Fowls, the only kind of poultry on the island, save a solitary gander left by Captain Vancouver a few months before, and which had become a 'pet' at Pare, were difficult to procure. Was more attention paid to rearing them, they would soon be abundant.

Among other articles, a quantity of *mahee*, which is breadfruit made, after fermentation, into a paste, was taken on board for the stock; this kept a considerable time and was very nutritious. Besides live hogs, a quantity of pork had been salted in the manner described by Captain Cook, which was found to answer equal to any cured in the European way.

Every hour served to convince me of the unfeigned sorrow of these gentle people at our approaching separation. For my *taio* I made a selection of every article likely to add to her comforts, but she had unfortunately fixed her affections on a fowling piece. Fully convinced that weapons of a destructive kind should, if possible, be withheld from these naturally peaceful beings, I resisted her solicitations for a considerable time, but her heart clung to it, and she became so urgent that I could not deny my consent any longer, provided it met our commander's approval. This, by perseverance, she effected, and the gun was received with the most greedy satisfaction.

Among other trifles she was left a small portrait of her *taio* with the dates of the arrival and departure of the *Providence* and *Assistant* at its back. And here, James, I cannot refrain from remarking with what friendly care and reverence a picture of Captain Cook by Webber (painted while at Tahiti in his last voyage) was preserved by Pomare. Nothing I suppose could tempt this amiable chief to part with it. Much did I covet the polygraphic secret, to steal the portrait of this immortal navigator, which was said by those who knew him to be a most striking resemblance. It has been customary for the different commanders of vessels visiting the island to note on the back of this picture the time of their arrival and departure. Some other tablet must now be found, as visits have been so frequent, no more space is left. We were not a little hurt at only seeing the bare mention of the arrival and sailing of the *Pandora*, as our anxiety was great to know what steps had been taken to secure the wretched mutineers of the *Bounty*. In some degree we were relieved from this doubt by the communication of the chiefs.

Mideedee, who has before been mentioned, determined about this time to accompany us to England. Indeed there was, I believe, scarcely an individual that would not with a little persuasion have embarked with us. The friends of poor Mideedee, however anxious, have vainly looked for his return among them. Voluntarily he quitted his own thoughtless countrymen in search of more enlightened ones, but in a few short weeks after setting his foot on the British shore, a British grave received him.

Several men, late of the *Matilda*, now embarked for a passage home, but four or five remained by choice on the island, one of whom was a Jew convict that had come in her from Sydney. To those who remained Captain Bligh, with great consideration, addressed a letter exhorting them to peace and good conduct, but if unfortunately, after the departure of the *Providence* hostilities should take place, to give their assistance to the royal party. Old Ha'amanemane, the high priest, was charged with this letter, who, notwithstanding his confidence in our commander, brought it to several of us to know if it was *maita'i* (good) which on being assured, gave him great relief.

15th

In a morning, the remainder of the plants were taken on board, amounting, with those already embarked, to –

Breadfruit	780 large pots	The major part contained more than
or uru	301 small pots	one plant. Many of them, three or
	35 tubs	four plants.
	26 boxes	
Avee or	8 large pots	
Tahitian apple	17 small pots	
Mattee	5 large pots	A beautiful red dye is produced with
	1 small pot	the mattee and ettow. The juice of
Ettow	2 large pots	the berry of the former and leaf of the
	4 small ones	latter.
Ayyah	4 large pots	A fruit in some degree resembling the
	31 small ones	avee
Raiah	10 large pots	A superior kind of plantain
Nahee	2 large pots	
Peeah	7 large pots	The root of the peeah is made into a
		delicious pudding.
Rattah or	18 large pots	
chestnut	17 small pots	
Other rare	8 small pots	
plants	2 tubs	

If you refer to this 'Plan and Section' of the garden on board the *Bounty* (which is among your father's books) it will give you a more perfect knowledge of our method of stowing the plants than anything I can say. It may, however, be observed that as well as the great cabin of the *Providence*, both sides of the after part of her quarterdeck were fitted at Tahiti for the same purpose, leaving narrow gangways next to the skylight for the movements of the crew.

Accompanied by a vast concourse of natives, our commandant of the post, with Pearce and his marines, in the afternoon marched to Point Venus, where boats were in readiness to embark them. When they put off from the shore, three cheers were given by the crews and returned by the more numerous islanders, who shed many a tear on the occasion.

Before the day closed Captain Bligh sent me to fill a few casks of water. Not a native was to be seen; grief had drawn them to the other side of the Matavai. It was the first evening for more than three months that Point Venus had not been the scene of festivity and good humour. Our encampment was deserted; a flagless staff bespoke its evacuation, and great was my relief from such a cheerless spot, when I returned to my associates on board.

The ship was unmoored and launch hoisted in the next morning. Many improvements, as well as to the other boats, had been made during our stay to render them more safe in case of accident to the ship in the subsequent part of the voyage, which was by far the most perilous. And as the crew was increased – one of the *Matilda*'s boats was taken on board.[2]

Both vessels were tumultuously crowded with natives of both sexes, heavily laden with various farewell presents for their English *taios*, who not ungrateful to the kindness of these good people, were equally liberal in return. Young Tu was about us the whole day nearly, in his canoe, but as usual could not be persuaded to come on board; the only instance where an unlimited confidence was not placed in us, and we were willing to attribute it to the custom of not entering any house but his own.

There was no *heiva* or merriment in the evening. Many at sunset took their leave with a tearful eye, while others continued on board the whole night, unwilling to lose the last attentions of such of our shipmates as they were attached to.

17th

Numbers of canoes were around us by early dawn bringing yet more provisions. The ship being so crowded we could hardly move. In the offing there was a strong trade wind, but to the great delight of the natives, Matavai Bay was becalmed. After dinner the anchor was weighed when, with the assistance of the boats, accompanied by our consort, we reached the sea breeze.

As we increased our distance from the shore, the natives reluctantly quitted us. Many vainly strove to follow in their canoes, expressing their sorrow by loud and reiterated lamentations, while some who had particularly attached themselves to the vessels or the post, were seen tearing their hair, and heedless of the pain, wounding their heads with a shark's tooth as on the death of a relation.

Pomare, Ari'paea, 'Itia, and several chiefs continued on board all night, during which a safe situation was kept in the offing. It might be almost said that we had the whole court on board; yet such was their good faith, the cruise did not at all alarm them.

18th

Early in the morning, the vessels stood in towards Pare. Captain Bligh had bountifully supplied his *taio*, Pomare, and his other visitors with a variety of useful articles, and what particularly delighted the king regent, our commander was so strongly solicited for a musket, he could not resist giving one. This increased Pomare's 'armoury' to about a dozen, for the supply of which he had a considerable quantity of ammunition. Besides those in his possession, there were about fifteen more in different parts of the island. Unfortunately, in the use of them, the natives are by no means ignorant.

The parting between Captain Bligh and his friends was kind and affectionate. They separated in the heart-felt conviction of having no want of harmony and good will to reproach themselves with.

It was my lot to convey the chiefs on shore. The boat was heavily laden with their various presents, serving in some degree to dissipate their sorrow; yet could not poor 'Itia imprison her tears, and had I encouraged such an infirmity, verily do I believe that, however 'albeit unused to the melting mood'* the whole boats crew would have admitted the sorrowful infection. Reaching Pare, a vast number of the inhabitants were assembled to take the last look of their English friends. An old lady, who had been ceaseless in her visits to the ship, brought cocoanuts and other fruit to refresh the boats' crew. Captain Bligh was anxiously waiting our return, which made my farewell interview with these happy islanders, but short, yet was it so distressing a one, I was glad to hurry from the scene. Old Torano's heart was full, and pressing my hand, she could only say, 'God bless you on the deep'.

Among the multitude, many were seen with whom we had been in constant habits of cordial intimacy and mutual kindness. When we left the shore not a word was heard, but every look beamed silent solicitude and concern for our safety, nor till long after the 'less'ning boat' was safe on board and by the weather helm the ship obedient was 'cast to sea', did they turn slowly from the beach to their peaceful habitations.

My pen is now about to quit this delightful isle. Yet ere it does, a few more crude observations, which may not have found a place in the preceding sheets, shall be hazarded under a conviction that, from your knowledge of the early habits and avocations of the writer, you will pass over with indulgent eye the inaccuracy of diction which cannot but too often occur. Such is almost inseparable from our 'calling'. Wishing it were otherwise will avail nought; you must therefore take the 'will for the deed'. For the present, farewell. George Tobin

---

* 'albeit unused to the melting mood': *Othello*, act V, scene ii. Fielding also used the line in *Tom Jones*, book V, chapter 3, paragraph 19.

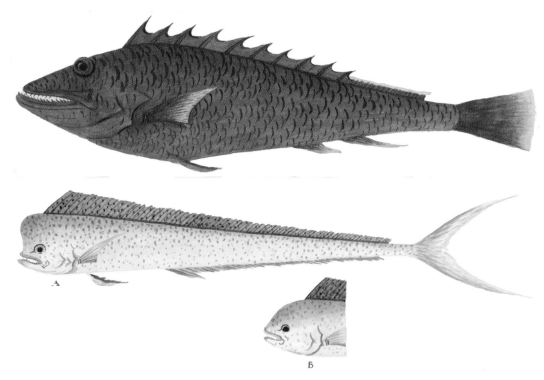

this page, from top: 18 Fish of Tahiti, aihoua
19 Dophins:
A Male
B Female (according to seamen)
20 A fare tuapapa'u, with the corpse on it, Island of Tahiti

previous page: 17 On Matavai River, Island of Tahiti, from recollection

21 *Matavai Bay, and the Island of Tetiaroa, from the hills south of the bay, Tahiti*

22 *In the district of Ha'apaiano'o, Island of Tahiti, looking towards Matavai*

23 *The marae at Pare, Island of Tahiti, looking towards Matavai*

24 *A double canoe, with the atua (god) and provisions on the prow, Island of Tahiti*

25 *Marae Point, at Pare, in Island of Tahiti*

below left: 26 *Parakeet of Tahiti, veney*
below right: 27 *Parrot of Tahiti, ah ah*

this page, from top: 29 Canoe of the Island of Aitutaki
                      30 Torres Straits – the general 'order of sailing'
                      31 Torres Straits – the Providence and Assistant obliged to fire at the
                      canoes

facing page: 28 Figures, called etee, Island of Tahiti, carved on a tree

following page: 32 Kupang, in the Island of Timor

CHAPTER 7TH

The Tahitians

Men and women of Tahiti.—Cleanly to a degree.—Early risers.—Children swimming.—Ra'atiras or gentlemen.—Dress and ornaments.—Hair.—Scissors.—Teary.—Mourning dress.—War mat.—Long nails.—Population.—Arioi Society.—Polygamy.—Government monarchical.—Ari'is.—Tavinis.—Labour of the females.—Cloth.—Women do not eat with the men.—Fishing lines, hooks, &c. &c.—Weapons.—Not warlike.—Heiva, dance now called hoopaowpa.—Musical instruments.—Language.—Short vocabulary.—Songs.—Priests &c. &c.—Missionaries.—Laws.—Diseases.—Harwood administers to them.—Insanity.—Suicide.—Not remarkable for longevity.—The late Captain Clerke.—Europeans left on the South Sea islands.—Account of natives visiting Europe.—Mai.—Natural deformity rare.

Thetis, near Savannah March 1797

On a retrospect of the preceding sheets, it seems that I shall bid fair to weary you, and therefore, the sooner they are brought to a termination the better. Yet cannot I quit these children of nature, about whom there are still a few more fragments to 'organise', without a confession that of late, I have derived no small degree of satisfaction in 'trying back'. You are not ignorant with what brittle materials the writer is constructed, and who has long fruitlessly courted a motto, which most of his neighbours seem, without much exertion, to be in possession of: to 'take things as he finds them'. But t'wont do – nor will it to the 'end of the chapter'.

Ever, instead of pushing straight forward in the highway, is he serpentining it to one side or the other, nor without stumbling into dilemmas of an esurine complexion,* requiring more philosophy to surmount than has been portioned to him from above. Yet, perhaps it is owing to what in our squadron is called the 'blue devils', where many long faces have been long looking out for promotion.

The men of Tahiti are of the middle stature; seeing them continually among our countrymen, there seems no better standard to compare them by. The Tahitian is not more muscular and strong, but in activity and pliancy of limb he exceeds the Englishman. By nature and habit they are indolent to a degree. Plenty is here as conspicuous as in any part of the globe. And when an Indian has only to visit a neighbouring tree to supply his wants, or should he covet more favourite food, paddle a mile or two in his canoe for fish, we cannot be surprised

---

*   esurine complexion: a voracious nature.

at his hatred to exertion. To what view is it exercised in Europe, where this enviable indolence is unknown? By the rich from ambition – and by the poor, unfortunately, from want – here it is not required, and the activity of these islanders is only seen in the hour of festivity and sudden occasion.

The countenance is free and open, nor scarcely ever furrowed with care or reflection. If there is any characteristic in their features, as in those of most Indians, it is a flatness of the nose, yet so trifling as to occasion scarcely any distention of the nostrils, but this among themselves is admired, and encouraged by a pressure when in a state of infancy. Their mouths are in general large, but in regularity of teeth they rival the universe. A dark penetrating eye is to be seen in the whole of them, in the women tempered by the most feminine softness, but (which is the case with every description of people of colour that have fallen under my notice in various distant parts of the world) the white has not that clearness common to the European. The hair of both sexes is in general black, and rather coarse, but in many instances it was red and brown. The women have been represented as considerably under the middle size, but this I could not discover. In symmetry of person, they are equal, particularly where age has not made its approaches, to the most critical imagination, was not the contour of the figure hurt, by the largeness of the feet, owing to their not being any way confined. Warrianow – nor have I forgotten our Hottentot at the Cape – was a most interesting figure. She would, indeed, have been a *bonne bouche* for the academic table at Somerset House.*

They are cleanly to a degree, both sexes generally bathing thrice a day in fresh water, and it is somewhat remarkable that, except the children for amusement, the salt water is never frequented but from necessity, and at these times, if a river be contiguous, they make a point of washing in it afterwards. It is common to see the children at five or six years of age amusing themselves in the heaviest surf with a small board on which they place themselves outside the breaking, whence they are driven with great velocity to the shore, fearless themselves, nor are the least apprehensions of accidents entertained by their parents.

We are taught in England that bathing during the sun's heat is attended with dangerous effects. The Tahitian is a stranger to this doctrine. At the back of our encampment we had daily, when the sun was on the meridian, numbers of the softer sex refreshing themselves in the Matavai by the hour, as fearless of suffering from it, as unconscious that in a more refined country it would be considered as highly indecorous and subversive of morality. Very true, our fastidious damsels bathe enveloped in a machine.† Yet, if my memory be right, I

---

*   Between 1776 and 1780 Somerset House was redone and became the headquarters for the Royal Academy of Art, the Royal Society and the Society of Antiquaries.
†   In order to shield swimmers from public view during the eighteenth and nineteenth centuries, wheeled vehicles containing dressing rooms brought the swimmers to the water's edge before they entered the sea.

have somewhere read – and it is, I believe, to be found among the archives in Doctors Commons,* of an English *ari'i* being so vain of the finely moulded limbs of his wife that he could not refrain giving his *taio* a peep, through one of these machines, at them. Surely this was more like the pliant obliging South Sea islander than the jealous selfish Englishman.

They rise with the sun, and the hour of repose is not much after it has set, though they were sometimes found keeping 'later hours'. On these occasions the nut of the candle tree serves for light, the manner of using it being very simple. It is about the size of a chestnut, containing an oily matter. Several of them being perforated, are stuck on a small reed which is lighted at the top, and as the first nut is expended, the next supplies the reed with oil and so on to the bottom. It is (I believe) from this nut that the stain used in tattooing is prepared.

The *ari'is* and *ra'atiras* (gentlemen) sleep on a mat with a small wooden pillow for the head in the form of a stool. In travelling, which is chiefly by water, a portable house or shed is fixed on the prow of the canoe, scarcely large enough for two to sleep in. The *tavinis* sleep on the bare ground in the open air, wrapped in the country cloth, but in rainy or severe weather, every chief's house is open to them.

The dress of both sexes is of their own cloth, and different kinds of matting, the *tavinis* scarcely using anything but a girt round the middle. The *ari'is* and *ra'atiras* are more extravagant in their apparel. In common, a piece of the thickest cloth, about three yards long and one in breadth, in the middle of which there is a hole for the head to pass through, is worn over the shoulders, the ends falling before and behind, leaving the arms at free scope. Sometimes a girt of matting or rope is worn over this, round the loins. The women dress with the finer cloth in many fanciful ways and have generally a small bonnet (*taupo'o*) made of the leaf of the *wharra* (wild pine) as a protection from the sun. The male sex seldom cover the head, but the hair is encouraged to acquire a considerable length, being either fastened in a bunch at the crown, or hanging loose down the back. It is frequently anointed with cocoanut oil (*monoi*) as a perfume, as well as to promote its growth. The beard, except on the point of the chin, where it is allowed to grow, is eradicated; a few, indeed, were seen with it on the upper lip.

The women wear their hair shorter, but in various ways. They are as strict votaries to fashion as our own fair countrywomen and have as many little interesting tricks of accidentally displaying their dress and figure. The superior orders are seldom without a fly flap of cock's feathers, serving to draw your attention to the prettiest hands conceivable. At other times their taper fingers are employed plaiting the palmetto leaf into a manufacture for hats. This last they were taught by Europeans, and it is now become quite an article of trade. It was the *ton* during the visit of the *Providence* to wear the hair in furrows like the waves of the sea (*are miti*), and which had a pretty effect; yet was it seriously

---

* Doctors Commons: the society of ecclesiastical lawyers in London. They dealt with church courts on matters such as defamation, adultery, fornication and incest.

wished that the means by which it was effected had been removed. For, since the introduction of scissors (*paoti*), these good girls have ever been clipping – one thing or the other – full as inviting, without being clipped. The finest eye lashes and arched eyebrows in the world did not escape.

The prettiest ornament is a *bandeau* of the Cape Jasmine (*teary*). In the morning after laving* in the stream, and anointing the hair with cocoanut oil, a flower of the *teary* is stuck in the lobe of each ear, which preserves its fragrance the major part of the day. Great pains are taken in the culture of this plant. The ear is also ornamented by many with a pearl-drop many of which, of a good size but inferior quality, are found about the islands.

There are many peculiar dresses worn on religious, warlike, and festive occasions. The mourning dress is the richest, the apron of it consisting of above two thousand small regular pieces of the bright part of the pearl oyster shell. The helmet is decorated, in the form of a glory,† with the tail feathers of the white, as well as the red-tailed, tropic bird. Some hundred of these feathers are on one dress, and when it is considered that there are but two feathers in each bird that will answer, the labour must be great in procuring them. My good father has one of these mourning dresses in England, that 'Itia gave me and which I was fortunate to get home in excellent preservation. An examination of it will satisfy you more than any description I can give. You will also see the *taumi* (war mat or gorget) and several other South Sea articles.

Among other customs may be mentioned that of the superior people, like the Chinese, suffering their nails to acquire a greater length than those in a more subordinate situation.

The island has all the appearance of an extensive population,[1] and if every part is as well inhabited as from Ha'apaiano'o to Teahupoo, which embraces a distance of about twenty miles, there must be forty or fifty thousand, and there seems no reason why it should not be supposed the case, as every part is fertile and productive near the sea. Plenty sheds forth its blessings to such an extent that agriculture is nearly as little known as required, but with very little exertion the soil would support double the number above mentioned. It is chiefly on the low plain encircling the rising hills near the sea (and which is a forest of breadfruit that grows without planting) the native fixes his residence. The rest of the island, by far the greater part, is scarcely ever seen by him; yet its soil is equal to produce almost every tropical fruit and grain. Except the *Arioi* village at the foot of Orohena, I never saw either hut or signs of cultivation four miles from the sea. In fact, generally speaking, the natives reside on the margin of it.

Yet have you been given to understand that they are in dread of over-population, to prevent which and keep an equality of the sexes, every other female is destroyed at its birth. I can only say that such a custom never came within my knowledge or observation, and on reference to the chiefs on the

---

*   laving: washing, bathing.
†   a glory: a circle.

subject, they uniformly declared that the children of the *Ariois*, whether male or female, were the only ones doomed to this early fate. Nor could they be persuaded of the inhumanity of the custom. An observation may be hazarded, which is that there appears no reason why the females should exceed in number the other sex. They are both subject nearly to the same accidents, the same diseases. War, which in some countries may occasion a disparity, is here but little destructive. The sacrifices, indeed, we were told were always of the male sex. But they so seldom occur that joined to the very few slain in battle, it cannot make so great a difference in the sexes as that the destruction of females is necessary to keep up the balance without. And this is too intricate a research for your humble servant – and indeed to the profound, who with critical eye explore the dark crevices of nature – little more than an amusing speculation.

It could be proved that at Tahiti a greater proportion of the female sex are really brought into the world, and here I cannot keep from saying that in my walks about the island, where houses have been teeming with children, there ever appeared an equality. Besides, in an island where polygamy is encouraged and indulged in by most of the chiefs and better sort of people, indeed, by everyone whose circumstances and inclination lead him, it is difficult of belief that means should be taken to limit it. I may indeed be told that where polygamy is general in a country, more females are born – but I am wandering from my narrative, nor without bidding fair to get out of my depth.

Yet, one observation shall not be withheld, as it aims at controverting the above position of more females being born. If a physical cause be assigned for it, should it not apply to the animal creation? It does not appear to be the case. When our sea stock of chickens are brought on board, there are generally an equal proportion of either gender; this is also the case with our hogs, our sheep and our goats. Yet the man who sold them declares that there is only one sovereign chanticleer in his farm yard; and the same of the quadrupeds. He then ensnares a covey of partridges. Still do I see an equal number of either gender, although it is well known the old ones paired early in the spring and that the male bird is free from the charge of infidelity. How is this?

The government of Tahiti is monarchial, and perhaps in no part of the globe is the hereditary prerogative of royalty more zealously attended to. At what age the heir apparent becomes *ari'i tane* (king) or assumes the reins of government, I did not learn, but until it takes place, a regent is appointed, generally the father; yet all kingly respect is paid to the young prince. I could not understand when he was to cease being carried on men's shoulders. To marry into an inferior family is considered as an indelible disgrace. Ari'paea and Vaetua, uncles of Tu, subdued by the power of ignoble beauty, were in this dilemma. The wife of the former had brought him a child, which he dared not acknowledge, passing it for a friend's who had placed it under his charge, and by this evasion probably saved its life.

Although the power of the *ari'i tane* is allowed by the chiefs to be absolute and unlimited, yet in their different districts, they have considerable influence with the lower orders. Insurrections are not unfrequent. The bold persevering conduct of Poeno and Tapiru is a recent instance, and which terminated in the royal party not being able to secure the muskets, these chiefs conceiving them as their property from a prior possession on their being first landed from the *Matilda's* boats.

Besides the *ari'i tane*, there are three classes of people, *ari'is*, or chiefs, *ra'atiras*, or commoners, and *manahune*, or lower orders indiscriminately, whether as servants to chiefs or not. In general, attention and respect is observed towards the chiefs, yet is there a cordial familiarity and friendly intercourse among the whole, which argues that they do not think there is that difference in mankind most among us are taught to believe. It is common to see groups of every description merrily conversing without the chilling spirit of rank intruding to restrain their social talk. Yet detach the more subordinate from such intercourse, they will feelingly reiterate the name and praises of their *ari'is* with unadulterated heart-felt pride and delight. Their *ari'is*, whose ears are ever open to their complaints and habitations to give them shelter.

In an island where the women boast so many charms and have such influence, it is extraordinary that there are many occupations assigned them much better adapted to their more robust 'lords and masters'. Towards low water they generally repair with a basket to the reefs in search of different marine productions, none of which are rejected by the palate of the Tahitian. I shall hardly be credited in saying that I have seen a lovely girl of fourteen or fifteen devouring a sea egg without the aid of cookery, with the keenest appetite and satisfaction.

The manufacturing of cloth falls also chiefly to the women. Never having been present at the whole process, I can only say that it is made from the bark of trees, chiefly that of the paper mulberry, which is cultivated for the purpose. Pieces are made several yards long without any visible joining, being beaten out with a wooden instrument on a plank to that extent. It is of various kinds and although a comfortable protection in dry weather, it will not bear much exposure to water. The thickest sort is formed by pasting close together two, three or more pieces. It is dyed of various colours; red, brown, yellow, and black, but I saw none either blue or green. The yellow dye is from turmeric, which is found in most parts of the island. With the juice of the *mattee* berry, and leaf of the *ettow*, a bright red is produced. Both these plants were taken on board the *Providence* and (I believe) reached our colonies in health. Means probably may be found of rendering the colour indelible – which are unknown at Tahiti. When they wish to affix any pattern on the cloth, it is done by the impression of a leaf or anything else they prefer, after being first wetted with the colour fixed on.

The white cloth acquires its fine colour from a long exposure to the air. Some of it was so very soft and flexible that the officers wore it for neck-cloths, nor without a close examination could it be distinguished from muslin. As well as cloth, matting is made of a very soft and beautiful texture, which is occasionally worn around the loins, falling before like an apron.

The women are prohibited eating in the presence of the other sex, yet it does not seem to proceed from a motive of delicacy on the part of the men, but in their considering the females as too subordinate to associate in one of their chief gratifications. But, without looking to the motive, I cannot but confess that the separation of the sexes among these people, while satisfying the calls of hunger, met my most cordial approbation. Surely it is an occupation that needs not congregating in any country, or indeed, but what should be got over without publicity of any kind.[2]

Fishing lines and nets, some of the latter of a great size, are made with much strength and neatness, a shrub* and the husk of the cocoanut being chiefly used for the purpose. Their hooks are variously formed of bone, wood, or shells, those used for ground fishing, not being barbed, but when a fish is once hooked, to disengage itself is nearly impossible. Nor can I help thinking that hooks of this form might be used with better effect in our Newfoundland fishery than the common European ones. I am aware that they might not catch so quick, but from experience know that vast numbers of cod are lost, as well as much time, from their so easily loosening themselves after reaching thirty, forty, and fifty fathom from the bottom. So partial are these islanders to their form that it was common to see nails manufactured by them into such kind of hooks, on which they placed a much greater value than on the barbed ones brought from England. The larger ones with which the shark is taken, is made of the *toa* tree, a hard kind of ironwood, some of them being full two feet in length. A different sort, barbed, are used as an artificial fish for dolphin and bonito, being made of the bright part of the pearl oyster shell, bone and hog's bristles.

Their warlike weapons are the spear and sling, the former being from ten to twelve feet in length, of *toa* wood, and used missively, as well as in the manner of a club. In discharging stones from their slings they are very dexterous. A few short heavy clubs were brought on board that came from a neighbouring island.

The soft voluptuous disposition of these people but ill qualifies them for hostile operations, nor do they indeed at all boast of being warlike. On the contrary, they acknowledge their inferiority as *tarai-aro* (warriors) to the inhabitants of many of the islands near them, particularly of Bora Bora. Doubtless it is fortunate for them that Bora Bora is so much to leeward as to preclude its people from invading Tahiti, between which islands there is no great degree of good will.

The bow and arrow are by both sexes used only as a recreation, large parties frequently meeting to try their skill; 'Itia was considered to excel in this amusement. Another pastime is that of wrestling, where much strength and agility are displayed. They also divert themselves in a game with a breadfruit, somewhat similar to football in England.

The *heiva* has been mentioned already (latterly indeed called *hoopaowpa*) which word seems to apply to all their diversions as well as to dancing. There are

---

* Probably the plant called *wikstoemia coriacea*.

many itinerant parties of dancers and musicians of both sexes, who, like our strolling players, visit the different districts, being ever well received and taken care of by the chiefs.

The musical instruments are rather destitute of soft sounds, being only a rude sort of drum, a fife which is played through the nose, and a trumpet, used on religious occasions, formed by a bamboo pipe fixed to a large conch shell.

In their dances short sentences are repeated, in which the performers all join, and they were not a little pleased at our ignorance of most of them, it being in general the 'scandal of the day'. You must not from this infer that it is a language difficult to acquire, being perhaps, of all others the most accessible. It is as soft and pleasing as the disposition of the inhabitants, being nearly free from every dissonant sound and composed chiefly of vowels. Some of our letters, C, G, J, L, S, K, Q, X, Z, seem unknown. Great quickness is used in speaking when the parties are much interested, and more gesticulation than in most European countries. The R is the only letter which at all makes the language guttural, and it often occurs. You shall have a short vocabulary, by which you will be able to judge of the language better than from anything in my power to say.

Airooroo	The hair		*Etta*	The chin
Aiootoo	The lips		*Etooa*	The back
Aiu	The nose		*Evaha*	The mouth
Aireroo	The tongue		*Eno*	Bad
Ah'Imacca	The eye lashes		*Etey Etey*	Small, little
Tu'Imacca	The eye brows		*Eree*	A chief
Aiee	The neck		*Eree dahy*	A great chief, or king
Aromaye	Come, or bring		*Heneeo*	The teeth
Aimah whytey	I don't know		*Hoomey,*	
A'vy	Water		*Hoomey*	The beard
A'ourey	Iron		*Hooha*	The thigh
Aai	The breast		*Irai*	The forehead
Aimah	No		*Maiu*	The nails
Boa	Hog		*Momoa*	The heel
Boamo	Goat		*Monooey*	Cocoanut oil
Baubo	A native who came home with us		*Maneeo*	The toes
			Medey	The sea
Babooey	A musket		*Miti*	Good
Bobooey, Etey, Etey	A pistol, or little musket		*Meari'i, Meari'i*	Let me see?
Bohooey, da hy	A cannon or great musket		*Mow*	To seize
			Mow	A shark
Dahy	Great or large		*Mow*	
			Tawmowtow	A shovel-nosed shark

Tawmowtow	A bonnet	*Pomaurey*	The king regent, father of Otoo
Maa	To eat		
Maade Tata	A cannibal, or man eater	*Rema*	The hand
Marama	The moon	*Rattera*	A man of middling rank
Mahanna	The sun	*Taponoo*	The shoulder
Mahanna Topa	After sunset	*Tarreea*	The ear
		Toorey	The knee
Ooree	A dog	*Tabouai*	The foot
Ooree Pevarrey	A cat	*Tamou*	Plaited human hair worn like a turban
Ooree Tata	A monkey, or dogman	*Towrow*	A rope
Tata	A man	*Tawmey*	A gorget or war mat for the breast
Ooroo	Breadfruit		
Oboo	The belly	*Towtow*	A servant, or man of low degree
Otoo	Name of the king or eree dahy		
		Towrowmey	Chaffing, and pressing the limbs
O'tahytey	Name of the island		
Orepaia	Uncle to the king	*Tepey*	A knife
Otow	Grandfather to the king	*Tai Aiva*	Name of Whidooah's wife
Obereroah	Grandmother to the king		
Oparrey	The district west of Matavai	*Whidooah*	Uncle of Otoo
		Waureddey	Angry
Mideedee	A native who came home with us.	*Whyhereddy*	Pomaurey's younger wife
		Waheyney	A woman
Mideedee	A child	*Whitey*	Yes, or I know
Papareea	The cheek	*Yavy*	The leg
Peeto	The navel	*Yava*	An intoxicating liquor
Peerey Peerey	A virgin	*Youra na T'Eotooa*	God bless you[3]
Peerey Peerey	A plant like the burdock		
Pahee	A ship or vessel	*Matow*	Fear, or afraid
Paupa	The hip	*Topa te Medey*	To jump into the sea
		Mariddey	Cold

Doubtless you will find this vocabulary sufficiently extensive. You shall therefore have in addition some of our names as they struck my ear when pronounced by the natives, with two or three songs:

Bligh	Beihe
Bond	Boney
Guthrie	Tooteray
Pearce	Pearthey
Harwood	Harwootey

Providence	Proverenthy
Vancouver	Fannytopa
Christian	Titieano
Edwards	Etwartey
Tobin	Topeney

There were some in the ship whose names the organs of speech of these people could not approach so as to bear any similitude. Gilespie, one of the petty officers, in particular. To Holwell they attached the term 'All well' (losing the L) the words passed by our sentinels after dark.

The following were among other lines generally repeated at our afternoon *heiva*. The two first are of thirteen syllables, the emphasis, and not without some degree of symphoory,* being on the eighth in each line:

'Miti Miti Miti, Miti te peeir oboo'

2nd

'Miti Miti Miti, Miti te mato peya.'

Another of nineteen syllables:

'Teta meitey, teta mea; Teta meitey, towro Owaurro'

The former are (I was told) in praise of the large water fall on Matavai River, and also of the officers' cabins, where indeed, these cheerful damsels were sometimes known to rest their wearied limbs after the exertions of the *heiva*. The Tahitians are not destitute of the best of attributes, gratitude, no wonder then that they thus sung the praises of what administered to their comforts.

The priests have not yet been noticed. They did not appear to be numerous. Ha'amanemane, an old chief of Raiatea, the *taio* of Pearce, we always understood to be at the 'head of the church', but however orthodox in his devotions, few of the laity were so licentious and depraved in their habits. It is impossible for me to speak with any degree of certainty as to their religion. Idolatry is so far followed that they worship through the medium of images, scarcely a house being without them, and when taking a journey, being sufficiently portable, they are never left behind. They recount various deities, of the sea, the woods, and several others, all of which are appealed to on different occasions. It would not seem that they congregate at stated periods to offer their devotions. I have heard old Ha'amanemane after dining with us, no other native being in company, repeat a long prayer with great quickness for the space of half an hour. Death certainly cannot be considered by them as an immediate or 'eternal sleep', as, for a considerable time, until the flesh decays and the bones are finally placed in the *maraes*, the dead are supplicated with viands and articles of dress.

It was as ridiculous as fruitless, in my humble opinion, attempting to make them acquainted with our religious tenets. Yet has such a plan been frequently talked of, and indeed it was in contemplation to send out missionaries in the

---

*   symphoory: growing or grown together.

Providence to convert these amiable people. Several have since (I hear) actually reached Tahiti without being well received, the native begging them to depart and promulgate their doctrines elsewhere.*

I am neither brave or fashionable enough to be a sceptic. Few indeed are the former, whatever they may profess. Yet, believing as I do, I cannot reconcile to myself either the wisdom or goodness of extending Christianity to distant worlds full as virtuous as ourselves. Doubtless, in this feeling I may be wrong; still, I cannot put it away. Besides, how is it to be effected? From what has fallen within the scope of my observation on this side of the Atlantic, where the numbers of missionaries are rapidly increasing, their doctrine seems wholly to be terror. Mercy is almost wrested from the Almighty, and not his attribute, while the chief theme is thundering damnation into the ears of their eagerly listening flock. That there may be many truly pious and worthy characters among the sect of Methodists (than whom no others have embarked on this converting South Sea voyages), I am willing to believe, but much fear it will be found that there are too many worldly and mercenary fanatics.

What the exact creed of the Tahitian is, it is not in my power to explain. Yet is it charitable to believe it a good one – if faith and good works travel in amity with each other. In the latter, these islanders are 'eminent beyond compare'. They encourage a lesson of morality and good will among one another that puts civilised religion to blush. Let us then – still I may be in error – in the name of Providence have done with missions of the kind. Take a retrospect of their sanguinary exterminating consequences in many a large portion of the world and humanity will tremble. The Tahitian needs no conversion; he divides what he has with the stranger, as with his neighbour.⁴ He administers to, he anticipates their wants. Can he be taught more, and still retain these amiable and generous qualities?

Doubtless some of their customs ought to be abolished, and let us hope that at no very distant period they will, whether by the aid of missionaries or not. I will drop the subject, with a belief that you will acquit me of any intention of being loose or licentious in the preceding observations. God knows it is the farthest from my heart. So often have I 'traced a Providence at sea, and saw his wonders on the mighty deep' that it is impossible for me to doubt.

> An Atheist sailor were a monstrous thing,
> More wonderful than all old Ocean breeds.

I am only hazarding an opinion – crude enough no doubt – on the plan of converting my old friends at Tahiti. Have we not a great deal to do 'at home?'

Of their penal† laws I am hardly able to speak. What in many countries would be deemed crimes, here meet no penalty. I rather believe that the life of an

---

* In 1797 James Wilson commanded the *Duff*, which brought missionaries to Tahiti.
† penal: criminal.

individual cannot be affected, let the guilt be what it may. In the sudden impulse of passion and resentment, I have seen a chief inflict a blow on an inferior without resistance but was never witness to anything like systematic corporal punishment. It has already been observed that the most worthless in society are selected for oblation to the deity on different occasions, yet even here, the devoted object is kept ignorant of the blow that awaits him. Although in the preceding pages, several instances of theft are mentioned, I am disposed to believe, and this opinion is confirmed by the report of the chiefs, that it seldom occurs among themselves. We cannot be much surprised that the novelty of European articles should tempt them to err. The rigid moralist will not find it difficult to discover that in our visits to these unoffending people, with the advantages of education and refinement – if such they be – and the taught conviction of right and wrong, we ourselves have been sometimes caught tripping. The balance, I rather fear is against us.

Their diseases are not numerous, and they are happily ignorant of those ravaging ones, the small pox and measles. Consumptions are not uncommon, for which like ourselves, they seem aware that there is no remedy. But what they suffer most from are diseases of a scrofulous nature. Many instances fell under my observation where it had made dreadful inroads on the human frame, the poor sufferers only looking to death for a termination of their misery. They attribute most of their complaints to the visits of Europeans, and that some of them were imported by us, perhaps it would be difficult to disprove.

The venereal disease, that cursed scourge on mankind, has here spread its baneful influence to a melancholy degree, by whatever channel it might have been introduced. On this question much sedulous disquisition has been exercised, yet seemingly with naught conclusive. Nearly two centuries have elapsed since the discovery of the islands by Quiros, but the natives date the origin of this cruel disorder at a more recent period, the visits of Captain Wallis and Monsieur Bougainville, the former in 1767, the latter in the following year. Save to the idly curious, it is of little import which of the two left this sad token among them; instead of disputing how the disease reached the island, humanity cries aloud that to heal their sufferings ought to be the consideration. We owe them every friendly and humane exertion, nor can it be doubted but that professional men might be found whose hearts would dilate in embarking on so laudable a purpose. This, indeed, was a mission the God of all, the protector of the Christian, as well as of the dark untutored savage, would approve. Here, although not ignorant of simples* that yield relief in their milder complaints, here their wretched obscurity calls feelingly for succour.

Our worthy messmate, Ned Harwood, with his ceaseless philanthropy, acted the part of the 'good Samaritan' to these poor islanders. But his healing relief was of short continuance.

---

*   simples: medicines.

A few instances of men suffering from insanity were observed, but in no case so as to render coercion necessary. I was led to enquire whether suicide was ever known among them and was informed it never happened but from insanity, the instances being very rare. The gloomy, ceaseless, overwhelming discontent and despair, so often the inmates of more reflecting and civilised breasts, and which covets dissolution for relief, is here never seen. Of the motives, indeed, to this desperate act among Europeans, they are happily strangers. The European perhaps has not more sensibility than the native of Tahiti, but there are reflections inseparable from the indulgence of such sensibility, the latter has never been taught to feel. If we could examine into the history of such among ourselves who have embraced self-murder as a termination of their woes, it would be found too often to have proceeded from the corroding conviction of guilt, doubtless more frequently than from any other impulse. Many, indeed, carry their history with them unknown but to a superior power, from a silent feeling to others left here to buffet it a little longer. The Tahitian is a child of nature, not plagued nor perplexed with too much thought. Her impulses he unreservedly follows, feeling, not reasoning about it, that she is the true guide, and that passions and affections were given him as a road to happiness. Nor to be chilled by the sapient decrees of profound legislators, who aim – yet impotently – by human institution to subdue their all-powerful voice.

The few preceding remarks bear not at all upon the turpitude of self-murder. They are only hazarded as an opinion, why it is more frequent among ourselves than with these people, thereby deducing that their system of life is wiser than our own. Without it argues wisdom to seek another world when this becomes burdensome. But few are bold enough to try an experiment – and which 'cannot be tried a second time' – so full of doubt and obscurity.

It would not appear that they are remarkable for longevity. One of the oldest of our visitors was Tue, grandfather of Tu, the *ari'i tane*, yet he did not seem above seventy; but as their method of keeping time, which is by moons, made any enquiries, except on recent circumstances, rather perplexing, I only speak of the age of Tue from conjecture.[5]

Our people were allowed to go on shore in rotation, but there was no instance of desertion; yet perhaps this was more owing to a conviction that the chiefs would deliver them up, than from want of inclination. It has been already observed that some of the *Matilda*'s crew remained on the island by choice. And here I cannot help noticing, on the authority of Captain Bligh, that Captain Clerke of the *Discovery* when last at Tahiti in 1777 with Captain Cook, had formed the intention of remaining there, and that on the day of their departure he went on board the *Resolution* to intimate such a wish to his commanding officer who, having been appraised of the circumstances, avoided a meeting, instantly proceeding with the two vessels to sea. Captain Clerke had been an invalid from the beginning of this arduous voyage and had encouraged a flattering hope that the genial climate of the island would have again restored him to health. You are aware that he died on the coast of Kamchatka about two years afterwards, not having reached the meridian of life.

Such Europeans as have voluntarily been left on any of the South Sea islands, however partial to the manner of the inhabitants, have generally availed themselves of opportunities to return.[6] The natives, I have no doubt, would act the same after remaining any considerable time in Europe, so powerfully do our affections cling to the soil where we first drew breath. Much is it to be lamented that of the South Sea islanders who visited Europe and other countries, only one returned. The death of poor Mideedee, who came home in the *Providence*, has been mentioned. Baubo, who we left at Jamaica not long after, met the same fate.[7] Tupaia and his boy, Taiata, fell sacrifice to the pestilential climate of Jakarta in the *Endeavour*. Ahutoru, who embarked with Monsieur Bougainville in 1768 after passing some time in France, sailed on his return, but only reached Mauritius or Réunion where he died. Hitihiti, it is true, from visiting the Tonga Isles, New Zealand and other places returned safe, after being absent about a twelvemonth, to Raiatea. Mai, it would appear, is the only one who after passing some time in Europe, returned to his own country.

However confident in our kindness, and unsuspicious of neglect having been exercised towards such of their countrymen as at different periods embarked with us, it cannot but appear extraordinary to the natives that death or other circumstances should so continually have prevented their coming back. Mideedee and Baubo were in the highest state of health when they took the last farewell of their native friends and relations.

Many accounts were current respecting Mai, but they all accorded in his having died a natural death at Raiatea, his native isle. A chief of that island stated that the firearms of Mai, of which he had a couple, gave him much importance, and that on the locks getting out of order, by continual use, it was his custom to present the musket, while a *tavini* with a lighted stick set fire to the priming. This poor fellow while in England certainly passed the time much to his gratification, but by no means so as to acquire any information likely to be of benefit to his country. Had Mideedee lived, there is no doubt but Captain Bligh would have had him instructed in some useful kind of handicraft, if indolence, which is inseparable from their people, had not proved an obstacle.

Among the several thousand who visited shipping and the post, I observed only one person labouring under natural deformity, from which it is fair to infer that such cases are rare on the island.

The mean of 9 sets of observations of the ☿ & ☽ (George Tobin) gave the longitude of Matavai Bay[8] 210°..35'.5" east or 149°..24'.55" west viz:

May 14th 1st Set	210..39'.15"
May 28th 2nd	210..31'.45"
June 13th 3rd	209..57'.30"
June 14th 4th	210..26'.45"
June 14th 5th	210..28'.30"
June 15th 6th	210..41'.15"

June 25th 7th	210..53'.45"
June 26th 8th	210..20"
June 28th 9th	211..17"
	1895..15'.45"
Mean longitude Matavai Bay –	210..35'.05" east

Captain Cook in 1769, on observing the Transit of Venus   210..27'.30"
Captain Bligh in the *Bounty* 1789 the result of 50 sets of observations 210..33'.5"

The 9 sets, above, vary in a considerable degree; the 3rd and the last so much as 79 miles, which strongly points out the necessity of taking a number of observations on such occasions.

The variation of the compass on board in Matavai Bay, the
   mean of 30 sets of Azimuths with 3 different compasses
   chiefly by Captain Bligh 1792   4°..58' easterly
Degrees by 9 sets on Point Venus   5°..47' easterly
         ½   10°..45'
         Mean variation   5°..22'.30" easterly

CHAPTER 8TH
July–September 1792

Pass Moorea or Eimeo.— Another Tahitian on board besides Mideedee, his name Baubo.—Very good lookout kept.—Island Aitutaki.—Intercourse with the natives.—Language somewhat similar to the Tahitian.—No harbour appeared.—Women dance the heiva.—Some account of the Bounty mutineers.— Want of journal.—Make the Mayorga Islands.—Fiji Islands.—Intercourse with the natives.—Christened the islands alphabetically.—Canoes.—Sir Joseph Banks.—A mutiny nearly taking place in the Endeavour, 1769.—Paradise Island.—White and ocean water, the terms at the Bahamas.—Alphabet expended, begin naming islands numerically.—Proceed westward.— Vanuatu.—South coast of New Guinea.—Noddies, boobies &c. &c.—Zeal of Lieutenant Portlock.—Armour for the boats' crews.—See the reefs eastward of Torres Straits.—Enter the straits.—Boats employed.—Affair in the cutter with natives.—Canoes.—Various islands.—Anchor frequently.—Eight canoes approach the vessels and consequence.—Two men wounded in Assistant, one mortally. Arrows &c. &c.—Proceed westward.—Lookout Island.—Dangerous anchorage.—Enter the Indian Ocean.

Thetis, coast of Virginia – April 1797

18th

Leaving Tahiti a course was shaped to the westward, passing Moorea (or Eimeo) at a few leagues' distance. It appeared to be surrounded with reefs. The valleys exhibited plenty, being well supplied with breadfruit, cocoanut and other useful trees, the mountains rising above them in the most picturesque forms, one in particular on the northwest part of the island bearing a close resemblance to the steeple of a church.

It was now found that there was another Tahitian on board besides Mideedee. Baubo had, in a manner, concealed himself in the ship, yet perhaps not without the knowledge of some of his English friends. He had ever attached himself to the botanists Messieurs Wiles and Smith, to the latter in an affectionate degree and was determined to follow his fortunes across the ocean, nor could this poor fellow have fixed his faith on a more worthy man. But Baubo never reached England. On the arrival of the *Providence* at Jamaica it was decided that Mr. Wiles should remain there to superintend the plants. And Baubo, knowing that his presence could not but be of service to 'the cause', joined him with every hope ere long to make the last stage after the plants were permanently established, yet with great regret at the separation from his friend, Mr. Smith. At Jamaica by his great good humour he had become a favourite with all the neighbourhood. He had been inoculated with Mideedee at St. Vincent's for the small pox and with every favourable effect. What his disorder was afterwards at Jamaica I did not learn, but some time after our return to England, his death was announced in the newspapers.

The most difficult part of the voyage was now opening, and until we reached the Indian Ocean by Torres Straits, each night was passed in an anxious 'lookout'.

23th

The latitude at noon was 18°..47' south, longitude by account 159°..21' west. Before sunset the island, Aitutaki, was seen about six leagues distant.

24th

Early in the morning bore up for the southern part under easy sail, from which, at the distance of four or five miles, are some keys with trees on them, connected by a reef appearing to encircle the island. Many natives were on the beach and in canoes about the reef. On hauling our wind off the western part, three canoes containing in all about a dozen men, after our making signs of friendship, came along side. Nails and every implement made of iron were enquired for with the greatest avidity, in return for which they bartered the only ornament about their persons, a pearl oyster shell hung to their breast by a collar of plaited human hair, in the manner of a gorget. They also disposed of some spears about twelve feet in length, the sharp point being of a very dark hard wood and jagged like a turtle peg. Whether these spears are used as weapons of war, or to procure fish, we could not determine. One man had a club formed of the *toa* tree of Tahiti.

They were muscular and well formed, and in colour the same as the Tahitians. But I believe nothing has been yet said on the subject, I must therefore go back again and observe that it is a clear olive, yet varying much in shade, more so perhaps than is to be observed in England between the darkest and fairest skins. But of whatever tint, brown or copper, there is a transparency, if the expression may be used, different from what is to be seen among people of colour in our own colonies. Nor did we always look in vain for the blood 'mantling' in the cheeks – certainly not gifted with the lily or the rose – of some of these island beauties. The male part of the royal family were darker than most of the natives (young Tu, indeed, was an exception, being more of the colour of his mother) with coarse black hair, in some flowing loosely of great length down the back, others having it cropped quite short.

Tattooing is practised by them, but the breech, so common in the island we had left, was free from these stains. One among our visitors had every part of his body marked with scars from one to three inches long, which did not appear to be accidental. Some had their faces daubed over, not a little proud of it, with a kind of red pigment. Their beards were not wholly eradicated, but cropped short.

With the comfort of cleanliness they seemed unacquainted, being by no means free from vermin. One man wore the exact dress of the *ra'atira* or gentleman of Tahiti; that of the others was simply a piece of island cloth passed round the loins and brought up between the thighs.

Their language bore some affinity to that of Tahiti, yet neither Mideedee or Baubo allowed it to be the same. On the canoes first approaching, we called to them *haere mai* (come here, or bring) which they perfectly understood.

As the vessels drifted to the westward, the natives were anxious to get away, and while we were in the act of wearing, put off in the canoes, leaving two of their countrymen on board, nor could all our waving and calling bring the canoes back again. This brought us to the necessity of making the two take to the water, in the hope the canoes would pick them up, but no attention was paid to them. And one became so very exhausted that had not Mr. Portlock in the *Assistant* taken him on board, he most likely would soon have been drowned. The brig then stood in shore and stopped the canoes.

The conduct of these islanders on this occasion gave us but an unfavourable opinion of their humanity, nor could our kind and gentle Tahitians help expressing their indignation in the most feeling manner against those in the canoes for deserting their countrymen.

The island appeared destitute of harbours, and from the very light colour of the water within the reef, it could not be many feet deep. The dark blue line of 'ocean water', as it is termed by the Bahama pilots, formed a striking contrast; and particularly on being viewed from the masthead, where we sometimes went (not indeed as is now the case, when the 'hands are turned up to make sail' – to reconnoitre the chase) to get a more enlarged range for the eye. It was my first trip aloft on these occasions after quitting Tahiti and as well as a commanding view of Aitutaki, our floating garden was particularly attractive. I might add that, besides the breadfruit and the other plants to be seen on the quarter deck and in part of the cabin, a great deal of the rigging was crowded with plantains, cocoanuts, and other fruits and vegetables, which had been taken on board for ourselves and stock. Some consumption, it is true, had eased the shrouds and stays, but still a 'birds' eye' view gave the *Providence* nearly in a garb of green, attended by her *Assistant* in the same gay livery.

Aitutaki is three or four leagues in circuit, of fertile appearance, and abundantly supplied with cocoanut trees, amid which were the huts of the inhabitants who, in proportion to the extent of the isle, were numerous. It was remarked that numbers of the cocoanut trees had lost their foliage and some broken off nearly half way down the trunk, probably from high winds.

As we sailed past the island, it was easy with our glasses to see the women dancing the *heiva* on the beach in its full latitude. The signs made by them for a closer intercourse with the ships being by no means repulsive but inviting.

Their canoes were formed with much neatness, and so very narrow that without the outrigger it would be impossible to prevent their overturning. The sail was a piece of cloth about the size of an handkerchief fastened by the corners to two spears, held upright by one of the crew. Some canoes within the reef contained ten or twelve persons.

At Tahiti we had learnt that many of the mutineers of the *Bounty* had been secured by Captain Edwards of the *Pandora* about a year before our arrival. Yet as the fate of the others was still unknown, particular enquiries were made at this island but could only learn that some vessel had been there not long before us. This doubtless was the *Pandora*, Captain Edwards having examined Aitutaki without success in his voyage homewards. Captain Bligh ever entertained an idea that the mutineers would visit this island.

Where these wretched men may be, if in existence, we have yet to learn. The Tahitians stated that, Christian (*Titieano*) returned there with a plausible tale of some accident having happened to Captain Bligh and such of the officers and crew who were not in the ship. Here the *Bounty* remained but a short time, and then sailed for Tubuai, an island above an hundred leagues to the southward. On her arrival at Tubuai, little stock of any kind was found there, which induced Christian to again seek Tahiti and lade the ship with such articles as would be useful in his intended settlement. Still no suspicion was entertained by the natives of the mutiny, and after taking on board a quantity of hogs, fowls and goats, he again departed and arrived safely at Tubuai, accompanied by several natives. But the inhabitants were by no means desirous for his remaining, opposing it by every means in their power. Several rencounters took place, Christian having entrenched his party in the hope of forcing a settlement. But after remaining about three months and dissensions arising among themselves, the plan was relinquished, and the *Bounty* returned a third and last time to Tahiti. The armourer, Joseph Coleman, whom Captain Bligh in his distressing narrative states as being 'kept contrary to his inclination',[*] I have since conversed with. When he assured me that Christian was so intent on fixing his party at Tubuai as to have begun a drawbridge, the hinges being actually completed.

The ship was no sooner anchored than most of the mutineers went on shore, where they were again received by the chiefs with cordiality and goodwill, but a suspicion soon arose in the minds of the natives that foul play had been used to Captain Bligh; possibly insinuations to that effect were made by some of the crew. This so much raised the indignation of Ari'paea and other chiefs that they determined to attempt getting possession of the ship, and in which they said many of the mutineers offered to cooperate. Christian by some means received an intimation of their intentions, and aware of the danger of delay, waited only until night when he cut the ship's cable and stood to sea. There were with him seven or eight of the crew, about an equal number of Tahitian women, two men,

---

[*]   W. Bligh, *A Voyage to the South Sea ...*, London, 1792, chapter XIII.

and a child or two.* The ship was plentifully supplied with all kinds of provisions and stores.

The remainder continued at Tahiti until Captain Edwards, who in the *Pandora* was sent in search of the mutineers, arrived there in March 1791. Two of them indeed were killed previously: Churchill, the master at arms, and Thompson. It appeared that one having shot the other in a quarrel, the native friends of the deceased instantly revenged themselves on the murderer. At the *marae* in Pare there was a skull, which the natives reported to be Thompson's, preserved with much care.

After reading the preceding account (which was collected from the natives), you will no doubt encourage various conjectures respecting the fate of Christian and his followers, so have I, but to be still in darkness. It seems that Captain Edwards, in May 1791, discovered a yard and some spars at the Palmerston's Isles in latitude 18°..2' south, longitude 163°..9' west, marked '*Bounty*', yet this is not even a proof of that ship having been in the neighbourhood. It has been mentioned that some articles from the wreck of the *Matilda* whaler were found at Tahiti, a distance of three hundred leagues from where she was lost, only four months before, and the *Bounty*'s spars most likely had drifted to the Palmerston's Isles from her wreck, whether purposely destroyed by Christian or accident. His persevering efforts to form a settlement at Tubuai naturally leads us to believe that a similar attempt was made elsewhere, which if accomplished, was the more free from discovery by the destruction of the ship. But, to return to a voyage more auspicious than the *Bounty*, which my pen shall drop, at all events for the present, however much I may think of it. Yet may it as well be remarked that the *Pandora* was wrecked about four months after quitting Tahiti on a reef in latitude 11°..22' south, longitude 143°..38' east, near the eastern entrance of Torres Straits, when four of the mutineers (and thirty-five of the crew) were drowned.

It has been observed that, owing to our journals being in 'requisition', I had but some loose scraps remaining to lead me along. This already appears in the *Providence* reaching Aitutaki without any of the Society Islands having been noticed. It is true they were passed at so great a distance, we had no communication with their inhabitants.

August 1st

The course was continued westward. In the night, land was seen to the west, northwest. The vessels were instantly hauled by the wind, and kept working with as much sail as they could bear. The weather was dark and squally, but fortunately had cleared for a short time to give us a sight of the land, towards which the vessels were steering a direct course.

---

* and a child or two: eight mutineers and six islanders from several different islands went with Christian to Pitcairn Island. Fewer women than men went along and there were no children on the voyage, though many were born on Pitcairn.

2nd

As the day broke, the land bore from southwest by west to west by north half north, four or five leagues distant. Bearing away, it was passed at three or four leagues' distance. The latitude at noon was 18°..29 south, longitude corrected from time keepers 176°..34' west. The northeast part of the island bearing south 73° east, west cape south 19° east. A high mountainous island south 42° west and another island north 29° west, 11 or 12 leagues distant. The shore appeared bold, in most parts rising in cliffs from the sea and well clothed with wood. Cocoanuts were growing in the lower grounds. No inhabitants or huts were observed, or smoke, or anything to indicate its being peopled. At sunset the ships were hauled by the wind, and kept their situation through the night by tacking.

3rd

At day light bore away, and in a few hours lost sight of the land. The latitude at noon was 18°..20 south, longitude by time keeper 176°..25' west. These three islands, it seems, were discovered by a Spaniard in 1781, who gave them the name of Mayorga Isles.*

5th†

The *Assistant* leading in the forenoon made the signal for land. At noon the latitude was 18°..26' south, longitude by time keepers 178°..59' west, when Sunday Island, which acquired its name from the day, and which was the most eastern of the Fiji Islands seen by the *Providence*, bore south 48° west, eight or nine leagues distant, two other islands being in sight from the masthead in the west, southwest and west by south. The weather was remarkably pleasant with a fine southeast trade wind. Soon after, extensive breakers were observed in the northwest quarter, and before four o'clock, more in the southeast. Shaping a course between them, more land appeared to the southward. Towards sunset, having reached close under Sunday Island, more breakers were discovered six or seven miles to the northward. A very comfortless night was passed between the island and these breakers. Natives had been seen on the beach before dark, and fires were burning on the upper grounds, probably to alarm the neighbouring isles of our approach, and some hours before daylight a canoe, in which were two natives, came along side with cocoanuts, but their fears were such that they soon paddled away. Another canoe, when the day opened on the 6th, visited us, her crew consisting of four men, requiring but little solicitation to come on board, where they exchanged their cocoanuts and a few weapons for iron, with which article they were thoroughly acquainted. Our shipmates who had been at

---

* Mayorgya Isles: part of the Tonga Isles, Vava'u Group.
† August 5th: International Date Line crossed on this day, heading west. Dates now as Tobin recorded them.

the Tonga Isles thought these people to be of the same race. Some of their weapons were exactly the same. That there is an intercourse between them can hardly be doubted, some large sailing canoes which were afterwards seen among Fiji Islands being equal to navigate with safety between the two groups.

The natives are of common size and well formed, their colour a duller brown than that of the Tahitian, and the hair, which was daubed with a kind of black paste, of a more wooly texture. With the Aitutakians they are equally filthy. None had their beards eradicated, nor does the custom of plucking the hair from various parts of the body prevail, which last circumstance gave great disgust to Mideedee and Baubo. There appeared to be some similarity in their language and that of our passengers; on naming tattoo they instantly repeated it, pointing at the same time to a man who had a few marks on his heel; the others were without any. Each man had two joints of either the right or left little finger missing; one, indeed, had lost them from both hands. At the Tonga Islands such a custom is followed on the death of a relation which may be adduced as a presumptive proof of their having communication with each other. The lobe of the ear of one man was perforated so that an egg might have been passed through, it hanging down nearly to the shoulder. Except a girt round the middle, they were not encumbered by dress of any kind, and their only ornaments were a breast plate of the pearl oyster-shell and necklaces of a smaller kind.

Their canoes are formed of a single piece of wood of dark red colour, very sharp at both ends, about eighteen feet long and three in breadth with an outrigger on one side supported by three projecting pieces, serving to carry their fishing spears on. None of the sailing canoes were near enough for any accurate account to be given of them.

Sunday Island is surrounded by a reef on every part that came within our view, at about half a mile distant. The hills were bare and arid, but near the sea cocoanuts were growing in plenty, as well as the *toa* tree of Tahiti. Could a passage be found through the reef, landing would be easy, as there are several sandy beaches between the cliffs. No habitation of any kind was observed; probably our visitors were on a fishing excursion from a neighbouring isle.

6th

Proceeding westward more islands appeared. The latitude at noon was 18°..28' south, longitude by time keeper 179°..46' west, Sunday Island bearing south 69°, east six or seven leagues distant, having other islands in the west and northwest. The variation per amplitude in the afternoon 9°..16' westerly. A large sailing canoe was observed following the ship, the people in her using every exertion to overtake us, but we had the mortification to see her return without effecting it. On such occasions it was regretted that the grand object of the voyage forbade any delay, as otherwise much information might have been gained, instead of the cursory view allowed us in passing many islands. The very fine cluster (which became so numerous after our departure from Sunday Island that they were christened alphabetically) at this time around, which were part of the same seen by Captain Bligh in his launch in May 1789, would have taken many months sedulous employment in a nautical survey of them. But our apprehension of losing the monsoon wind, before reaching Torres Straits, would not admit of the smallest deviation from a direct course. And it was only in the daytime the vessels could be put to their utmost speed, as when darkness closed on them, their safety depended on proceeding with the utmost care and caution.

The plants, although in a flattering state, had experienced some mortality, and there were many months trial of various climates for them yet to encounter; so that no time could be spared in attending to other pursuits but in a passing way; yet is Captain Bligh so prompt at every kind of nautic science that the relative situation of such of these islands as were seen by the *Providence* may be depended on. There is very little doubt but that more extend to the north and the opposite quarter than came within our view.

With our glasses it was discovered that the canoe contained full a dozen people, and there appeared a kind of shed on it similar to what has been described at the Tonga Islands; more cannot be said with certainty. Although we had a fine breeze, she had considerably the advantage of the ship in sailing. At 8 o'clock the vessels were brought to for the night.

Shortly after quitting Tahiti, a warrant officer was added to each watch, and, as well as for reefs and shoals, a vigilant eye was kept upon the crew. Not that their conduct created any particular degree of suspicion, but they had passed some months at a South Sea Island and in the full swing of its indulgencies. They might possibly look back to them. And here, I cannot help remarking a circumstance mentioned by our commander a short time before, that 'he heard Sir Joseph Banks tell the king at Court, a similar case to what took place in the *Bounty* was in contemplation, and nearly put in practice on board the *Endeavour*; a person then under government being principally concerned in it.'* All however went on right in the *Providence*, nor could any crew, as well as that of her *Assistant*, have conducted themselves better throughout the whole expedition.

7th

Several islands were in sight as day broke; when the vessels bore away to the westward with a fine trade wind being at noon in latitude 17°..42' south, longitude by time keepers 179°..42' west. Four islands now in sight were called, Guernsey, Jersey, Alderney and Sark.

---

* James Magra (or later Matra), a member of the *Endeavour* crew, reputedly told this story to Banks.

8th

The latitude at noon was 17°..52' south, longitude by account 179°..55' east, thermometer 73¼°. Islands being in sight from north round by the west to south, southeast, the later eleven or twelve leagues distant, from which quarter a swell came. Shortly after, the *Assistant* leading, we bore away to make a passage between V (Gau) and U (Nairai)* the wind having failed us in the intention of weathering the former. The cry of breakers from the masthead produced a short alarm which was soon done away, the apparent danger proving to be a gleam of sunshine on the water. The vessels passed on the northern side of V (Gau) at the distance of three or four miles. Towards sunset the western part was doubled, leaving U (Nairai) on the right hand, which with our glasses, was distinguished as a very similar island.

Numbers of natives were collected about the hills and reefs of V, (Gau) indicating by waving and other tokens an anxious desire for us to communicate with them. Many carried a long spear, particularly those on the reefs, which led us to suppose they were for the purpose of striking fish.

Three canoes resembling those of Sunday Island were at this time launched, their crews paddling strenuously to overtake us, but the ship outsailing their exertions, disappointed us of a visit. It was noticed that, as well as the common paddles, a long one over the stern was used in a similar manner to the Chinese scull. The men were ornamented with the pearl oyster shell breast plate. Some of them wore a kind of white turban, which, with a girt round the middle, were their only encumbrance, being otherwise in a state of nature. One man was particularly desirous of drawing out attention to a piece of scarlet cloth, from which it would seem that they had been before visited by Europeans.[1]

From the fertile and picturesque aspect of the island it acquired the name of Paradise. Its circuit is from eight to ten leagues, surrounded, like most of the South Sea islands, by a reef, within which the water did not reach above the natives' knees. There appeared to be an opening through the reef on the lee side, but the day closing as we passed, this was left undetermined.

These encircled islands have been before noticed, yet I cannot help adding that among the Bahamas and the opposite Florida shores where the *Thetis* has recently been, the appearance of the sea is very similar. She not long ago anchored near the Island of Providence in less than forty feet 'white water', so very clear that every fish could be distinguished at the bottom, while but a short half mile from her stern no soundings could be found in the 'ocean water'. But to return to a scene where our avocations differed widely from those of the present hour.

Paradise Island is diversified by hill and dale; and agriculture appeared to have made advances unknown to the indolent Tahitians, the valley and sides of

---

*   Tobin left blank spaces in parentheses after each of the islands called by letters. Where identification is possible, the names have been added from Isaac Oliver, *Return to Tahiti*, Honolulu: University of Hawaii, 1988.

the hills being laid out in plantations, fenced in the most compact manner. Plantains were in great abundance, and, if our glasses did not deceive us, a great proportion of yams and sweet potatoes. The higher hills were wooded to their very summits, the fern tree being among it in numbers. The habitations were in general on the sides of the first range of hills, in appearance like the cottage tracts of England, ten or fifteen being situated together. On an eminence on the west part a crowd of natives collected where they displayed flags from cocoanut trees, probably to signify our approach to the neighbouring isles, and as soon as the day closed, fires were made and kept burning until the next morn, when our distance was so much increased that every hope was given up of acquiring more knowledge of this delightful island.

9th

At noon more islands were in sight, the latitude being 18°..30' south, longitude by account 178°..56' east. The vessels were kept under a press of sail to weather the most southern land, but breakers ahead soon obliged them to tack. A sailing canoe made an effort to reach us, but soon put back to Island Number 1. In christening these islands the alphabet was now expended, obliging us to continue them numerically. There was in the evening a long swell from the southward. The wind throughout the night was from the east, southeast; the vessels were frequently tacked until daylight, to keep a safe situation.

10th

The weather was dark and unsettled, the wind from the eastward. Flying fish and various sea birds were seen. At noon the latitude by account 18°..31' south, longitude by account 179°..04' east. Much sail was carried the whole afternoon to weather Number 2, variation 9°.55' east. The swell from the southward increased, which indicated the ocean was getting more open in that quarter.

11th

Hazy weather prevented our seeing far. The sun was obscured at noon, but the dead reckoning gave the latitude 19°..24' south, longitude by account 178°..23' east, Number 3 bearing from north 22° west to north 10° east. A high promontory, forming the western part of Number 3 (as well as of Fiji Islands, seen by the *Providence*) north 16° west, four or five leagues distant. Leaving Fiji Islands the course was continued to the westward.

30th

At break of day mountainous land was seen in the northeast quarter, which was judged to be the southern coast of New Guinea, or islands contiguous to it. The course was now west, northwest, with a fine southeast trade wind. At noon a good observation gave the latitude 10°..05' south, longitude by time keepers 146°..49' east, the land bearing from north, northeast, to northeast half east, eleven or twelve leagues distant. Various sea birds were around the ship, particularly noddies and boobies, their slothful habits being such that, after settling about the decks and rigging, our seamen caught them with ease. The noddy I never recollect to have seen but in the neighbourhood of land, and navigators ever exercise more than usual vigilance on their appearance. It is about the size of a pigeon, of a dull brown colour, except a white spot on the top of the head. The booby is a much larger bird with a bill in some measure resembling that of the gannet. Rock weed was also seen, another indication of being near a coast.

The course was continued west, northwest and west by north until noon the next (31st) day, the *Assistant* leading several miles ahead, which vessel from her small draught of water always took the post when danger was apprehended. Nor could it possibly have been in better keeping. I think I now see the zealous and persevering Portlock at our little consort's top gallant masthead, his eye travelling in every direction. The latitude was observed in 9°..27' south, longitude by account 145°..25' east. Signal flags had been prepared for all the boats as we approached Torres Straits, as well to denote soundings or danger when detached from the ships, as the approach of natives. To guard against their arrows, Captain Bligh had dresses fitted for the boats' crews of the thickest Tahitian cloth of many folds in the form of those used by the *ra'atiras* of that island, which did not interfere with rowing, while great protection was given to the more vital parts. Just before sunset, the signal was made for breakers, which soon appeared from southwest by west to west by south, two or three miles distant. Night closing on us prevented their extent being correctly ascertained. The vessels were instantly hauled by the wind, when with ninety fathom of line, no bottom could be found. The discovery of this reef before dark was a fortunate event, as the course we were steering would probably have led the vessels into some difficulty. At midnight tacked, and until day break, kept making short boards* to secure a safe situation.

September 1st

We now bore away with the intent of passing to the southward of the reef, but just after breakfast more breakers were seen on the lee bow, on which the ships were hauled by the wind, but being unable to weather the danger, were soon tacked. At noon the latitude was observed in 9°..37' south, longitude by time keepers 145°..14' east, by account 145°..03' east. There was no land in sight, but breakers, from the masthead, in the north, northwest, which in the afternoon were left to the southward. At 6 they bore south, seven or eight miles distant, when it not being judged prudent to proceed westward in the night, the wind

---

*   making short boards: tacking (changing directions) frequently.

was hauled, and the vessels tacked every two hours. At four in the morning on putting about, the broken water had the same bearings as before dark, but at not above a fourth the distance, a proof that the current had been from the northward.

2nd

At daylight bore away, at which time the reef was just discernible from the masthead in the south. The course until noon was west by southwesterly, thirty-four miles, when the latitude was observed 9°..26' south, the variation in the morning 5°..31' easterly.

A signal had been made by the *Assistant*, just before the sun was on the meridian, for breakers, which were soon seen from the masthead in the west, southwest and west by north. These we hauled to the southward of, a sandy key at one o'clock bearing southwest, at which time an alarm was given of discoloured water close under the bows. The sails were instantly thrown aback, and on sounding, a bottom of grey sand and coral was found with sixty fathom of line. The wind continued from the southeast and east, southeast throughout the night, the vessels being tacked every two hours, keeping in about fifty fathom water.

3rd

At early day an officer was sent in a boat with sounding signals to lead ahead of the *Assistant*, and shortly after we bore away making a course west, northwest and northwest by west about eighteen miles, when signals were made to denote danger. The tacks* were immediately hauled on board to the northward. At noon the latitude was observed 9°..06' south, breakers being in sight from north, ½ west, to west, northwest. After noon the wind died away. At four o'clock a sandy key was discovered and soon after an island, A (Darnley Island) of moderate height in the southwest. At sunset it bore southwest by west, and the sandy key south by west ¼ west. The anchor, a short time after, was dropped in thirty-seven fathom on a sandy bottom, the tide setting to the west, about one mile an hour. At midnight it turned to the east. The vessels rode very secure during a night of less anxiety than we had experienced for some time.

4th

At day break the anchor was weighed. At the sandy key bore south ¼ west, four or five miles distant, shoal water from some parts of it. The boats and *Assistant* leading, the course was continued westward.

---

*   tacks: a rope, wire or chain and hook used to secure the windward clews or lower square sail corners to the ship's windward side when sailing close hauled.

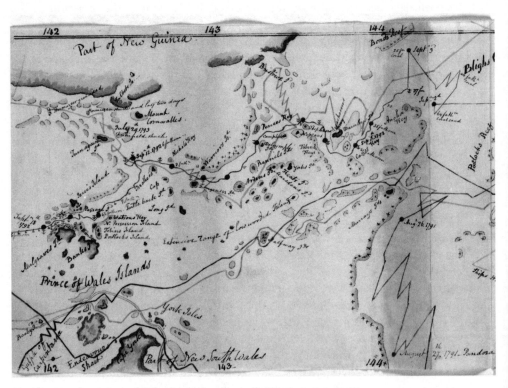

Map 6 *New Guinea and the Torres Straits*

145   146 East Long.ᵈᵉ

Enhance Sepʳ 1792

9 South Latᵈᵉ

Part of New Guinea

Seen from the Providence and her Tender Part. Aug.ᵗ 30ᵗʰ 1792

Capt Cook in the Endeavour. Aug.ᵗ 1770

Lieut Bligh in the Bountys Launched
May and June 1789

August 31. 1792

Aug 24ᵗʰ 1791

Sept 1 1792

The single and line Near the Track of the Providence and Tender Ken August and Sept.ᵗ 1792

Investigator in 1802

Eastern holds

10 South Latᵈ

Providence and

August 30ᵗʰ 1792

Pandora from Otaheite in 1791

Assistant from Otaheite in 1792

Cumberland Schooner from Wreck Reef in 1803

amuzee and Chesterfield in 1793

June 20ᵗʰ 1793

N.B. The Pandora was lost on the next day (Aug 23ᵗʰ) about 11 Leagues to the Southward on the continuation of the Reef.

145   146 East Long

The want of materials will prevent my trying your patience much more with bearings, distances and other nautic phrases. You are now fairly entered into this labyrinth of rocks and shoals, but to get you regularly through them, I am at a loss. Yet, were I briefly to say that after about three weeks of danger and difficulty, the *Providence* and her little leading *Assistant*, by the great care and caution of their commanders, entered the Indian Ocean over a bank with less than four fathom water on it, several occurrences would be left untold. Let us then get on by patchwork.

After running a few leagues westward, shoals again obliged the vessels to anchor. On looking around from the masthead, the colour of the water promised a passage in the southwest quarter.

5th

Before dawn Mr. Nicholls, the master, in the whale boat and myself in the cutter, left the ship to explore. When finding it practicable for the vessels to pass, a signal was accordingly made, but they were at so great a distance, I was fearful it could not be distinguished, and therefore directed Mr. Nicholls to make every effort to reach them with the report of a passage, while the cutter followed him. Making a direct course and sounding occasionally in some places, no bottom was found with thirty fathom of line, then suddenly come on coral banks with not five feet on them. The bottom here had a beautiful appearance, with a great variety of tints from different marine productions, particularly what is generally known as the sea fan.

Four large canoes were soon observed shaping a course towards the boat from Island A and their rapid approach made it necessary to be on my guard, having only a young gentleman, Mr. Bushby, and the boat's crew, while our pursuers were numerous. The whale boat was so far advanced towards the ship that I had the mortification to find a signal I made for assistance was unnoticed. The leading canoe soon reached our wake, about a quarter of a mile distant, the people in her waving flags for us to stop. The wind and tide were adverse, but we still kept on our course towards the ships, at this time about five miles off.

The second canoe had lowered her sails and was paddling to windward, having considerably the advantage of the cutter's oars. From their strenuous exertions, it remained no longer a doubt that they were determined, if possible, to have intercourse with us, and seeing it utterly impossible to avoid it by flight, every preparation was made to repel any attack they might make. She soon hoisted her sails and edged down to cut us off, waving and making signs for the boat to stop, but remote as we were from the ships, and having heard but an unfavourable account of the inhabitants of these straits, I considered this too great a risk and continued our course. Paddling close across our bows, a man held up a cocoanut, which was given from a kind of an enclosed place in the middle of the canoe. On observing this, I directed him by signs to carry it to the ships, which was by no means satisfactory, and in a moment the whole crew were busy about the enclosure furnishing themselves with bows and arrows which had hitherto been concealed from view. This allowed me the opportunity of observing that there were more men than had at first been apparent, several having been hid. There were, in all, about fifteen, without the least article of dress whatever, except that the arms of some were covered with a sort of matting, or cane work, which we afterwards conjectured was to aid them when using the bow and arrow. Two of them now took a deliberate aim at the stern sheets of the boat, about twenty yards distant, while the rest were stringing and preparing their bows with great expedition. As it appeared that they only waited to be ready for a general discharge of arrows, and as any misfortune or loss on our part must inevitably have placed us in the power of the other canoes, which were closing fast, self-preservation prompted me to fire a volley of musketry among them, and to which I have little doubt, from what occurred but a few days afterwards near the Islands O and P, we were indebted for our safety. Yet, had they rallied and attacked the boat in conjunction, our opposing efforts, perhaps, would have been but impotent against such numbers, with weapons nearly as destructive as firearms.[2]

Our musketry caused great consternation among them, the whole striving to shelter themselves under the railing of the enclosure, and of which we availed ourselves by fresh charging, and then using every exertion with the oars. They soon withdrew from their retreat, but after viewing us some minutes, seemingly undetermined how to act, made sail for Island A (Darnley Island), the other canoes soon taking the same direction.

It is probable that some were hurt by our fire; the coxswain seemed confident that one of the two who had taken aim, fell, as if mortally. The signal was, of course, repeated for assistance, fearing we might again be pursued, and not long after my messmate, Guthrie, came to us well armed in the pinnace.

On the part of our shipmates, the greatest vigilance was ever observed when the boats were absent on discovery, that succour might be sent if necessary. Yet on this occasion Baubo had a claim to our gratitude, who dreading some trouble from the natives, had stationed himself in the maintop, from whence he discovered the firing.

An opportunity soon after offered of examining the canoes of these straits with some correctness. They were from about thirty-five feet to fifty in length, formed (no joining at least being perceptible) of a single tree, about two deep. The extreme breadth was near the head, being double that at the stern, where it did not exceed two feet. A kind of forecastle was raised and laced to the main body in the manner of the canoes at Tahiti. The stern rose in a curve about a foot and an half, from which part two poles projected, one over each quarter, being hung with shells and other ornaments, and to an upright staff was a flag of rushes. About one-fourth from the bows, a platform was fixed, extending to midships. This projected from each gunwale three or four feet, at the extremities of which was a bamboo railing as many high. On this platform the sails and weapons are kept, the former being made of matting; but probably its chief use is to shelter the crew in battle. Outriggers extended from each side about six feet, ornamented with bunches of shells. In managing the sails, as well by the wind as before it, the natives were very expert, as also in striking the masts which are of bamboo. But the most remarkable part of these vessels was a leeboard* used in the same manner as by the Dutch fishermen in the North Sea and many other parts of Europe.

The knowledge we had now gained of their celerity, as well as the unfriendly disposition of their crews, rendered every caution necessary to guard against surprise. But though in the very detached duty of the boats, apprehensions were entertained, we could not admit of a possible suspicion that their temerity would ever lead them to be hostile to the ships. It very shortly proved otherwise.

Leaving Island A (Darnley Island), the boats and *Assistant* leading, the course was continued westward. Early in the morning, or on the preceding afternoon, it was the occupation to search for a channel, when after a short stage of a few leagues, as the sun declined towards the western horizon and thereby obstructed our view, the vessels were again anchored for the night.

A (Darnley Island) appeared about three leagues in circuit, of a moderate height, and in some parts woody. Where free from trees it was barren and parched; yet was it by far the most fertile to the eye of the many passed in these straits. On every part that came within our view, it was surrounded by reefs and shoals. Not far within the beach, among the trees, a few huts were noticed.

More islands were now passed, but of little extent; all well supplied with wood, some of the trees being of considerable height and magnitude. Mangroves were growing in the water near the shores of many of them.

The natives in canoes had now visited us, from which circumstance most probably they were ignorant of the affair with their countrymen and the cutter. They remained but a short time along side, appearing full of fears and an anxious desire to get away. Besides those who came to the ship, we passed about twenty on a sandy key not above as many yards in extent. They were huddled together in a group, seemingly to view the ships, and from their sable skins in contrast to the light sand were taken with our glasses for large birds or animals.

Sailing close past F gave us an opportunity of seeing about forty more, two women being of the party. The men were not the heavier by dress of any kind, and the covering of the other sex was scarcely a short apron of rushes. A dog was following them, the only quadruped seen, yet it would appear from the tusk of a boar being afterwards brought on board, that such an animal must be known to them. On this island were a few huts similar in form to a beehive, the eaves shelving very near the ground. They were detached a few yards from each other, and encircled by close railing.

The vessels anchored near H, and a dog being seen on the beach, left little doubt of it being inhabited. In the afternoon several natives were observed

---

*   leeboard: a moveable board that extends some distance below the water line on the side of the vessel away from the direction from which the wind is blowing.

coming round the south part armed with bows and arrows, which they soon put away, wading into the sea and waving green branches to us. A little before sunset Captain Bligh sent Guthrie and myself in the whale boat and cutter with nails and other articles in hope of cultivating their good will. They evinced no fear at our landing, meeting us up to their middle in the sea, with fresh water in a large shell, which they called *whabow*, and asking in return for *toorey* which was ceaselessly repeated with greedy eagerness. A coarse kind of plumb was also brought by them.

Both sexes readily dismantled themselves of their few ornaments of shells in exchange for *toorey*. It is rather remarkable that the word in use for iron the whole way from the Society Isles to the straits is nearly the same, however the appearance, manners and general language of the various islands may differ. At Tahiti it is called *auri*, nor at Aitutaki and Sunday Island was the term different.

Aware that the disposition of these people was by no means pacific, we returned before the night set in, much to their dissatisfaction, as they were desirous of detaining the boats on shore, some force being necessary to prevent their being dragged higher up the beach. Among other articles procured, were some very neat fish hooks made of turtle shell and necklaces of the Panama.* At this island were the remains of several huts close together, but enclosed by a railing as at F.

9th

At early day break the natives were on the beach waving green branches for us to pay them another visit, but seeing no boats approach, they soon launched a canoe and paddled towards us. By this time the vessels were under sail, when, after following us some time, they reluctantly put back.

More canoes were seen under sail about an extensive reef to leeward, as we passed I, K, L, and M, all small, low and woody. On M there were a few huts and a canoe hauled on the beach. Several sea snakes, from five to ten feet in length, were seen, apparently asleep on the surface of the water until disturbed by the motion of the ship. They were all ringed – black and yellow.

About this time more natives visited us, three or four. After much persuasion, quitting their canoes and coming on board, where they remained but a short time, expressing by their countenances and every limb the greatest distress until they left us. No solicitation could induce them to go lower than the quarterdeck. Iron, which as before was called *toorey*, they received with unbounded satisfaction.

This visit allowed me a very correct view of their persons. They were of the middle size, rather delicately than well formed, of a colour similar to the Negro, with short curly hair, but not of a close woolly texture, nor were their lips more than ordinarily thick. The *septum nasium* of the nose being perforated and a ring

---

* Panama: screw pine.

worn inside, prevented our telling its natural shape. One of these rings was procured, large enough to go on a man's little finger. Their beards were not in any degree eradicated, and their teeth were of a very foul colour. There was a considerable projection of the brow, the eyes being small and much sunk in the head. The ear being divided, the lobe reached below the chin, the upper part being decorated with small bits of cane stuck through it. In both sexes the left shoulder was burnt or scarified in the shape of an epaulet, and some had this mark on the right. None were tattooed, but a sort of red pigment was rubbed over various parts of their bodies, as well as grease and filth, insomuch that, after swimming, they came on board perfectly dry. Except two compact cases of cane-work fitting the arm tightly the whole length above and below the elbow, which we conjectured was of some service in using the bow, they were in a state of nature. One among them indeed, perhaps a chief, differed from his countrymen in having a shell fastened to a girdle round the loins, for the same purpose that in remote times a fig leaf was used. Their ornaments were shell necklaces, with tassels of different coloured cord, strung with the same kind of red seed called *jumbee* beads, now so much in fashion in Europe, besides bracelets of cocoanut husk on the legs and arms. Among other articles, a mask was procured from them which is probably used in battle. The only women I had a tolerable view of were two at H. They had no covering but a short apron of rushes. Different from the men, part of the hair on the crown of the head was shaved close. Mideedee was in a boat with us, and though not notorious for being insensible to the many charms of his own nankeen coloured countrywomen, expressed great disgust at these sable damsels; nor indeed without reason, for in good truth, they were neither formed to 'raise envy in woman or desire in man'. 'Twas in vain we here looked for the bewitching countenance and delicately moulded figure of the ductile Tahitian. All seemed cheerless and debased. The parched soil on which the wretched inhabitants of this wretched country dwell appeared every way unproductive; a few cocoanuts and plantains were noticed, but the breadfruit, the yam, the *taro*, and other edible plants, the support of the healthy South Sea islander, is here looked for in vain. Fish, it would seem, must be the chief sustenance, and in which the straits abound, particularly turtle, as wherever we landed their bones were found near the remains of fires, and the ships passed many in the water.

Whether the natives are cannibals has not yet been ascertained, nor did we wish to learn by putting ourselves in their power. That one of our seamen seriously believed them so, appears from a letter to his friends in England which fell under my perusal. In giving an account of the attack made on the *Assistant*, he says 'Fires were prepared on the beach by the women, who were licking their lips in hopes of making a meal of us.' And this, for anything I know to the contrary, might have been true enough.

This affair happened between O and P on September 11. Six canoes from P having been joined by two from O, containing in the whole about an hundred persons, approached the vessels without any suspicion being entertained of their hostile intentions. Our consort was at some distance, when she was observed to make the signal for assistance, and about the same time opened a fire on the canoes surrounding her. One of the boats was also engaged. At this time two or three canoes were about the *Providence* and others closing, their crews by the most friendly, yet treacherous signs, inviting us to P where a number of natives, chiefly females, were collected around several large fires. Our visitors held up large bamboos containing water which, as at H, they called *whabow*, but none came along side. The arrows procured on a former visit were of such a murderous shape, it became necessary to guard against their effects; therefore some muskets were fired in hope of dispersing the canoes, on which their crews made a wild and dreadful yell, instantly returning some arrows, none of which fortunately reached on board. Still they evinced no disposition to withdraw, and continued to discharge more arrows, but without effect from the distance. Two or three four pounders were now fired, one of which charged with grape shot took immediate effect on a canoe, the natives in her, save one who was wounded, instantly leaping into the sea with great terror; and it is hardly conceivable their wonderful exertions to get away, by throwing themselves forward, nearly half their bodies above the surface, at an amazing rate. It was observed, as indeed is the case with most Indians, that they swam by using a hand alternately in the manner of a paddle, different from the common European way.* Another gun made their whole squadron retreat, when seeing us discontinue firing, they picked up the disabled canoe and paddled to their women at P.

On closing with the *Assistant* we had the mortification to learn that, without any provocation on the part of our countrymen, the natives had discharged a volley of arrows at her, wounding two of the crew, one of them mortally,† nor did the other perfectly recover the use of his arm the whole voyage homeward.[3] It can hardly be supposed that these miserable people were acquainted with the effect of firearms who attacked the *Assistant*, and the little fear the others evinced at the musketry from the *Providence* surely serves to strengthen this opinion. Had they known of the firing from the cutter on the 5th near Island A (Darnley Island), the dread of again being exposed, would most probably have kept them at a distance. Yet is there little doubt but that this was a premeditated plan of hostility, nor is it possible to say what might have been the issue had the whole force acted against our little consort, as she was too remote to have received any immediate succour from the *Providence*.

The small party, who were in the cutter on the 5th, while they feelingly lamented the loss on board the *Assistant*, derived no small degree of relief by this rencounter between the natives and the shipping, as the captain, on the former occasion, had by no means approved of what had taken place. The present transaction brought a thorough conviction to his mind of the truly desperate

---

*   This is one of the earliest descriptions of what became known as the Australian crawl or free-style swimming.

†   mortally: William Terry was killed.

people he had to deal with in these straits, and of his good fortune in no loss having attended the boats while distantly exploring a channel, on which hazardous service they were so long employed.

In a narrative of the proceedings of the *Pandora's* boats, in August or September 1791 (after her shipwreck) towards Timor through Torres Straits, the hostile disposition of the natives is noticed. Captain Edwards stopped at one island where the inhabitants brought him a small supply of water, in exchange for knives and other articles, but on his refusing to go on shore for more water, which was placed on the beach, they discharged a shower of arrows at the boats. Fortunately none of the crews received injury, but an arrow fell between the captain and third lieutenant with such force, as to go through the boat's thwart formed of oak plank an inch thick. Some muskets from Captain Edwards put them to flight.

That the native of these straits live in amity with each other is sincerely to be hoped, else, naked and exposed as they are, war with such destructive weapons must be dreadful. Their bows are of split bamboo, above six feet in length, the string being a strip of cane. The most robust of our people, as well as Baubo and Mideedee, tried ineffectually to string them; yet the natives by no means so muscular, did it with little apparent exertion. They carry their arrows in a quiver on the back. These are of various kind, some being nearly as long as the bow, barbed with fish bone, or pointed with the tail of the sting-ray, or hard sort of ironwood; but you have specimens in our museum. Slings and heavy clubs were also observed.

To guard against their arrows, it has before been noticed that Captain Bligh had fitted armour of Tahitian cloth for the boat's crews. Mideedee, who did not at all relish the appearance of these sable gentry, always took care, when he went in a boat, to put it on. Baubo, less gentle, cared little about such a precaution. Baubo was of Christian's party when he attempted a settlement at Tubuai, and ever recounted their exploits at that island with wonderful satisfaction. The population of the straits did not appear to be great. The novelty of vessels passing, it is fair to suppose, brought all the inhabitants to the sea shores, yet throughout the whole navigation I do not believe five hundred were seen.

More islands and reefs were passed, the vessels as usual being anchored as the sun in the afternoon obscured the western view.

Turtleback Island is of a moderate height, rocky and clothed with wood to the summit. The Cap is an island with large detached rocks to the top, bare of wood but on the west side, where it terminates in a sandy spit, its circuit about two miles. The Brothers have rocks on the summit like those of the Cap, apparently left bare by the soil having been washed away. No huts or natives were observed on either of these three islands.

At September 17th the vessels were anchored about 7 miles from Possession Island, which acquired its name from Guthrie having been sent by Captain Bligh to take formal possession of these straits in the name of our royal master. Our messmate reported that there was very good landing, five or six fathom water being close to the beach. From this anchorage lands were in sight.

Leaving Possession Island, we passed some others where little verdure was to be seen, though their summits were not free from wood, and on the low grounds trees with a light coloured bark were noticed. Huge rocks were scattered about in such a manner as to leave little doubt but that this country had undergone some violent convulsion of nature, or perhaps, they had been rendered bare by the washing away of the soil in heavy rains.

In our way from Possession Island to Hell Gates (an anchorage so called by us from its being somewhat similar to a place of that name between Manhattan and Long Islands in America) about fifteen natives were seen, and near them on the beach poles with white flags, apparently as signals for us to stop. They were like the rest seen in the straits, entirely naked. As the ships passed, several waved green branches to us, as at H. No hut or habitation was seen.

The channel, as we advanced westward, appeared so full of reefs and shoals that the vessels were anchored and boats sent on their daily occupation of searching for a passage. The tide was running with such strength that it was with difficulty the ship 'brought up'. By our longitude we were well convinced that the Indian Ocean was at no great distance, however intricate the channel to it. The boats proceeded to an island (Lookout Island) about three miles to the northwest, but at a slow rate from the strength of an adverse tide. As natives had been seen in the neighbourhood, the crews were ordered to be on their guard while Guthrie and myself proceeded to the summit, from whence, as far as could be distinguished with our glasses, it was bounded to the northward by shoals and small island keys round by west to the southwest where they joined the southern lands, but the eye was cheered by the appearance of one small passage in the west, northwest, which was speedily communicated by signal to our anxious shipmates, when the vessels again weighed anchor. The tide was by this time setting so rapidly to the eastward, they made scarcely any progress, though assisted by a favourable breeze. The sun was nearly sinking in the horizon ere they reached abreast of Lookout Island when the clouds gathered and the atmosphere became unsettled and full of threats. To continue westward after the night set in amid this labyrinth of dangers was impracticable, so that our only trust was the 'ground tackle' on this rough and unpromising bottom. After looking for a spot as free as possible from rocks, the anchor was dropped in 8 fathom water. The night was passed in much anxiety; it blew a strong gale, and the tide set violently, but both vessels 'rode it out' without loss or accident of any kind.

The boats at early day were again sent to explore, when to the great joy and relief of everyone, a passage, after much search, was discovered over banks with less than four fathom water on them, and in a day or two the vessels safely entered the Indian Ocean from this truly intricate and dangerous navigation.

Lookout Island, like the Brothers and some other islands passed, is an assemblage of huge rocks to the summit, with scarcely any soil, yet some trees were growing of a tolerable size bearing a pod with red seeds similar to those in the West Indies called by the Negroes *jumbee* beads. The wild pine (*wharra* of Tahiti) was observed, but of the dwarf kind. At every step our admiration was called to a variety of beautiful shrubs, which in this remote quarter of the globe, save to its ruthful* inhabitants, are 'born to blush unseen,

> And waste their sweetness in the desert air.'†

The track of a canoe on the beach assured us that the natives had recently left the island; their pathways, indeed, were easily distinguished, but neither hut or habitation of any kind. About the remains of fires, turtle bones were scattered, and on a rock, the skulls of several of these animals were piled with great regularity as if sacred to some occasion. No water was discovered, but, as many land birds were seen of the pigeon and parakeet kind, most probably it is to be found at no great distance.

The shore abounded with herons, curlews, and various kind of sand larks. The reptile tribe were lizards, and an incredible number of large grasshoppers or locusts. Among the bushes we were much annoyed by the bite of a large green ant, whose nests were attached to the branches. The skin of a snake was found above nine feet in length, which appeared to have been recently quitted by its tenant. Various kinds of shell fish were about the beach, one in particular from its excellent flavour served our party to 'fare sumptuously' on, and without any bad effects. It was of the oyster kind, adhering so firmly to the rocks as to be with difficulty disengaged. It is true that we looked in vain for porter to our oysters, and even of 'Adam's Ale' were at a sadly 'short allowance'.

---

*   ruthful: lamentable, piteous.
†   The quotation is from Thomas Gray (1716–71), 'Elegy Written in a Country Churchyard', ll. 55–6.

CHAPTER 9TH

October 1792–August 1793

Arrive at Timor.—Dutch brig.—Transactions at Timor and departure.—
Double the Cape, homewards.—Arrive at St. Helena.—Short stay.—
Transactions, &c. &c.—Arrive at St. Vincent's—Leave part of the plants.—
Mideedee and Baubo inoculated.—Arrive at Jamaica.—War with France.—
Detention at the island.—Fit out a tender.—Mideedee sick.—Visit Mr.
Raymond.—Leave Jamaica.—Arrive in the Downs.—Proceed up the
Thames.—The plants sent to Kew Gardens.—Captain Bligh.—Promotions.—
The ship paid off &c. &c. &c.

Thetis, coast of America June 1797

The vessels now (October 1792) entered the straits of Roti, and thence, passing
Semau and part of Timor, came in sight of Kupang Bay and a brig at anchor near
the town. Nearly ten months had passed since an European vessel had been seen
from the *Providence*, save her little *Assistant*, and you cannot but suppose that the
appearance of this 'square rigged' one afforded us great satisfaction. We soon
after anchored in 22 fathom water, when the cutter was despatched to acquaint
the governor of Kupang of our arrival and to procure a pilot. Two or three
Malayan boats passed us in the course of the day, carrying an extraordinary large
sail, apparently of matting. On rising early the next morning, Guthrie had
returned from Kupang with Captain Bouberg of the Dutch brig, and the
melancholy intelligence of the shipwreck of the *Pandora* at the eastern entrance
of the straits through which we had so providentially searched our way. This
circumstance has been before noticed, but it is right to add that Captain
Edwards, with the preserved part of the crew, left Timor for Europe by way of
Jakarta about a twelvemonth before our arrival. The anchor being weighed,
Captain Bouberg conducted us safely to Kupang, where it was again dropped in
16½ fathom water, off shore of a mile.

Kupang is of no great extent, but its situation remarkably pleasant, a fine
stream, on whose banks are the mango, plantain, breadfruit, cocoanut and other
trees, running through the town. A fort of no great strength, but in good repair,
commands the mouth of the river. Including military, the Dutch inhabitants did
not reach an hundred, yet they felt the greatest confidence in their security,
notwithstanding the many Malayan powers in the neighbourhood, none of
which bear them any good will. During our stay, a Malayan chief was banished
to Jakarta for life on a charge of disaffection to the Dutch government. This
unhappy wretch was sent a prisoner on board Captain Bouberg's brig. I was

present when he was removed to her. His wives and offspring attended him to the seashore to take their last heart rending farewell. It was a scene truly distressing to humanity, but the hand of power imposed it and beyond the hope of change. While amid the tears and agonised embraces – never alas again to be known – of those who had hitherto felt happiness, but as he felt it, was this devoted victim hurried, to worse than death – an eternal separation from all he loved. Nor does it appear that the Malayans are the only nation subject to the will of the Batavian flag on this island. There is a Chinese settlement adjoining Kupang whose inhabitants, double in number to the Dutch, patiently allow their gates to be closed on them every night and, without a murmur, submit to the most oppressive taxes. These people were particularly studious to procure firearms from us to barter with the Malayans for slaves.

Bees' wax and sandalwood, brought to Kupang from the distant part of Timor and the neighbouring isles, are the chief articles of exportation, but on a very small scale indeed, yet two vessels come annually from Jakarta, partly laden with India and European goods. Of the sandalwood, a considerable quantity is used by the Chinese on religious occasions.

Most of the Dutch were married to Malayan women, a mongrel race filling all the houses. The town boasted but a solitary European female, the clergyman's wife, whose attachment to her husband led her to this distant spot. Some of the Malayans were not destitute of beauty – if such there can be, without the lily or the rose – and, in their forms they were most interestingly delicate, with such a profusion of long dark hair as to have reached the ground if not confined, in the most fanciful ways. They are of neglect, jealous to a degree unknown in colder regions and have been known to administer poison to their husbands on their quitting the country for Europe; such strong fears being entertained on this head, that it is in general done by stealth, leaving to the Malayan nymphs 'to sigh alone'. We were informed of slow poison having been given to a truant husband at Jakarta, the effects of which did not appear until his arrival in Holland, when he was so alarmed that he embarked on his return to India without loss of time, nor ever made a second experiment of putting the healing qualities of his wife to the test. How much cooler do our own matrons act in voting the 'green-eyed monster' obsolete by the aid of indifference, or perhaps retaliation, when their 'good men' are caught receding. The natives about the town appeared to be a wretched race of half formed beings, and hateful custom of chewing the betel nut, which causes a red saliva to be constantly exuding from the mouth, adds to their disgusting appearance. Yet this constitutes their chief solace and pride, the greatest pains being taken to have their betel equipage, which hangs over the shoulder, as grand as possible. In this bag the various ingredients used with the nut are kept. Both sexes indulge in it, even the pretty women at the governor's table were unacquainted with the fascinating powers of a naturally white set of teeth, ceaselessly taking from their purity by this offensive compound.

It was the study of Mynheer Vanion to render our short stay at Kupang as agreeable as possible. A gentleman who moves like a little potentate in this distant corner of the globe, yet is it accompanied by the most cordial hospitality. Several times within these few years it has fallen to the lot of this worthy governor to relieve our shipwrecked or distressed countrymen. He was kind enough to allow us the perusal of a journal kept by Bryant along the eastern coast of Australia to Timor, after escaping in a boat from the settlement of Sydney in March 1791.* In this journal there was an interesting account of his various distresses and escapes from natives. It appeared that not far northward of Sydney, Bryant found coal of a good quality within a few feet of the surface of the ground.† In what latitude I cannot charge my memory. This enterprising man had with him in the boat a female partner and her two children who, he observes, bore their sufferings with more fortitude than most among them. It never came to my knowledge what became of Bryant after his departure from Timor for Europe in a Dutch India ship with Captain Edwards and the *Pandora* crew. At Kupang it was said that the period of his transportation had expired. Perhaps he wished to avoid returning at all to his own country by the desperate step which he took with his fellow convicts to reach this foreign settlement.

Mynheer Vanion, besides his house at Kupang, had a cool retirement on the banks of the river at Pantassey, a short walk from the town. We were, some of us, at his table daily where there was ever an honest welcome, but we murmured internally at the custom of sitting down with the sun on the meridian and rising with the cloth. Yet, if we did rise with the cloth, fault rested with ourselves if we did not get a sufficient quantity of tolerable claret, as in no part of the world is this serious business of drinking – save sitting long at it – 'better ordained'. The glass once filled, so may it remain, but the instant the contents are removed down your throat, a servant again fills it to the brim. Before and after meals, several beautiful Malayan girls of twelve or thirteen years of age, dressed uniformly in white, make a circuit of the company with water in which are sprigs of orange or some other fragrant tree, and a salver with sandalwood powder on it to use as a perfume after ablution. The procession has a pretty effect. Both their hands being engaged, a napkin is fastened to the shoulder of each of them for the use of the guests. As in most eastern countries, the afternoon is passed in repose. Towards sunset they rise, and in smoking, cards, music, coffee and afterwards supper, nearly the whole night is passed, a few hours only being allowed to recruit for the approaching day.

Our crew were supplied with beef of two kinds, the common large Indian buffalo, and another not much above half the size. Few other refreshments were to be procured, particularly vegetables which was attributed to a long continuance of dry weather. This we subsequently found to have been the case at

---

* William Bryant and his wife, Mary, escaped from Sydney in March, 1791. Upon her return to England, Mary became something of a celebrity, 'the Girl from Botany Bay', and received a pardon, thanks in part to James Boswell. Her husband and children died before they could return.

† Newcastle, New South Wales became Australia's first coal mining location.

St. Helena, and indeed it would seem that scarcely any rain had fallen the whole year between the Equinoctial Line and the southern tropic in the track passed by the *Providence* and *Assistant*. It was almost in vain that we courted showers to assist our stock of water, which reduced the crew to a scarcity allowance as they approached Torres Straits, notwithstanding the *Providence* stowed an hundred and ten tons, and our *Assistant* in proportion. But the plants as well as ourselves required moisture. It is true there was a machine on board for distilling sea water, but, if I recollect right, fifteen gallons was the greatest quantity ever produced in a day, nor was it by any means free from a brackish quality.

An anxiety to reach our destined port soon hurried us away. The parching winds between Australia and New Guinea had caused much mortality in the garden, but the plants were yet numerous, and in a flattering state, and to land as many as possible in our own colonies demanded every degree of care and attention. It was with anxious apprehension we looked toward the inclement weather almost inseparable in doubling the African cape where, if the vessels passed it even in sight, the plants would be seventeen degrees south of their native soil, exposed to the baneful effects of the polar winds which frequently, even in the summer season, blow with considerable coldness. Some very fine mangoes and other plants were here taken on board.

The crews had been unavoidably hard worked in watering, which joined to the deleterious effects of an inferior kind of arrack, increased the sick list considerably, but by care and attention this was of short continuance.

The variation of the compass in Kupang Road per mean of several set of Azimuths with different compasses (not by George Tobin) was 1°..1' westerly.

Some aquatic birds by seamen called St. Helena pigeons were now (December 17, 1792) seen, a certain indication of being in the neighbourhood of the island. More than sixteen months had passed without any communication with our own country. Indeed, we were altogether ignorant of what had taken place on the Grand Theatre of Europe, for at Timor little information was to be collected; you will therefore well understand our feelings at again seeing the British flag flying on *terra firma*.

Sailing almost within the surge beating on St. Helena's rugged shores to secure an anchorage, you pass a small fort where a board is affixed instructing the commanders of vessels (in various languages) to 'send a boat on shore before they anchor'. The town soon after opens to the view, situated in a chasm formed by two dreary mountains, having batteries on them commanding the anchorage, the one on Ladder Hill to the westward, of considerable strength. A neat church rises above a row of trees nearly parallel with the beach and higher up some scattered palms and cocoanut trees wave above the houses. The landing place, on which there are cranes and every convenience for trade, is in general easy of access. Water for the shipping has been conveyed by pipes to this quay, but it can be procured at other parts of the island if required. The barracks and hospital are at the upper part of the town, and near them some ground was preparing for a public walk and kitchen garden for the military. A road on either side leads to the country, but the acclivity to Ladder Hill is so great that, to use a nautic phrase, many tacks must be made to reach the summit, nor without a stranger feeling some apprehension for the footing of the streets, until from experience he finds they clamber these craggy steeps with ease and security.

A ride of about four miles carries you to the county seat of Governor Brooke, passing to the right of a richly cultivated valley interspersed with farm houses, the more to be admired from the contrasted bare and rugged mountains that shelter it. Neither the house or grounds of Mr. Brooke were completed, but his elegant and enlarged taste cannot fail of rendering it a most desirable spot.

Though within sixteen degrees of the Equinoctial Line, the climate was here particularly mild and refreshing. The oak, the plantain, and bamboo were luxuriantly growing in the same group, but it was said that some of the more tender tropical fruits could not resist the coldness of the southern winds. Of the fate of some breadfruit plants left by Captain Bligh, I have seen no account, but there is reason to fear that the soil would not be congenial to them. Our botanists were by no means sanguine in the hope of their succeeding. Indeed the climate of St. Helena, though nearer the Equinoctial Line, is by no means so warm as at Tahiti, which was another difficulty for the plants to struggle with. It is beyond me to account why there should be this difference, but I cannot help hazarding an opinion that the air in the southern hemisphere is more cool and temperate northward of the Line. Over such parts of the world as your friend has voyaged between the tropics he has invariably found the northeast trade wind to be more close and oppressive than the southeast. Is it not probable that the difference is owing to the great bodies of ice so often seen at no great distance south of the southern tropic? The *Guardian*, it may be remembered, only twenty-three degrees south of the Tropic of Capricorn experienced a most melancholy disaster by striking on them, affording the zealous and persevering Riou* an opportunity of evincing that in no case, however desperate, should hope be put away.

Ice islands,† it is true, have been seen in the North Atlantic, but by no means in masses of such magnitude. In this ship on our passage from Plymouth to America in June 1794 we were some days among detached bodies of ice, but the largest did not appear to be a quarter of a mile in circuit at its base above the surface of the sea. The latitude was 40½° north, longitude 48° west. Some sketches taken of them will give you an idea of their form and appearance.‡ Probably this ice came from the neighbourhood of the St. Laurence, the Straits of Bellisle, or northern part of Newfoundland.[1]

---

*   In early 1790 Edward Riou commanded the ship *Guardian* that was carrying supplies to the convict colony in New South Wales when it struck an iceberg off the coast of South Africa and sank. Riou and other crew members survived.

†   ice islands: icebergs.

‡   Tobin did not include these sketches of icebergs in his collection.

At St. Helena nothing of the indolent languor and lassitude of the creole, or European settler in Hindustan, is to be seen, but sturdy old men, healthy children and fair ones who look 'the bloom of young desire'.* It is here, after toiling the most desirable moiety of life under the pressure of a parching sun, to amass the riches of the east, the returning nabob is first reminded of his country 'long left'. In a ride up the country, we were more than commonly pleased by observing the inhabitants engaged in a match of cricket with no small degree of skill and still more cheerfulness and vigour, and this at a season by no means the coolest, than which nothing further need be said in favour of the climate. Yet may it be remarked that some of Mr. Brooke's rooms were provided with a fire place to counteract the wintry chills sometimes felt in an island only sixteen degrees from the Equinoctial Line.

The great influx of strangers who, after the tossing of a long voyage, naturally covet a little rest on dry land, has induced the inhabitants to open their houses for boarders in the same way as at the Cape of Good Hope, but one's own language being spoken we felt more 'at home' than when under the roof of a Dutch landlord. The visitor to St. Helena forgets that he is paying twelve shillings a day for meat, drink and sleep in the conciliating manners of those who are the richer for it. He is generally a long while removed from the fairest part of the creation, nor can he help drawing a comparison between the brown or sable damsels he has left and the delicate red and white inter-blended in the cheeks of the fair inhabitant of this isle. Nothing helps a man to get in love so much as a long voyage. At least such have I found to be the case with most of my fellow voyagers, though perhaps few of them could assign a rational reason for it, and I verily believe no one was ever five days at this island without getting a wound from the eyes of some fair damsel or other. Yet probably not so deep, but that a cure was effected ere the northeast trade wind was passed on the return to England. A few at the island have received the advantage of a 'finish' at some of our fashionable seminaries in the British metropolis, but this fortunately is not common, nor did I discover any solid advantages they had reached over their friends educated on the island.

Including slaves, the island contained about two thousand inhabitants, besides five hundred troops belonging to the East India Company who were very well 'appointed'. From an early age the inhabitants are embodied in the militia, so that with the natural defence of its rugged coast, and the improving works of Mr. Brooke, the island may be considered as tenable against a formidable force. Signal posts have been established on several eminences, by which means communication is made of the approach of vessels.

A continuance of dry weather had considerably checked vegetation and occasioned great mortality among the cattle, our crew however, enjoyed a 'skin full' of fresh beef for their Christmas dinner, a viand they had almost forgotten the flavour of, without the buffalo at Timor, might be so called. Scarcely any

---

*   From Thomas Gray, 'The Progress of Poesy, A Pindaric Ode', line 41.

stock was to be procured or vegetables, but a few potatoes, some of which, I afterwards got planted at St. Vincent's in the hope they would succeed better than those from England or America. Although so far within the tropic, the potatoes of St. Helena have not the sweet flavour of those in the West Indies. Water cresses were procured in the greatest abundance at no great distance from the town by sending a few men daily to gather them.

From laws prohibiting its destruction, but at certain seasons, game was increasing fast on the island. Besides pheasants, partridges and rabbits, Guinea fowls and peacocks are to be found in a wild state. The coast and banks abound with fish. A small kind of Spanish mackerel were taken at the anchorage with hook and line. Turtle are sometimes caught, and while speaking of this nutritious food, we cannot but lament that the island of Ascension,[2] remarkable for producing them in numbers, is situated so directly to leeward, though at no great distance, the difficulty of beating up against the trade wind discourages the inhabitants of St. Helena from undertaking voyages to it. But, while we have possession of the Cape of Good Hope, or are in peace with whoever may be the inhabitants, this little island need not fear getting supplies from that land of plenty, and this may be necessary, should the regular storeships fail reaching the settlement from England.

To quit the place would be ungrateful, after the gratification afforded by it, and pass unnoticed the very curious museum of Major Robson, the lieutenant governor. Here, the persevering labours of many years are open to the inspection of every visitor, nor will the naturalist, the antiquary or the admirer of the rude implements of Indian nations, find their morning unprofitably spent in examining this collection. There are some Asiatic coins and images of great antiquity. The shells are scientifically arranged, the variety of dresses, ornaments and other articles from different newly discovered countries perhaps is not exceeded by any collection in the world. Indeed Major Robson has opportunities of continually augmenting them from vessels that touch at St. Helena in their way to Europe from many distant parts of the globe.

We here learnt the state of affairs in Europe, that the success of the French had extended their views to a system of 'equality over the face of the earth', and that a war with England was far from improbable. The *Providence* and her little tender were not fitted for hostilities, and we could not but wish for peace to continue until the plants were safely deposited in their destined ground, after all the anxiety and labour that had been bestowed in nursing them.

As well as public news, I was gratified on our arrival in finding letters from the family, but there is, in the demolition of the containing wax, something so trying after long absence that a pause always takes place ere the fingers 'do their office'. Our dearest friends may be no more – or estranged by separation. A single line may chill expectations which have filled the heart for many a tedious month. Such are the fears that intrude. Happy those who have never realised them. Nothing of the kind was imposed on me. On the contrary, the kindest assurance of affectionate remembrance and an ardent hope for my return.

It might be said that we were travelling post the whole way to the West Indies which admitted but of a short stay at this singularly romantic little spot. A considerable degree of time had been lost in 'doubling the Cape' by strong and adverse winds, against which the ships were struggling a full fortnight and would have been driven far eastward, had not a current from that quarter checked it. It is rather remarkable that during this tempestuous weather, the plants suffered but little.

In our passage from Timor to this island we buried one of the marines, a man advanced in years, whose constitution was much impaired by intemperance. He acted as steward to our mess which gave him but too many opportunities of indulging in this sad propensity. Our cook died afterwards on the passage to the West Indies. These were the only men who fell by disease until our arrival at Jamaica, above eighteen months after our departure from England; and, in general, a degree of health was enjoyed by the crew not often to be found among the same number of persons on shore.

Baubo condemned in angry terms our throwing the corpses overboard, saying it would be cold (*to'e to'e*) for them, and that they ought to be hung at the jib boom end 'till the ship reached port, adding that the sharks would eat them.

Both the Tahitians were frequently on shore and highly delighted with the buildings and fortifications, but the military band, at the relief of guard, afforded them more gratification than anything they had yet seen. The mistaken hospitality of someone was the means of Mideedee getting much intoxicated, of which he was so much ashamed, as for several weeks to be continually expressing his sorrow at it. In a walk up Ladder Hill with this gentle islander it was amusing to observe the critical examination some old soldiers made of him. At length one asked a comrade, 'And what do you suppose will be done with him on his arrival in England?' 'Why you fool,' he answered, 'what should I suppose? Why he will be put in the Tower to be sure for a rare sight.' As such a decision was pronounced by the artillery man in pure innocence of heart, I did not feel so displeased at their disposing of our friend with the wild beasts of the creation, as at Jamaica some months after, when it was observed with profound solemnity, and by one of the higher rank than the St. Helena soldier, that 'he would no doubt undergo the inspection of the Antiquarian Society in London'. But, had not the 'grim tyrant' clutched poor Mideedee ere he had barely reached our isle, his friends, and they were many in the *Providence*, would in gratitude have administered to his happiness and comfort, nor treated him like an old coin, or rare quadruped from the wilds of Africa.

The variation of the compass, taking the mean of the observations on board (not by George Tobin) – 15°..31' westerly. The vessels made a very fine passage from St. Helena to St. Vincent's in twenty-seven days, when a proportion of the breadfruit and other plants were landed and deposited in the botanic garden, a short distance from the town of Kingston. If I recollect right, there were about three hundred of the former, being nearly half that reached the West Indies.

The hospitable inhabitants had been anxiously looking for the arrival of Captain Bligh, and during our stay were studious to render it agreeable by every attention.[3] You know that I was here 'at home', but my shipmates, who were strangers, soon felt the same.

The attempt giving any account of a place so often described, and if I mistake not, visited by yourself, is unnecessary. It shall only be observed that, if Tahiti was in a state of sugar cultivation, with a few buildings about the middle hills, it would have much the aspect of great part of St. Vincent's, particularly where the land is low near the sea. A collection of plants were here furnished us by Doctor Anderson, chiefly for the royal gardens at Kew, but several were to be left at Jamaica.

The small pox was prevailing in the island, which induced Captain Bligh to have Baubo and Mideedee inoculated. The confidence they placed in him quieted any apprehensions they otherwise might have entertained; yet could they not well reconcile the idea of voluntarily inflicting disease, when told that it was commonly practised. They received the infection favourably, but afterwards at Jamaica suffered much from illness; indeed Mideedee's health and cheerfulness had been on the decline a long while, nor can it be said that he ever enjoyed the former, except for three or four months from his first becoming our shipmate.

Early in this month (the 5th of February) the vessels arrived safely at Port Royal, and soon after the remainder of the plants were landed, except a number of the stronger ones which we afterwards carried to Port Morant for the botanic garden at Bath, no great distance from that harbour. Our floating forest was eagerly visited by numbers of every rank and degree, and in fact it was a most gratifying sight, however much reduced in numbers. The poor Negroes, for whose benefit the voyage was chiefly promoted, were loud in their praises of 'de ship da hab de bush' and were constantly paddling round her in their canoes. But she was soon to come into 'the Line' with a more warlike appearance, and to the great annoyance of my peaceful cabin, where a new visitor in a four pounder was placed. This arose from the arrival of a packet with the news of war having been declared against Great Britain by the French nation. It totally altered our plans. The Commander-in-Chief despatched his cruisers against the enemy, while the ship that 'had the bush' was honoured with a broad pendant,* previously to which indeed, she had (on the report of an attack being intended by the *Sans Culottes* on Jamaica) been brought into the 'Line of Battle'.

This was in April. Some plants which had been taken on board for Kew Gardens were again landed. Any difficulties hitherto encountered were light when compared to this listless uninteresting situation. Prizes were arriving daily, nor could we help feeling sore at being detained as a mere guard-ship, without consideration to the immediate object of the voyage. The prospect of taking home a convoy did not serve to make us more contented, and this we were anticipating. The *Providence* still being a fixture, we became very clamorous for a

---

* broad pendant: signifying that Bligh had become commodore of a fleet of ships.

tender to cruise about Hispaniola which was at length complied with by the Commander-in-Chief. A prize schooner was accordingly fitted and victualled from both vessels and sailed on a cruise for three weeks. She was christened the *Resource*, having forty men with six three pounders, six swivels, and plenty of arms for boarding. Guthrie commanded her, and your correspondent would have been his first lieutenant, but the commodore* had an objection to more than one commissioned officer being absent from the *Providence*. The outfit altogether was, indeed, in a manner 'under the Rose'.

Fortune did not attend the *Resource* as she returned without having made a single capture, although every zealous effort was made by her commander. The truth is, she was a day 'after the fair'.

The very high wages given by the merchants caused desertion among our crew which could hardly have been expected; in short, we may date our detention at Jamaica as the most untoward part of the voyage in every respect. It has been mentioned that Baubo and Mideedee suffered from illness at this island, nor were the officers and ship's company exempt from it; a very promising young gentleman by the name of Hind fell a martyr to the yellow fever in a few days. Your friend was attacked with dysentery, but by attention and the aid of a good constitution soon 'weathered' it.

In the hope that a change of air might be of service to poor Mideedee, Captain Bligh allowed him to accompany me on a visit to a Mr. Raymond near Port Henderson. The heart of this worthy man was gratified at the thoughts of affording him relief. His house, horses and carriage were at Mideedee's disposal and a temporary amendment took but, 'twas a false promise. The very day on which the pendant was struck on board the *Providence* at Woolwich, and we all quitted her for our different families he, poor fellow, struck his pendant to be no more hoisted. His remains are in the church yard at Deptford.

Our much esteemed messmate, Harwood, wrote at a moment in the genuine sorrow of his soul, the following epitaph for him:

> Stranger with solemn step approach, and know,
> A fav'rite son of nature sleeps below.
> From that fam'd Queen of Southern Isles he came
> Fair O'Tahytey; fir'd by British fame
> And *Providence* each deep safe wafted o'er,
> Yet only gave to hail the promis'd shore,
> For here could life alas! no more supply
> *Than just took around him and to die*

Little did this poor islander's host imagine he was on the eve of paying the same debt. Yet so it was ordained; for er'e we quitted Jamaica, Raymond was beckoned away. In the last letter I received from him, he says 'and how is Mideedee? May he be restored to the inestimable blessing of health, and return in

---

*   commodore: Bligh.

safety to his native isle.' It was a warm and pious wish – but our poor Tahitian reached neither.

The muse in a few lines on this unexpected event listened to our worthy doctor. Raymond had often pointed out to us, when but a few weeks before high in health, a particular tree under whose umbrage he wished his gross materials to be laid when animation quitted them. We passed with him, Ned, very many happy hours, and well do I remember that his singularly eccentric, yet gentle manners, gained him your warm admiration, nor did they differ much from your own. Four lines before me in your handwriting, say:

> Here gentle Raymond lies; the stroke of death
> A soul more worthy ne'er depriv'd of breath;
> While those, who now deplore his fate survive,
> He'll live, where living, he most wish'd to live.

But our medical messmate had not always occasion to be in the *penseroso* mood. Not many weeks after leaving the British coast, the boards of our round house* were pencil'd with the following kind wishes for its occasional visitors:

> Here may ye never, social souls complain,
> Of constipated gut or costive brain;
> Here, may ye sit secure, in thought profound
> And no wry faces make, the *world around*,
> Here, if the muses coy, should ever deign,
> To smile upon the disembogu'ring swain,
> Sacred to Cloacina† and the nine,
> Here let him freely scrawl the comic line
> So that we all experience when we —,
> Both mental and corporal delight.

An effort was soon after made by another of our circle, but the poetic soul of the doctor could but ill brook this neighbourly intrusion of 'prose run mad' from the 'costive brain' of — nor could he help replying as follows –

> On reading Mr. B[on]ds verses –
> O'Son of dulness; by the muse not warm'd,
> Whose soul, poetic pathos never charm'd;
> How couldst thou *Godolph* with distracted brain,
> Disgrace the log-house by thy dog'grel strain;
> Where errors gross, and metre false appear.
> And discord dire, to wound the tuneful ear.
> How would her Cloacina, blush, to see,
> Her poets Corner so disgrac'd by thee,
> Her poets Corner, where she hop'd to find,

---

* round house: w.c.

† Cloacina: The Roman goddess of the sewer system.

> The pure impromptu's of poetic mind.
> Not now, one son of genius will be found
> To grace with genuine wit, this hallow'd bound;
> For who dr'ze think, or human or divine
> Would think his *verse*, fit company for thine?

Yet was — sometimes more happy; for instance, on observing a pair of whales in dalliance

> Two Whales were seen upon the sea,
> Wagging their tails in extacy.

Which Harwood could not but admit to be full of pathos and sublimity.

A retrospect of this, and various similar warfare, ever accompanied by good humour, fills me with the most pleasing reflections. In good truth nothing like it afloat has since fallen in my way. Yet is the society of the *Thetis* more interesting than in general is to be found on board ship.

In the short time Mideedee was at Mr. Raymond's, he learnt to ride with much confidence, accompanying us on a visit to Stoney Hill barracks. After his return on board to evince his gratitude, he sent Mr. Raymond a present of Tahitian cloth, and this he begged from his English shipmates. It was with the greatest difficulty he was persuaded to take milk during his illness, so strong is the aversion of these islanders to it. In temperance he was far superior to Baubo, who required no pressing to take wine or spirits in any quantity, whereas, particularly after his excess at St. Helena, Mideedee rather avoided both. There was a jealousy between them which we much lamented and vainly strove to conquer, particularly on the part Mideedee. Yet he ever considered Baubo as the lowest order of his countrymen, which was indeed the case, nor without arrogating much to himself for being one of the queen's favourite servants. Baubo bore his illness with less temper than his countryman, having many quarrels with an old Negro nurse who attended him. One day when she was over solicitous for him to eat, after making several ineffectual attempts to explain to her that he required nothing, in rather an angry tone he said, 'I do not want to eat, my belly is full', but taking her finger put it in his ear telling her 'she might perhaps find room in his head'.

It was not until the middle of June that we left Murfields, the *Antelope* packet and two merchant ships accompanying us. The plants for Kew had been taken a second time on board previously to quitting Port Royal, at which place everything was done to make the *Providence* and her *Assistant* as warlike as possible. In our way to the Gulf of Florida we touched at the Grand Cayman having with us, in addition to our little convoy, a dismasted merchant ship that joined company in our way from Jamaica. This ship was left here. Having taken on board some turtle, the voyage was continued round the western part of Cuba, and thence, through the Florida Gulf. August both vessels were anchored safely in the Downs, very little mortality having taken place among the plants; indeed of the two, we ourselves were greater sufferers from the cold than them, although in very height of summer. But to such as have been long between the tropics without having seen their breath, the warmest air on the English coast is at first sufficiently sharp.

The vessels soon proceeded up the Thames, first to Deptford, but shortly after dropped down to Woolwich. While at the former place, the plants were conveyed to Kew Gardens in a lighter, the whole being contained in six hundred and eighty-six pots and tubs, and among them a few of the breadfruit. Perhaps there never were so many plants deposited in the royal garden at one time from inter-tropical countries.

The ships being cleared of stores and provisions, were this day put out of commission. And, as has been before mentioned, poor Mideedee also this day struck his pendant. One of the last objects which called forth the feeling of this gentle islander was the number of our countrymen suspended on gibbets in chains on the banks of the Thames as we sailed by. His soul sickened and revolted at so sad a spectacle, nor perhaps did he ever so much wish to be again among his countrymen, where such sights are unknown, as at the moment these victims to civilised law first caught his eye.

Before we separated, 'all hands' had the satisfaction of receiving the captain's public thanks for their conduct during the voyage, with an assurance that his interest and interference 'as far as it went', should be applied to our advancement. In a former letter the subject of promotion has been touched on. I shall only observe that we had yet to wait, even our excellent first lieutenant, who as has been noticed was appointed to, perhaps, the worst ship in the British Navy. The health of the second was gone past recovery. As the last hope he was sent, poor fellow, to the Mediterranean, but it proved in vain. He died about the middle of 1795. The third, in about two months after wearing a plain coat, was appointed to this ship, where (except seven or eight months in the admiral's) he has been ever since, nor without hopes ere long of quitting the 'white lapel'.* Yet, if he is still to tarry longer in a gunroom and not be the supreme on deck in no ship, nor with any commander, could he possibly be more happy and satisfied than in the *Thetis*. Still he looks back to the ship 'da hab de bush'.

I must now conclude, yet ere I do, it may be satisfactory for you to know that we have received accounts from the West Indies of breadfruit being permanently established. Like other fruits of the island, they are now sold publicly at the markets of Jamaica.

Ten years have elapsed since this humane undertaking was suggested to our gracious sovereign by the West India planters through the medium, if I mistake not, of Sir Joseph Banks. Many unlooked for obstructions have intruded to prevent its earlier accomplishment. These, however, did not damp the zeal of its promoters, who must ever feel the most cordial gratification from their persevering efforts in 'doing good'. That the introduction of this nutritious food into the sugar colonies will be attended with the most beneficial effects to the

---

*   The lieutenant's uniform had white lapels.

toiling Africans can hardly be doubted. Most of the edible plants in the West Indies are known to suffer and frequently to be wholly destroyed by the violence of hurricanes. This, we have reason to believe, will not be the case with the firm and prolific breadfruit tree, but that in the course of a few years, it will become the chief sustenance of a large proportion of our fellow creatures, whose lot in life loudly calls on our sympathy and consideration.

Farewell, the ship is fast approaching her port, where (as the first lieutenant) plenty of employment is laid out for me. Should a safe conveyance offer, these 'crudities' shall take a passage across the Atlantic for your perusal; or perhaps I may keep them 'till we shake hands. Some drawings are attached to them, and here I believe you have not been told that an artist, Mr. Kirkland, was to have accompanied the expedition, but who was left in ill health at Haslar Hospital. This obliged us all to work with our pencils as well as we were able.

I am, my dear James,
   Very faithfully and affectionately
      Yours, George Tobin

Thetis off Nova Scotia
July 18th 1797

Officers &c. &c. on board H. M. S. Providence on her quitting England, August 1791

Names	Quality	How since disposed of 1831
William Bligh	Post Captain	Died in London (vice-admiral) December 12, 1817
Francis Godolphin Bond	1st Lieutenant	Post-Captain – On half pay
James Guthrie	2nd „	Died (a lieutenant) 1795
George Tobin	3rd „	Post-Captain on half pay
William Nicholls	Master	
Edward Harwood	Surgeon	Died in London 1814
Edward James	Boatswain	
John England	Gunner	
John Flow	Carpenter	
Thomas Gilespie	Master's Mate	Died a lieutenant in 1800 or 1801
John Impey	Master's Mate	Post-Captain on half pay
Thomas Walker	Master's Mate	Died
George Holwell	Midshipman	Died (a lieutenant)
George Kilsha	„	
John Bushby	„	Died (a post-captain) 1810
Robert Ogelvie	„	Drowned in the *Swift* sloop in 1797
William Hind	„	Died during the voyage at Jamaica, 1793
Matthew Flinders	„	Died (a post-captain) in England, 1814
John Head	„	Died (a lieutenant) in 1804

William Askew	„	Killed (a lieutenant) by accident
Robert Ridgeway	Surgeon's 1st mate	
Douglas Whyte	Surgeon's 2nd mate	Died at Rosetta 1802 of the plague
Edward Hatful	Captain's clerk	Purser in the navy: Died in Canada, 1829
Thomas Pearce	Lieutenant of marines	
Mr. James Wiles	Botanist	
Mr. Christopher Smith	„	

Officers &c. &c. on board the Assistant on her quitting England August 1791

Names	Quality	How since disposed of
Nathaniel Portlock	Lieutenant & Commander	Died September 12, 1817, a Captain of Greenwich Hospital
George Watson	Master	
Richard Frankland	Surgeon	
David Gilmore	Master's mate	Died a commander 1829
John Gore	Midshipman	Died a rear-admiral
J. R. Lapenstiere	„	Post-Captain
Thomas England	„	
Andrew Dyce	„	
Francis Mathews	„	Died
James Campbell	„	
Joseph Sherrard	Clerk	
Andrew Goldie	Gunner's mate	
David Myers	Carpenter's mate	

(Copy) *Gentleman's Magazine* September 1811 Died Lieutenant R. B. Hopkins. He was one of the circumnavigators in the H M S *Providence* at Stoke Abbot, eldest son of the Reverend W. Hopkins.

Extract from the Reverend R. Polwhele's 'Traditions and Recollections &c&c' published in 1826. (George Tobin 1827)

Captain Bligh to the Reverend R. Polwhele
Durham Place Lambeth
December 21 1803

I hope yet to be able to publish my last Voyage in which I secured the Bread fruit plants to the West Indies.

Author's Notes

Chapter 1st

1 We had a rendezvous open for volunteers at the sign of the *Round About* in that refined port of Wapping, New Gravel Lane but in a month entered only five men notwithstanding our bills were well passed in praise of Tahiti and its inhabitants. The vessels however were not detained a moment for want of crews.

2 This most excellent officer and well-informed man, suffered great injury in his person by an explosion of gunpowder on board a prize where he was in the American War.

3
>   *On the Petrel, or Mother Cary's Chicken.*
> When the bold Petrel wines his flight,
> O'er Ocean's wide and 'trackless deep';
> How does he rest his foot at night?
> Where does the little wanderer sleep.
> I cannot tell if the wanderer sleeps
> Or how he may rest his foot at night;
> Perhaps he a constant vigil keeps,
> But I've always rued 'his boding sight'.
>
> For I ne'er saw his active flitting form,
> Sweeping with dusky wing the wave,
> But I've ask'd the tempest's rising storm
> And thought of the seaman's wat'ry grave.
>
> Off the blue sea rises proud and high-
> tend the st'ring clouds precede the gale;
> Then you may note the dark Petrel fly,
> Stemming the breeze with his pinion sail.

Naval Chronicle Vol. 37

>   *Sonnet to the Petrel or Mother Cary's Chicken*
> Bird of the Storm – for ever hovering nigh!
> But *most* when tempests shake the watery plain,
> Child of each clime in Neptune's boundless reign,
> The burning tropic and the polar sky –
> Following this mazes oft through liquid space,
> Wondering ask, what power uphold thy flight,
> What – through the sent ask'd ether, guides thy sight?
> And where when wearied is they resting place?
> As though (vain thoughts that *He* who made me *man*
> And in my ample bosom pour'd a *soul*;
> Had not protected his creative-plan,

And breath'd his spirit through the mighty whole;
And to thee, wanderer o'er the troubled tide
Powers suited to the state, with bounteous hand supplied.

Naval Chronicle Vol. 32

4   Gannets the same.

Chapter 2nd

1   In the early part of the present war the 82nd Regiment landed nine hundred and eighty men at St. Domingo, six hundred and thirty of which were buried in ten weeks. See Bryan Edwards *History of St. Domingo.*

Chapter 3rd

1   What we considered Frederick Henry Bay, in February 1792 was soon after explored (in May 1792) and named D'Entrecasteaux Channel. We lived (Francis Godolphin Bond, George Tobin and others) at this red mark ☉. Labillardière* says it is separate from Adventure Bay by a narrow strip of land 'not more than 200 toises at its greatest breadth'. Six feet to a toise.
2   Except in the Southern Hemisphere.
3   Quartermasters roasted in the cockpit for their 'own good'.
4   E. informed me (April 1819) that he planted on the Morant Keys near Jamaica in the year 18— a number of cocoanut trees. I saw trees on them in May 1809 and before we could distinguish the land. George Tobin.

Chapter 4th

1   A highly valued friend of your father, Lord N—k, paid me a visit on board the *Providence* before our leaving England. When he observed on being introduced to our first lieutenant, that Mr. Bond would have to give two nails to the fair of Tahiti.
2   It was well known at Tahiti.
3   There are (I believe) doubts who discovered the Island of Tahiti, but Quiros in 1606, seems to have the fairest claim to it, if Sagitaria and Tahiti be the same Island. In the narrative of that voyage, the editor said 'They had sight of an island (February 9th 1606) to the northeast. They passed it leaving it to windward being in latitude 18°..40' south. They passed the day with some rain, till the next, February 10th, when from the topmast head to the no small satisfaction of every one, a sailor cried out land &c. &c. and in several places columns of smoke arising, which was a clear sign of inhabitants, whence they concluded that all their sufferings were at an end. &c. &c. They fetched abreast of it ordering the *Zabra* to go to look for a port while the *Capitana* and *Almirante* kept turning to windward in sight of it' . . . Quiros, it appears, passed

---

*   J.J.H. Labillardière, *An Account of a Voyage in Search of La Pérouse* . . ., London, 1800.

the night of the 10th in 'the offing, but when morning came, they found themselves about eight leagues down the coast; this gave great disquiet to all, as it was impossible to return back and see the Indians, but discovering the land abreast to be the same they had left, it was great satisfaction to every one as they knew it was inhabited.'* The night of the 11th, as the preceding one, was passed in the offing and the next day, February 12th, they ran along shore to the northwest observing the sun in it in 17°..40' south. Presently leaving it, they sailed &c. &c. No mention is made of the longitude of Sagitaria; but the latitude accords tolerably with Tahiti; if Quiros passed its south side as does the latitude of Mataiea, the island, he must have seen on the 9th to northeast when in the latitude of 18°..40' south. Mataiea is in about 17°..55' south, and can be seen at a great distance. If we invert the northeast bearings and allow for the probable inaccuracy of instruments two centuries ago, the situation of Quiros from Mataiea on the 9th, (that is southwest from it) accords pretty well with the discoveries of Tahiti on the succeeding day. Speaking of a chief who came on board at Sagitaria, the narrative says 'The chief then went on board his Paragua and setting sail navigated towards a small islet. Quere? What islet could this be? Was it one of the small keys on the south side of Tahiti? Or was it Moorea which is a few leagues on a western direction from Tahiti?

4   The island of Tahiti is the only part of the world which I have ever visited without noticing the hawk or kite species (Quere St. Helena?) It is also somewhat remarkable that there are no snakes of any kind, or frogs, or toads.

Chapter 5th

1   Impossible in drawing to give the colour.

2   Mr. Whyte (as well as Mr. Ridgeway) was promoted shortly after the return of the *Providence*. He died in Egypt in 1802. He had embraced an opinion that the plague was not contagious, and inoculated himself twice for it without any effect. On making a third trial which communicated the disease, it caused his death in two or three days. But *vide* an recount since met with.

George Tobin 1803

I always understood that Mr. Whyte had inoculated himself twice for the plague, in Egypt, without receiving the infection. But, the following account is from the *Quarterly Review*, December 1825. George Tobin 1826

The experiment (Dr. Whyte's) and the result are thus related in a letter from Mr. Rice, then doing duty in the pest house at El Hammed to Mr. (Now Sir James) McGregor:

    Viz. – 'Dr. Whyte came here last night January 2nd 1802. Soon after he came in, he rubbed some matter from the Bubo of a woman on the inside of his thighs. The next morning he inoculated himself in the wrists with a Lancet with matter from the running Bubo of a Sepoy. Dr. Whyte continued in good health on the 5th and all day on the 6th till the evening, when he was attacked with

---

*   Alexander Dalrymple, *An Account of the Discoveries Made in the South Pacific Ocean, Previous to 1764*, London, 1767, Vol II, p 45.

Rigors, and other febrile symptoms. He continued to have shiverings, succeeded by heat and perspiration, much affection of the head, tremor of the limbs, a dry black tongue, great thirst, a full hard irregular pulse, great debility, and great anxiety. He still persisted that the disease was not the Plague and would not allow his groin or arm pits to be examined. He became delirious on the 8th and died on the 9th in the forenoon.'

3   In 1789 Mr. Samuel, clerk of the *Bounty*, saw from the mountains of Tahiti the Islands of Huahine and Mataiea, which are nearly in opposite directions, seventy leagues apart.

4   Stewart's girl.

5   Whole of it breaking through in the *Bounty*.

Chapter 6th

1   Forster, in May 1774 says 'In the evening we let off a few Sky rockets and some air-balloons.' Vide Forster's *Voyage* Vol. 1 Page 101. George Tobin 1828, but Quere:– Had any balloons been exhibited as early as in 1774? Even in Europe?

2   The boats were able to contain all the crew in case of shipwreck.

Chapter 7th

1   Captain Cook estimated the inhabitants at two hundred thousand. In 1797 Captain Wilson in the *Duff* at rather above sixteen thousand. In the *Transactions of the Missionary Society* 1804, at only eight thousand. And in Turnbull at a still inferior number. The *Annual Register* 1804, speaking of the reduction in the inhabitants of Tahiti, observes, 'We believe the principal reason to be wars between themselves and the neighbouring tribes; a tremendous epidemic which not long since raged with peculiar mortality; the abominable crime of infanticide, and the paucity of females to males; a paucity so extreme, as that the latter are supposed to exceed the former in the proportion of ten to one. Whence we may infer that infanticide is far more frequently perpetrated upon female, than male children.'

2   Perceval, speaking of the Ceylonese says (1803) 'While at meals, they seldom converse with each other; they seem to look upon the whole business of eating, as something rather required by necessity, than very consistent with decency. While drinking, they never turn their faces to each other.'

3   This expression is used by the natives to each other when anyone sneezes, exactly as we say 'God bless you' in England.

4   Where all partake the earth without dispute,
            and bread itself is gathered as a *fruit*;
            Where none contest the fields, the woods the streams,
            The Goldless Age, where Gold disturbs no dreams,
            Inhabits or inhabited the shore;
            Till Europe taught them better than before,
            Bestowed her customs, and amended theirs,
            But left her vices also to their heirs.

> Away with this! Behold them as they were,
> Do good with Nature, or with Nature err.
>
> From Lord Byron's 'Island' 1823

5   Yet Foster says, (in 1773) '*E Happai* (which was *Otow*'s* name at that period) was a tall thin man with a grey beard and hair, seemed to be of a great age but not entirely worn out. *Otoo*, Son of *E Happai*, seemed about four or five and twenty.'

6   Yet, when the *Duff* touched at Huahine in 1797, a man by the name of Connor, one of the *Matilda*'s crew, declined embarking on board her. Connor had been among the Society Isles five years, but he supposed it had been eight. He could neither read or write and had nearly forgotten his native language. He first expressed a desire to be taken on board, but his affection for a child borne him by a woman of the island, superseded the desire and he remained in this distant quarter of the globe. (George Tobin 1802)

7   The death of three Tahitians is noted in *Gentleman's Magazine* 1803. '*Mydowe*, about seventeen or eighteen at the Moravian School near Leeds. *Oly*, about nineteen or twenty, at the same place, and *Mideedee*, another youth, who died some time before (but in what part of England is not mentioned) of a spitting of blood. These three victims to a less genial climate than their own left *Tahiti* about the year 1799 in a Southern Whaler and her prize.' In reading the account of these poor fellows, it was not without reflecting on the names as of one of them our old shipmate, Mideedee, who removed from all but a few English friends, paid the same debt but a few years before. Our Mideedee had been absent from Tahiti about seven years when the late one left the island. It would be satisfactory to know whether an account of our friend's death had reached the island at this time. If it had, his namesake had certainly a claim to resolution and enterprise in quitting his native isle on a voyage at least of obscurity. Mideedee signifies a child. Much is it to be wished that Europeans would leave these Mideedees to their own teeming soil and cheerful habits. I may be wrong, but the more I see and hear, the more I reflect, the stronger an opinion is fixed in my mind, that the aim of civilised nations to ameliorate the condition of those in what is called a savage state, is but in general, a fruitless one.

Twelve years are not passed since I was among the Tahitians, but I fear that were I now to visit them, I should not find them in an improved state. The public prints notice that great numbers of our countrymen from New South Wales have by various means found their way to Tahiti, that they have built several vessels and are employed on many more of considerable burden. From the contiguity of Tahiti to this Land of Convicts, its fine climate, productive soil and pleasurable habits, we cannot but suppose that emigration from Sydney will increase, nor is it a very remote calculation to imagine that this very fine island may become a European settlement, and the hand of power by degrees reduce the right owners to an abject state of servitude. We are already told of the chiefs having bestowed the productive district of Matavai to the missionaries, a class of men who purposely embarked on what is generally considered a humane errand and who cannot be supposed to cherish worldly considerations while converting

*   Otow=Tue.

the heathen. What may we not then expect from those of more dissolute and licentious manners? The island is capable of producing everything that is cultured in our West India colonies. It has good harbours, fine rivers, abundance of wood, and holds out but too great a temptation to the insatiable speculator on gain. (George Tobin 1804)

8 1792 July & the tide in Matavai Bay was very inconsiderable, not (I think) rising above a foot, and what is somewhat remarkable, it was high water about the middle of the day. It is in my recollection that the captain used to send a careful person to a rock near Venus Point to note it almost every day.

Chapter 8th

1 This might indeed have been the island cloth, as a red dye is common among them.

2 *Vide* Collins *Account of New South Wales*. The *Chesterfield* and *Hormuzear*, two ships from Sydney bound to India through Torres Straits, on the 1st July 1793 lost some of their men in this neighbourhood. A boat was sent on shore to an island, called Tate's Island in latitude 9°..39'.30" south, longitude 143°..00'.45" west. The ships were driven to leeward, but on their return on the 3rd no boat was found: but it has since appeared that five of the party out of eight were murdered by the natives, among them Captain Hill of the New South Wales Corps. The other three effected their escape severely wounded, and after suffering much from want of water and provisions, reached Timor on the 11th. When these men made their miraculous escape in the boat, the natives were dragging their murdered companions towards fires. (George Tobin 1803)

3 There were no symptoms in the wounded men of the arrows being poisoned.

Chapter 9th

1 The distance from Newfoundland, about 200 leagues south of Cape Rose, Newfoundland.

2 Ascension is about 685 miles from St. Helena in a northwesterly direction.

3 Carried away the main royal mast by luggery. The only spar lost during the voyage.

Index